Jedidiah Chapman, David Bostwick

Four Sermons on Christian Baptism

In which the privilege of believers, under the Gospel respecting the mode and

subjects of baptism is established and illustrated

Jedidiah Chapman, David Bostwick

Four Sermons on Christian Baptism

In which the privilege of believers, under the Gospel respecting the mode and subjects of baptism is established and illustrated

ISBN/EAN: 9783337114299

Printed in Europe, USA, Canada, Australia, Japan

Cover: Foto ©Lupo / pixelio.de

More available books at **www.hansebooks.com**

ON

CHRISTIAN BAPTISM;

IN WHICH THE

PRIVILEGE OF BELIEVERS,

UNDER THE GOSPEL,

RESPECTING THE

MODE AND SUBJECTS OF BAPTISM.

IS ESTABLISHED AND ILLUSTRATED.

PUBLISHED AT THE REQUEST OF THE HEARERS.

By *JEDIDIAH CHAPMAN*, V. D. M.
PASTOR OF THE CHURCH OF CHRIST AT ORANGE-DALE.

ELIZABETH TOWN:
PRINTED FOR THE AUTHOR BY SHEPARD KOLLOCK.

M,DCC,XCI.

ADVERTISEMENT.

THE following Sermons were preached at the particular Request of a Number of serious Persons, without the most distant Thought of their Publication. However, through the Importunity of the Hearers, seconded by the Desire and Advice of several Gentleman, who honored them with a Perusal, they are now offered to the Public, with no small Degree of Reluctance, in their plain, native Dress.

The Author has Nothing further to add, except his most ardent Wishes, that they may be useful in the Cause of Truth, and promote the Glory of God, in uniting, edifying and comforting his dear People.

SERMON I.

On CHRISTIAN BAPTISM.

MATTHEW xxviii. 19, 20.

Go ye, therefore, and teach all nations, baptizing them in the name of the Father, and of the Son, and of the Holy Ghost;—Teaching them to observe all things whatsoever I have commanded you: and, lo, I am with you alway, even unto the end of the world.

My dear friends, and beloved brethren,

IT is my prefent defign to addrefs you on the ferious and important fubject of Baptifm.—Treating this point, as God fhall enable me, in a courfe of fermons, I fhall endeavor to handle the fubject with great plainnefs and candor, not feeking fo much the applaufe of man, or the conviction of thofe who differ from us, as the eftablifhment of your minds in the truth. The words which I have now read are joyful, folemn words. They were fpoken in a very affecting fituation—they are fome of the laft words of our bleffed Lord and Saviour to his dear difciples. In the preceding chapter, we have an account of his crucifixion, and painful death on the crofs—In this, of his joyful refurrection and appearance to the apoftles, whom he imformed of his acceptance with God as the Mediator and Saviour, and of his great power in heaven and earth. He gave them the commiffion in our text—" Go ye, therefore, "and teach all nations, baptizing them in the "name of the Father, and of the Son, and of the "Holy Ghoft:—Teaching them to obferve all "things whatfoever I have commanded you: "and, lo, I am with you alway, even unto the "end of the world."

I fhall here mention feveral things of great importance to the fubject before us, in which all parties agree; and beg you will keep them in view through the enfuing difcourfes.

Firft, Our bleffed Saviour's command, in this text, is equally binding on all his minifters, in all ages of the world—that they are to preach the gofpel to every creature, and to teach all who are capable of inftruction, in all the doctrines he has revealed in his word.

Second, The minifters of Chrift are to baptize among the nations, " in the name of the Father, " Son, and Holy Ghoft," all thofe, and only thofe, who, according to his revealed will, are the proper fubjects of baptifm.

Third, All his minifters, by this, are bound to teach the nations to obferve and obey all things, whatfoever he hath commanded; all the laws, ordinances, and inftitutions, which, according to the fcriptures, are in force under the gofpel difpenfation.

Fourth, Let it be well obferved, that according to this promife, Chrift will be with *his minif-*

ters, to support and comfort them—to bless and succeed them in the glorious work unto the end of the world. These things being observed, I shall proceed to consider our text, with reference only to the sacrament of baptism—and shall endeavor to shew,

I. That baptism with water is an institution of Christ, to be a standing ordinance in his church to the end of the world.

II. I shall speak of the mode of baptism as it respects the controversy between us and our brethren called Baptists.

I. I am to speak of water-baptism, and shew that it is an institution of Christ, to be a standing ordinance in the church to the end of the world.

There is a baptism of the Holy Ghost, and with fire, agreeably to Mark i. 8. " I, indeed, " have baptized you with water, but he shall " baptize you with the Holy Ghost." Luke iii. 16. " He shall baptize you with the Holy Ghost, " and with fire." But its administration Christ has reserved to himself. We no where read of his commanding any to administer such a baptism. Some, indeed, since the apostles' day, have undertaken to do it; but we expect they will stand reproved in the great day of the Lord.

That baptism by water is an institution of Christ, is very evident from our text. " Go, says " Christ, teach, or disciple all nations, baptizing " them," &c. They are commanded to teach, and they are commanded to baptize. The same precept is also recorded, Mark xvi. 15, 16. "And "he said unto them, Go ye into all the world, "and teach the gospel unto every creature. He "that believeth, and is baptized, shall be saved; "but he that believeth not shall be damned."— We accordingly find the apostles, and primitive ministers of Christ, baptizing all whom they disciplined to him. On the day of Pentecost, when three thousand were added to the church in one day, the apostles called on them to repent, and be baptized. The Quakers, and some others, deny that baptism with water is to be continued in the church; but the contrary seems evident, from the very face of the command. The apostles, and succeeding ministers of Christ, were commanded to teach, to preach the gospel, and to baptize all nations; and in faithfully teaching and baptizing, Christ promises to be with them to the end of the world. Our blessed Saviour, likewise, expressly enjoins on the apostles, to teach his disciples to observe all things whatsoever he hath commanded them; but baptism by water was the command which had just then proceeded from his sacred lips. It is manifest that the primitive church received the practice from the apostles, and observed it as a command of Christ.

The design of baptism as a seal of the covenant, and badge of the Christian profession—its use as an initiating ordinance into the church, and its obvious signification, all plainly shew it to be a standing institution in the church, and to be administered with water, to all proper subjects, " in the name of the Father, and of the

" Son, and of the Holy Ghost," by all the faithful ministers of Jesus Christ.

II. I am now to speak of the mode of baptism.

Before I proceed, two remarks are worthy of particular notice.

1. As baptism is merely a positive institution of Christ, nothing, with regard to its mode, should be made essential, but what Christ has expresly enjoined. This observation must be too evident to meet with any opposition. Should any think this or that mode most decent, convenient, or significant, let them answer a good conscience, where the scriptures are silent; but let them not make it essential to baptism, unless it is expresly enjoined by Christ.

2. No denomination of Christians has a right to set up one mode of baptism as essential, and exclude all other modes without expres scripture warrant, or some positive proof, that it is the will of Christ, the great king and head of the church. The reason of this is plain. Since it is the prerogative of Christ to appoint the ordinances of his church, it must belong to him alone to determine, what should be considered essential to them. For any, therefore, to determine the exclusive mode of baptism, or make any thing essential to it, which Christ himself has not appointed, is not only very uncharitable to their brethren, but also a great presumption on the prerogative of Christ. Our brethren, the Baptists, my hearers, hold with us, that baptism must be administered, by a regular minister of Christ,

with water, in the name of the Father, Son, and Holy Ghoſt; but, they aſſert, that it muſt be done in the mode of dipping, or plunging the whole body under water, otherwiſe it would be no Chriſtian baptiſm. Let us now candidly examine this matter. The queſtion is not, whether dipping or plunging is baptiſm, but whether plunging or dipping is the only Chriſtian baptiſm. It is not ſufficient for them to prove in the cleareſt manner, that plunging is a proper mode of baptiſm; but they ought to prove, and muſt prove, if they do any thing to the purpoſe, that plunging is the only baptiſm by water inſtituted by Chriſt. Inattention to this circumſtance, I believe, has been the occaſion of much doubt and confuſion in the minds of ſome, if not the ſource of real impoſition, in this point, on many Chriſtians. But, I hope, your minds may be free from all ſuch impoſitions, and that you may be able, in the truth, to ſtand faſt in the liberty wherewith Chriſt has made you free.

Let us now, keeping theſe things in view, conſider the words of the inſtitution, as we have them in our text. " Go ye, therefore, and teach " all nations, baptizing them in the name of the " Father, and of the Son, and of the Holy Ghoſt. " Teaching them to obſerve all things whatſo- " ever I have commanded you: and, lo, I am with " you alway, even unto the end of the world," Here we have the plain command to baptize, but not any thing poſitive reſpecting the mode. Does this prove that plunging is the only ſcripture-baptiſm?—Would not one of the baptiſts have expreſſed it differently, if he deſigned to eſtabliſh dipping the body under water as the only mode of baptism? Since the Baptists assert, that the true meaning of the word baptize, is to dip or plunge under water, this must command some attention; but as it will lead us back to the original language in which the gospel was written, waters too deep for most of you, my dear hearers, I shall first lead you where you may see for yourselves.

1. We assert, that the word baptize does not now generally signify to plunge or dip any thing under water; nor is it any where confined to this signification alone, but among the Baptists.— They say, on the contrary, that we have perverted the word to support our own practice.— We therefore assert,

2. That the word baptize did not, in our Saviour's time, always signify plunging or dipping, Luke xi. 38. " And, when the Pharisee saw it, " he marvelled, that he had not first washed be-" fore dinner;" or, as it is in the original, that he was not first baptized. We all know that *baptizing* here does not mean the dipping or plunging of the whole body under water, but only the washing of the hands. But is the word baptize here misapplied and perverted? Who has done it?

It is also certain, that this word is used by inspiration to signify divers washing without any reference to the mode. Mark vii. 4. " And from ", the market, except they baptize or wash, they " eat not." The word *baptismous*, in this and the eight verse, deserves particular attention. Being in the plural number, it must signify various

B

modes of wafhing, of cups, pots, brazen veffels, and of tables. The word is likewife applied to the many kinds of ceremonial wafhings. Heb. ix. 10. " Only in meats and drinks, and divers " baptifms or wafhings." Some of thefe wafhings or cleanfings were performed by pouring, others by fprinkling, and fome of them could not be done by dipping or plunging.

There are many other places in the fcriptures where the word is ufed to fignify any kind of wafhing or cleanfing, even where there is no dipping. Some of our brethren, the Baptifts, may, perhaps, ftill infift, that according to the beft lexicographers and moft approved mafters of the original language, this word fignifies dipping or plunging only.

It may therefore be neceffary for their fakes, to pay fome farther attention to this matter; though if all the Lexicons in the world fhould confirm their appropriate meaning of the word, it ought to have no weight with you contrary to the known ufe of it by divine infpiration— However, for your better fatisfaction, I have examined a number of lexicographers, and find, that all of them allow the word *baptizo*, to fignify any kind of wafhing, or cleanfing with water. This matter, I believe, will be clear beyond all doubt, to any one who will take the trouble to examine Hefychius, Budeus, Scapula, Stephanus, and Dr. Leigh's Critica Sacra. They are all acknowledged to be great mafters in the Greek language, and they allow the word to fignify wafhing in general.

In their Lexicons and Commentaries, they fay *baptizo lavo*, which fignifies, beyond all difpute, washing in general—*baptisma lavatio, ablutio,* washing, ablution, which we all know may be done, and is often well done without plunging the body all under the water. It is of no force to say, that the word also signifies to wash by dipping, or plunging; because it then allows of other modes of baptizing besides dipping.

This is granting all we contend for in the text, that our blessed Saviour did not command and fix any particular mode of washing with water in the sacred institution of baptism, and that he does not require dipping or plunging, any more than sprinkling or pouring, but only baptism.

Some say, that the word *baptizo* is derived from *bapto,* which all allow to signify dipping or plunging only, as the dyers do when they mean to tinge, or form a bright color; and, therefore, it must have been the design of our Saviour to fix the mode of baptism by that word.—But this is nothing to the purpose. If our Saviour designed to establish the mode by the word, why did he not in the institution of baptism, make use of *bapto* instead of *baptizo,* which would at once have carried the allusion more strongly, and forever fixed the mode of baptism to plunging only, as the Baptists would have it?—It is more than probable that the word *baptizo* was used by our Saviour, and not *bapto;* because it carried the beautiful allusion of the other, but left his church at liberty to use the various modes of administering the holy ordinance according to the different climes and seasons—according to to the different circumstances and necessities— and according to the various infirmities of his dear people.

It was his maxim, "I will have mercy and not sacrifice."—But not to weary you with these remarks, we shall return to the law and testimony—I imagine you see that the mode of dipping as the only true baptism, is not enjoined by our Saviour in the words of the institution, where we should most certainly have found it, had it been his design—Let us examine scripture-example respecting the mode of baptism. There we have a right to expect some positive proof, that dipping is the only mode, especially since it is not positively and expressly enjoined in the words of the institution. But if all the examples of baptism we have recorded, were most evidently performed by plunging, it would no more than prove that plunging is one scriptural mode, or at least it would not alone prove, that it is indispensably necessary to baptism. The baptism of our blessed Saviour, by John, in Jordan, claims our first attention. Matt. iii. 16. "And Jesus when he " was baptized, went straightway out of the wa- " ter."—This may be true history, though he were not baptized by plunging. His coming up out of the water may have no respect at all to the mode of baptism; for it was manifestly after he was baptized. Here we might most surely have expected it to have been established, were any one of the modes of baptizing to be the only true baptism. But we are still left without any thing certain to determine, whether our blessed Saviour himself was baptized by sprinkling, pouring, plunging, or some other way.—Mark also says, " Jesus was baptized of John, in Jordan;" but respecting the mode, he is wholly silent.—He might have been baptized by either mode, especially as there was water enough for dipping—The fact that Jesus came up out of the water after he was baptized, cannot with any certainty prove, that he had been plunged all under the water upon that solemn occasion.

The next example is John's baptizing at Enon, John iii. 23. " And John was also bap-
" tizing in Enon, near to Salem, because there was
" much water there; and they came and were
" baptized." This does not even prove that John baptized by plunging, much less that dipping is the only mode of baptism. Where there were such multitudes of people as resorted to John, much water must have been necessary for their use, had he baptized by pouring or sprinkling.

John, notwithstanding all that appears to the contrary from the sacred history, might have used all the modes on different subjects, according to their sex, age, and circumstance. On the day of Pentecost, when there were three thousand added to the church in one day, it is not very improbable that any of them, since it is incredible that all of them, were baptized by plunging. The baptism of the Eunuch is another example recorded in scripture—We have a particular history of this in the 8th chapter of the Acts of the apostles—" And they went down
" both into the water, both Philip and the Eu-
" nuch, and he baptized him; and when they
" were come up out of the water, the spirit of
" the Lord caught away Philip." This is a very particular description of the solemn transaction upon which the Baptists much insist, as a clear and positive proof, that plunging is the only scripture-baptism.

But I hope, in a few words to shew, that this is so far from proving, that dipping is the only scripture-baptism, that there is not any certain proof whether the Eunuch himself was baptized by plunging, pouring, or sprinkling. Here let it be noticed, that the Greek preposition *eis*, does not always signify, into, as it is here translated, but is often translated, *to or unto*—and *ek* translated, out of, very frequently signifies, *from any thing*. Agreeable to this, the passage may be thus read—" And they went down both to the " water, both Philip and the Eunuch, and he " baptized him; and when they were come up " from the water," &c.

I may now appeal to any impartial mind, that if any one should read this history, who has heard of baptizing only by pouring water upon the person baptized, whether he will not immediately say the Eunuch was baptized in that way; and whether he who has never seen the ordinance administered only by sprinkling of clean water, will not as certainly conclude, that Philip baptized him by that mode?—But could this possibly be the case, if there were in the text any clear and certain proof in favor of plunging? We will now consider the passage more critically—" and they went down both into the water, both Philip and the Eunuch." The going down into the water could not be the baptism here recorded; because Philip must then also have been baptized, since they both went down into the water. But the plain fact is, that the going down into the water, is no part of the baptism here, but a distinct thing—" And he baptized " him." This sentence contains the baptism, and all that is certain about the mode in which it was adminiftered. After the Eunuch was baptized, it is faid, " they both came up out of the " water." Does this prove that the Eunuch was plunged? and why not Philip? Since he alfo came up out of the water. Should it be granted that the Eunuch was dipped, which is by no means certain, it will not eftablifh dipping as the only fcriptural mode of baptifm. Neither will it prove, that it is effential to the right adminiftration of the ordinance, efpecially as it is not made neceffary by him, who is the acknowledged author of the facred inftitution.

Let us now confider thofe particular paffages of facred fcripture, which are brought to prove that plunging is the only true mode of fcripture-baptifm—The firft I fhall take notice of is in Coloffians ii. 12. and the parallel text in Romans vi. 4. " Buried with him in baptifm, wherein ye al-
" fo are rifen with him through the faith of the
" operation of God, who hath raifed him from the
" dead. Therefore we are buried with him by
" baptifm into death; that like as Chrift, was raif-
" ed up from the dead by the glory of the Father,
" even fo we alfo fhould walk in newnefs of life." It is very clear that the defign of infpiration in thefe words, was not to eftablifh any particular mode of baptifm. It was to fhew, that all thofe to whom he addreffed himfelf, who were truly baptized into Jefus Chrift, had really the internal change fignified by baptifm. They were baptifed into his death, as the apoftle expreffes it. They were really dead, and buried with Chrift as to fin, and with him were rifen again; and

they alfo were really alive unto God, and could not defire to live any longer in fin.

This is true with refpect to all thofe who have this internal fpiritual change, by the wafhing of regeneration, and fprinkling of the blood of Chrift fignified by baptifm; though they were baptized only by fprinkling. They are trully and fpiritually baptized into his death—They " are buried with him by their baptifm into " death;" and they alfo " are trully rifen with " him through the faith of the operation of God, " who hath raifed Chrift from the dead."

Let us not, my hearers, be too ftrenuous, but candid and generous to our brethren, who feem to be a little ftraitened on this fubject. Let us allow, that the apoftle has reference to the external mode of baptifm. It will then prove that plunging is an allowed mode—But grant that it was an approved mode; grant that it was a mode of baptifm practized in thofe warmer climes; and, ftill farther, grant that it was the only mode practifed by the apoftles, even then it will not by any means follow, that plunging is the only Chriftian baptifm. It is not exprefsly commanded, and exclufively enjoined by our Lord and Mafter, in the original inftitution; neither any where elfe in the facred fcriptures, is it intimated to be his will.

Some, to prove dipping to be the only baptifm, have made ufe of 1 Cor. x. 2. " And were " all baptifed unto Mofes, in the cloud, and in " the fea." But it is probable, that they who imagine it to the purpofe, are ftill where our fa-

thers were, under a cloud, and have not yet paſſed through the ſea. Should any think it refers
to the mode of Chriſtian baptiſm, I ſhall only
obſerve, that the ſpray of the waters on the
right and left, and the miſt of the cloud above,
as they paſſed through the ſea, gently ſprinkling
them, do as aptly repreſent, to an impartial
mind, the mode of ſprinkling. But the apoſtle,
Eph. iv. 5. ſays, "One Lord, one faith, one
"baptiſm." It is true that we acknowledge but
one baptiſm by water, even *that* inſtituted by
our bleſſed Lord in our text; but ſtill there may
be different ways of applying the water in the
ſacred waſhing, ſuch as may anſwer a good conſcience, and may moſt aptly repreſent the manner of his death with Chriſt, as to ſin, and his
riſing again to ſpiritual life. The three modes
uſed in the proteſtant church, taken together,
may moſt fitly repreſent the out-pouring of that
all-powerful influence of the Holy Spirit, by
which the command comes home to the guilty
ſoul; by which ſin revives, and is overwhelmed in death. They may alſo repreſent that ſpiritual waſhing of regeneration and ſprinkling of
the precious blood of Chriſt, by which the ſoul
is cleanſed from ſin and guilt, and riſes with
Chriſt to a new ſpiritual life and comfort, thro'
faith, which is of the operation of God.

On the whole, it at leaſt is evident, that our
brethren the Baptiſts ought to be a little leſs poſitive on this ſubject, and more modeſt and charitable toward thoſe who differ from them in
that reſpect. They hold that without dipping
or plunging the body all under the water, there is
no Chriſtian baptiſm; eſteeming themſelves;

from this principle, the only Chriſtian church in the world: They will hold no Chriſtian communion with any of the proteſtant churches.

The Epiſcopal church adminiſters baptiſm by pouring, and thoſe of their communion uſe that mode. We think the mode of ſprinkling as ſcriptural as pouring or plunging; but yet we can uſe either mode as may beſt anſwer a good conſcience to him who is baptiſed.

The mode of baptizing, by ſprinkling clean water, we think was holden forth by the Jewiſh types, and clearly foretold of the Chriſtian church in Ezek. xxxvi. 25, 26. " Then will I
" ſprinkle clean water upon you, and ye ſhall
" be clean from all your filthineſs, and from all
" your idols will I cleanſe you.—A new heart
" alſo will I give you, and a new ſpirit will I put
" within you; and I will take away the ſtony
" heart out of your fleſh, and I will give you a
" heart of fleſh." It is expreſly promiſed to Chriſt, in Iſa. lii. 15. " So ſhall he ſprinkle ma-
" ny nations; the kings ſhall ſhut their mouths
" at him, for that which had not been told them
" ſhall they ſee: and that which they had not
" heard, ſhall they conſider." This mode of baptiſm is very expreſſive of our being waſhed and cleanſed from our ſins, filth, and pollution, by the precious blood of Chriſt, which is, therefore, called the blood of ſprinkling. Heb. xii. 22—24. " But ye are come unto Mount Zion—
" and to Jeſus the Mediator of the New-Cove-
" nant, and to the blood of ſprinkling, that
" ſpeaketh better things than that of Abel."—
1 Pet. i. 2. " Elect according to the fore-know-

" ledge of God the Father through fanctificati-
" on of the Spirit unto obedience, and fprinkling
" of the blood of Jefus Chrift."

Upon the whole, it is clear to me, beyond a doubt, and I ferioufly think it will alfo appear to every impartial mind, that it was not the defign of Chrift to confine his church in the adminiftration of baptifm, to either of the modes which have been mentioned. He, therefore, has given fufficient light in his word, to countenance the ufe of either mode, as the circumftances and neceffities of his people may require. To afcertain the proper fubjects of this ordinance, is a matter of much greater importance. I fhall, therefore, proceed upon that fubject, after making a few remarks.

1. Our brethren are moft certainly wrong and fchifmatical, in rejecting all other Chriftian churches, on account of their difference in the mode of adminiftering baptifm. They have no fufficient warrant to make dipping or plunging effential to the very being of baptifm.—We do not doubt that many of them think they are right; but it is very clear to me, that fuch have never thoroughly and impartially examined the facred fcriptures, or have not yet learned what that meaneth, "I will have mercy and not fa-
" crifice."

2. We may, and ought to own thofe minifters and churches which Chrift Jefus owns, and bleffes with his graces, prefence and influence in the adminiftration of his word and ordinances, agreeably to his precious promife in the text.—
We believe he thus owns fome of the Baptift

churches and ministers; and, if we make the comparison, we trust some of our ministers and churches are nothing behind them. Should we not then bless God together, and love one another as brethren? Who objects to this? Let him answer it to our Lord and master. But rather let him now, in love, receive the light and truth as it is in Jesus—let him learn to be less bitter and censorious—let him be more modest and charitable towards the church of Christ, and let him not make a schism where Christ makes no difference.

3. It is of great importance as matters now stand, that we all should critically and impartially examine the sacred scriptures on this point. Important for us that we may know and have our minds established in the truth; and be able to "stand fast in the liberty wherewith Christ has made us free." Important for the Baptists, that they may be less zealous in matters non essential; but more zealous in the things that make for the peace, and the edifying of the body of Christ in love; lest some of them suffer loss when they shall be saved so as by fire, and others stand reproved in the great day of the Lord.

SERMON II.

THE QUALIFICATIONS IN ADULTS FOR ADMISSION TO BAPTISM.

A C T S viii. 37.
And Philip said, if thou believest with all thine heart, thou mayest.

THIS was the anfwer given by Philip, an eminent preacher of the gofpel, to the Ethiopian Eunuch's requeft to be baptized. " See," faid the Eunuch, " here is water; what doth hin-" der me to be baptized?" Philip replied, " if thou " believeft with all thine heart, thou mayeft."— The Ethiopian anfwered, " I believe that Jefus " Chrift is the Son of God." Upon this profeffion he was baptized.

There are two queftions about the proper fubjects of baptifm. One refpects adult perfons— the other infants. Our text has immediate reference only to the former, and is a proper anfwer to that queftion.

We fhall, therefore, now proceed to confider, who, among the adults to whom the gofpel is preached, are to be baptized, or what qualifications in fuch are neceffary to baptifm. Let it here be well remembered, that as the facred fcriptures are the rule we muft neither increafe, nor

diminifh the qualifications therein prefcribed.—
I fhall, therefore, call your attention,

I. To the facred fcriptures on this fubject.—
And then proceed,

II. To prove the neceffary qualifications for adult baptifm, from the nature, ufe, and defign of the facred inftitution.

The enquiry now before us is, who among the adults, that live under the light of the gofpel, and are capable of hearing and underftanding its folemn and interefting report, are to be baptized?—The obfervations which fhall be made in this difcourfe, are to be underftood with reference only to thefe. The other queftion, refpecting infants, muft be diftinctly confidered in another place.

On this fubject, my brethren, we have the Bible open before us; but the text claims our firft attention, becaufe of its place at the head of this difcourfe; " If thou believeft with all thine " heart, thou mayeft" be baptized. This text muft be allowed to import, that if thou doft not believe with all thy heart, thou muft not be baptized—I may not baptize thee. It is evident that Philip here intended two things by his anfwer. 1. To refer the Eunuch to his own confcience before God. 2. To obtain fome credible evidence of the true ftate of his mind. The firft being clear, the Eunuch readily and folemnly anfwers the fecond in the following emphatical words—*I believe that Jefus Chrift is the Son of God.* What kind of faith is here required by the

Evangelift, is the only queftion that remains to determine the fenfe of the text; for it muft be fuppofed, that the Eunuch profeffed the fame faith which Philip required. Some imagine it to be only what is called an hiftorical faith—A common bare affent of the underftanding to the hiftory of the gofpel—fuch as thofe commonly have who are educated under its light. But how this can be called believing with all the heart, can hardly be conceived, fince the very difinition wholly excludes the heart.

Others fuppofe it is the faith that, in fome meafure, realizes to the mind the folemnity and importance of the facts holden up to view in the gofpel, which muft greatly affect the foul, and make the finner tremble; but does not imply any change of heart, or real conformity of it to the things believed.—But how can this be a believing with all the heart, which is, according to the fuppofition, a believing againft the heart!— Thus the apoftle fays, " The devils believe and " tremble." But let the fcripture explain itfelf, and we fhall not here be at a lofs. Rom. x. 9, 10. " That if you fhalt confefs with thy mouth " the Lord Jefus, and fhalt believe in thine heart " that God hath raifed him from the dead, thou " fhalt be faved. For with the heart man be- " lieveth unto righteoufnefs, and with the mouth " confeffion is made unto falvation." To believe in the heart, and with the heart, is a faving faith in fcripture-language; " For with the heart man " believeth unto righteoufnefs." It is alfo obfervable, that the true confeffion with the mouth flows from a believing heart; for thus confeffion is made unto falvation.

It is evident, that in order to baptifm, the Evangelift required faving faith in Chrift, and that of one alfo who was not a heathen. It feems, hence, clearly to follow, that of thofe to whom the gofpel is preached, no one is to be baptized but the believer, and he only upon giving credible evidence of his faving faith in Chrift Jefus. This agrees with the moft obvious fenfe of the commiffion, Matth. xxviii. 19. Mark xvi. 15, 16. " Go ye, therefore, and teach all nations, bap" tizing them in the name of the Father, and of " the Son, and of the Holy Ghoft. And he faid " unto them, Go ye into all the world, and " preach the gofpel unto every creature. He " that believeth and is baptized fhall be faved; " but he that believeth not fhall be damned."

It accords with the doctrine Chrift taught long before, fee John iii. 5. " Jefus anfwered, and faid " unto him, Verily, verily, I fay unto thee, ex" cept a man be born again he cannot fee the " kingdom of God. Jefus anfwered, Verily, ve" rily, I fay unto thee, except a man be born of " water, and of the fpirit, he cannot enter into " the kingdom of God."

It alfo feems to have been the uniform practice of all the apoftles, according to the infpired records of their conduct. Acts ii. 38—41 " Then " Peter faid unto them, repent and be baptized, " every one of you in the name of Jefus Chrift, " for the remiffion of fins, and ye fhall receive " the gift of the Holy Ghoft. Then they that " gladly received his word were baptized; and " the fame day there were added unto them a" bout three thoufand fouls."

True repentance neceffarily implies a change of heart; therefore to give up ourfelves to be baptized in the name of Jefus Chrift, as called upon in the text, pre-fuppofes a faving faith.— It pre-fuppofes that faith, which is connected with the forgivenefs of fins. But to clearly determine the matter, it is added in the 41ft verfe, " Then they that gladly received the word," which is the fame as believing with all the heart, " were baptized." Here it is manifeft that the apoftles baptized none of the many thoufands, who heard them preach on that folemn occafion, but thofe who appeared cordially to embrace the gofpel, Acts viii. 12, 13. " But when they be-
" lieved Philip preaching the things concerning
" the kingdom of God, and the name of Jefus
" Chrift, they were baptized, both men and wo-
" men. Then Simon himfelf believed alfo," &c. Simon was baptized only on the fuppofition of faving faith, and was rejected immediately when it appeared, that he was in the gall of bitternefs, and bonds of iniquity. I find no example in this facred hiftory, of adult perfons, who were baptized, but what confirms the fame thing.*

Upon the whole, it is very evident, that though the apoftles preached the gofpel to every creature, to Jews and Gentiles, yet they baptized no adult perfons, unlefs they made a profeffion of real religion, and gave credible evidence of faving faith in the Lord Jefus Chrift. Thus it appears from fcripture, that nothing fhort of true and faving faith renders an adult perfon a proper fubject of Chriftian baptifm.—I fhall now proceed.

* See the inftance of Lydia and the Jailor—Acts xvi. 15—34.

II. To argue the neceſſary qualifications for adult baptiſm, from the nature, uſe, and deſign of the ſacred inſtitution.

Under this head I ſhall endeavor to ſhew, from a variety of conſiderations, that faith in Chriſt, and nothing ſhort of it, qualifies an adult perſon for baptiſm.

This will appear, *firſt*, from the uſe of baptiſm as an initiating ordinance into the church. Our bleſſed Saviour, ſpeaking of adult perſons, ſays, John iii. 3. " Except a man be born again he " cannot ſee the kingdom of God." In the 5th verſe—" except a man be born of water, and of " the Spirit, he cannot enter into the kingdom of " God. And in John xviii. 36. " Jeſus anſwer" ed, my kingdom is not of this world. If my " kingdom were of this world, then would my " ſervants fight, that I ſhould not be delivered to " the Jews; but now is my kingdom not from " hence." The apoſtle alſo aſſerts, Titus ii. 14. " That Chriſt gave himſelf to redeem us from all " iniquity, and to purify unto himſelf a peculiar " people, zealous of good works."

If the church of Chriſt is to conſiſt of a peculiar people, ſeparated from the world—if a man muſt be born of the Spirit to enter into this kingdom, it muſt follow that baptiſm, which introduces an adult perſon into the viſible church, as a qualified member, ought not to be adminiſtered to any of theſe but upon credible evidence, that they are thus qualified. This is exactly agreeable to the anſwer of our queſtion, in the Shorter Catechiſm, which ſays, " That baptiſm is not to be administered to any who are out of the visible church, until they profess their faith in Christ, and obedience to him."

2. From the design of baptism, as a seal of the covenant of promise, both on God's, and on our part. In this covenant are promises to the church in general, and to the believer in particular, for himself and his children, as I shall shew on another occasion. But nothing short of faith in Christ brings an adult person into this covenant, and entitles him to the promises. The promises are yea and amen, only in Christ Jesus, agreeably to 2 Cor. i. 20. Since it is by faith only that a person, who acts for himself, or who, according to the gracious constitution, acts for others, agrees to the covenant, or takes hold of the promise, it is a great absurdity to administer baptism, which is a seal of the covenant to any adult unbeliever. Faith, therefore, in Christ, or an hearty agreement to the covenant on our part is absolutely necessary to baptism.

3. Adult baptism is a public solemn profession, that we do forsake our sins, that we renounce our idols, and give ourselves and ours to God through Jesus Christ. But no person actually does this except he has faith in Jesus Christ. Philip, therefore, said, " If thou believest with all " thine heart thou mayest" be baptized. Consequently true faith is a necessary qualification in adult baptism. But to sum up the whole, and bring it before you in one view—If adult baptism signifies any thing spiritual on the part of the baptized, if it seals to him any promise for himself, or for his children, it must suppose real faith. For example:

The washing away of our sins by the blood of Christ must certainly suppose faith in Christ, or else it signifies that which is not true. If it seals to adults the promised blessings of the new covenant for themselves, or for their children, it is only through Christ, and necessarily supposes faith. In whatever light we consider the subject, saving faith appears to be a qualification essentially necessary for adult baptism. All the instances of adult baptism, we have recorded in the sacred scriptures, are full on this point. They clearly shew, that the apostles, and primitive disciples of Christ did not baptize any to whom they preached the gospel, on the supposition of a mere historical faith, or because they were only seriously affected. Felix trembled, but was not baptized. And, no doubt, many others trembled under the powerful preaching of the apostles on the day of Pentecost; but we do not read that any of them were baptized, except those who gladly received the word. When the apostles went out to the Gentiles, they preached the gospel to vast multitudes; but we do not find that they baptized any adults, either men or women, except those who made a credible profession of their faith in Christ.

We have sufficient light, therefore, whether we look directly to the scriptures, or reason on the nature, use, and design of this institution, to shew us that faith is an essential pre-requisite to adult baptism; or that this ordinance must not be administered to any but through the qualifying influence of this grace. The reason is obvious. All the promised blessings of the covenant of grace are treasured in Christ for his church and people, and flow out to them only through faith. This alone unites us to him, and gives us a gracious title to the privileges and bleſſings granted to believers, either for themſelves or their children. The apoſtle addreſſed the multitude on the day of Pentecoſt, exactly in this connexion.

Preſſing on them the call to repentance, faith, and baptiſm, by this very argument, he ſaid, "Repent and be baptized every one of you in "the name of Jeſus Chriſt, for the remiſſion of "ſins—For the promiſe is to you, and to your "children." It is plain, that there is neither force nor propriety in this, unleſs repentance and faith were neceſſary to baptiſm, and to the enjoyment of the bleſſings and privileges of the goſpel church.

That which qualifies an adult perſon for baptiſm, gives him, through this ordinance, an equal right to enjoy all the privileges and bleſſings of the free citizens of Zion. But nothing ſhort of faith in Chriſt can give an adult perſon, before God, and nothing ſhort of a credible profeſſion of it can, in the view of the church, give him a right to the enjoyment of all theſe bleſſings and privileges. Faith in Chriſt, therefore, muſt be conſidered as an eſſential qualification for adult baptiſm—And, upon the ſtricteſt examination, this will be found to be agreeable to the practice of the church in pureſt times. It alſo has been the ſentiment and practice of the moſt pious and ſuccefsful miniſters of Chriſt in every age of the church—and it agrees with the confeſſion of the faith of our church, and I believe of all the beſt reformed churches in the world. This discourse shall now be closed with a few remarks.

1. Baptism is a solemn institution. It is undoubtedly of equal authority and solemnity with the holy ordinance, the Lord's supper. Some seem to have loose ideas of baptism, and of the qualifications necessary for its proper subjects, who, at the same time, are very superstitious respecting the holy supper. But, according to scripture, they are both on the same foundation—Both equally solemn and sacred. They have one author. They are seals of the same covenant; and they are both sacraments of the new testament, and require the same qualifications in adult persons—In both we have to deal with a heart-searching God; and we are to give up ourselves in covenant to him, through Jesus Christ, to be his for ever.—The sin of coming unqualified to both, is equally heinous—The prophanation of either is equally dangerous.—He who comes properly qualified to baptism, ought to bless God, and come cheerfully to the Lord's supper.

2. The true church is founded on the rock Christ Jesus. Since baptism is the initiating ordinance into the church, faith in Christ is necessary to baptism in adult persons. A credible profession of this faith is the ground upon which baptism is to be administered to any adult person. Accordingly we find that when Peter professed his faith in Christ, our blessed Saviour answered, (Matt. xvi. 18.) " And I say also unto " thee that thou art Peter, and upon this rock " I will build my church; and the gates of hell

"shall not prevail against it." There may be other churches, and indeed there must be other churches, who are not built on this foundation, and make not any, or a different profession.— They may be numerous and flourishing; but they certainly will be entirely consumed when every man's work shall be tried by fire.

3. The church of Christ ought to hold the ordinance of baptism, very dear and sacred. This not only signifies and seals to believers the inestimable blessings and privileges of the new covenant, but is the ordinance of admission into the church. Oh! how careful should the ministers and churches of Christ be in their conduct, lest this sacred ordinance be prophaned! They should always be vigilant, lest any should prostitute it to purposes foreign to the sacred design of its institution. The world should know that ministers have no right, but from Christ, to administer baptism to any. Every one ought to know, that it is not a matter of favor with them, which they may bestow at pleasure, but at their peril. The word of God is their rule: And we all know, or ought to know, that when this sacred institution is misapplied and abused, it is always attended with some of the worst consequences, both to the church and to the souls of men.

4. They who despise and wilfully neglect this ordinance, cannot be Christians. Though we do not hold that baptism is absolutely necessary to salvation; yet since it is a positive institution of Christ, and enjoined on his church as a standing ordinance, they who wilfully neglect it, they

who defpife it, are certainly chargeable with continued difobedience to him, and muft be confidered as deftitute of the diftinguifhing qualifications of Chriftians.

5. All thofe who are baptized are under moft folemn obligations to live holy lives—They are given up to God—They are fet apart for him—They ought to give up themfelves wholly to God and his fervice, and to live foberly, righteoufly and godly in all manner of converfation. For them now to live in fin, and to purfue the ways of the wicked, is to deny their baptifm; is to difown the God of their fathers, and to load their fouls with aggravated guilt. Be perfuaded then, all you of this chara&ter, to renounce your tranfgreffions, fpare your own fouls, and give glory to God through Jefus Chrift. Some of you have folemnly acknowledged thefe obligations before God and his people; and have fealed the covenant at the Lord's table: You ought, therefore, to love and ferve him, whom you have thus acknowledged to be your God and Saviour. Confider, Oh! confider how aggravated your fins muft be againft fuch folemn ties! Can you think any obligations fo facred, fo folemn, fo often confirmed, as thofe which you are under, to forfake all the ways of fin, to live to God, and to ferve him with your whole foul?

SERMON III.

INFANT BAPTISM.

GAL. iii. 29.

And if ye be Chrift's, then are ye Abraham's feed, and heirs according to the promife.

RESPECTING the eternal council of God the Father, and the defign of his grace towards our loft world, we are informed, John iii. 16. That " God fo loved the world that he gave " his only begotten Son, that whofoever believ-" eth in him fhould not perifh, but have ever-" lafting life."

To complete this glorious work of falvation; to redeem us from all iniquity, and purify unto himfelf a peculiar people; to deftroy fatan's kingdom and to bring glory to God in the falvation of finners—Jefus Chrift was appointed Mediator of the New-Covenant. It pleafed God, foon after the fall of man, to reveal this gracious defign, and fet up his church and kingdom on earth, which he has fupported in every age of the world. To the members of this kingdom, God has, at different times, promifed certain bleffings, and granted certain privileges gradually' difplaying the riches of his grace and goodnefs, in a variety of fucceffive difpenfations. The firft gracious intimation is recorded Gen. iii. 15.

where it is promised, that "The seed of the wo-
"man shall bruise the serpent's head." It pleased God more fully to reveal this glorious design
to Abraham. With him he established a gracious covenant; a covenant which contained certain promises. To him he also granted certain
blessings and privileges, both for his natural and
spiritual seed, (Gen. xvii. 7.) Upon this I shall
hereafter have occasion to speak more fully.—
God thus constituted him the Father of the
Faithful. He thus established his covenant, that
they should not only pattern his faith, but that
all his spiritual seed or children should also inherit the spiritual blessings and privileges of the
covenant of promise. This the apostle, more
than once or twice, expressly asserts in our context. "Know ye, therefore, that they which are
"of faith, the same are the children of Abraham.
"And the scripture foreseeing that God would
"justify the heathen through faith, preached be-
"fore the gospel unto Abraham, saying, In thee
"shall all nations be blessed. So then they
"which be of faith are blessed with faithful Abra-
"ham. That the blessing of Abraham might
"come on the Gentiles through Jesus Christ;
"that we might receive the promise of the Spirit
"through faith. For ye are all the children of
"God by faith in Christ Jesus."* Then he sums
up the whole in our text. "If ye be Christ's,
"then are ye Abraham's seed, and heirs accord-
"ing to the promise." That the promise here
mentioned, contained spiritual blessings and privileges: that God granted these to Abraham as
the Father of the Faithful; that it was one of
those blessings contained in this covenant of

* Verses. 7, 8, 9, 14, 26.

promife; that infants were to be received with their parents into the church, and have the feal of the righteoufnefs of faith adminiftered to them —that this blefling, or privilege of Abraham, is now come upon the Gentiles, through faith in Chrift, as is afferted in the 14th verfe—and that all who are Chrift's, are Abraham's feed and heirs according to the promife as exprefled in our text, feem to be inconteftable truths. The doctrine inferred from the words of our text, in this connexion, as the fubject of the enfuing difcourfe, is,

That believers under the gofpel difpenfation have a right to baptifm for their infant children, or that the infants of fuch are to be baptized.

To illuftrate and eftablifh this doctrine, it is propofed by divine affiftance to fhew,

I. That God did gracioufly grant unto Abraham, as the father of believers, that infants fhould be received into the vifible church with their parents.

II. That God commanded, that the feal of the righteoufnefs of faith fhould be adminiftered unto them.

III. That this great privilege is, under the gofpel, confirmed and continued to believers. Or that the infant children of believers are to be baptized.

I. I am to fhow, That God did gracioufly grant unto Abraham, as the father of believers, that infants should be received into the visible church with their parents.

That the truth of this may clearly appear, several things command particular attention.

1. At a time when religion was very low in the world, and when the visible church was almost extinct, God called Abraham out from the wicked world, in order to set up his church and kingdom in his family.*

2. When God had tried and proved Abraham's faith and obedience,† he established his covenant with him as an everlasting covenant, and set up his church in Abraham's house.‡ Here we see certain commands enjoined on Abraham; certain institutions for him to observe, and certain blessings and privileges granted to him for himself, and for his seed. These blessings were to continue in the church, and to descend to his children through succeeding ages. This was an everlasting covenant. " I will be a God to thee, " and to thy seed after thee."

3. Let it be strictly observed, that the spiritual blessings contained in this covenant, were granted to Abraham as a father to the faithful. They are summed up in these emphatical words; " I " will be a God to thee, and to thy seed after " thee." The Jews themselves understood it in this view, but confined the blessings, both spiritual and temporal, to Abraham's natural seed through the law. This gross mistake the apostle corrects, in the chapter containing our text,

* Gen. Chap. 12.   † Chap. 15, 16.   ‡ Chap. 17.

by clearly shewing, that they were designed for his spiritual seed also, through the gospel, whether Jews or Gentiles. The true state of the matter was this—The visible church at that time was almost swallowed up in a deluge of idolatry, and wickedness—but God was pleased to call forth Abraham, and begin a new dispensation of grace to his church. To display more fully his glorious design, he gave richer promises, and granted more ample privileges.

This was to be an everlasting covenant, Gen. xvii. 7. " And I will establish my covenant be-
" tween me and thee, and thy seed after thee, in
" their generations, for an everlasting covenant,
" to be a God unto thee and thy seed after thee."

4. In this dispensation of his grace to his church, he expresly granted unto Abraham this great privilege, that infants should be received into the visible church with their parents; and he ordered that the sign of the covenant should be administered to every male child at eight days old. The same day, in obedience to the divine command, was Abraham circumcised, and his son Ishmael.*

Here, my brethren, was something new and glorious—Abraham, through this covenant, no doubt, saw Christ, the glorious head of all his spiritual seed, and was glad, as our blessed Saviour observes.†

Under this dispensation you see that God appointed and commanded, that infants should be

* Genesis xvii.   † John viii. 56.

received into the church with their parents. Infants, by circumcifion as an initiating ordinance, were admitted into the church. Thus the apoftle fays, Acts vii. 8. "And he gave him the co-
"venant of circumcifion. And fo Abraham be-
"gat Ifaac, and circumcifed him the eighth day," &c.

It is very evident that the church once poffeffed this ineftimable privilege of giving up their children to God in the covenant of promife; and it is as evident that by the fpecial command of God, the faithful, in the only true church, enjoyed the fame through fucceeding ages. They alfo had many precious promifes for their children recorded in the facred oracles, all which are yea and amen in Chrift Jefus to believers.— Of this I fhall have occafion to fpeak more freely in another place.

II. I propofe to fhew, that God did command, that the feal of the righteoufnefs of faith fhould be adminiftered to infants. To prevent a difficulty from arifing in your minds, I would here obferve, that no fign nor feal, which is wholly legal, and refpects only temporal bleffings, can, with any propriety, be called a feal of the righteoufnefs of faith. Thofe who believe the facred fcriptures, cannot doubt, that God commanded circumcifion to be adminiftered to infants of eight days old.*

It is commanded, that not only Abraham muft circumcife his own children, but it is exprefsly commanded, that his feed after him muft be cir-

* Genefis vii. 10—12—14.

cumcifed in their generations. So ſtrict was the command, that every uncircumcifed male child was ordered to be cut off from God's people, becauſe he had broken the covenant. Some, perhaps, may ſay, that this is nothing to the purpoſe, for circumciſion was a carnal, legal, bloody ordinance. They may ſay, that it was a covenant of works, and could have no reſpect to Chriſtian baptiſm. But, my hearers, let your minds be calm and attentive. As for ſuch ranters, let them take heed leſt they be found to oppoſe the apoſtle, and contradict the ſpirit of inſpiration. Circumciſion was a ſeal of the righteouſneſs of faith, The very ſame circumciſion which God appointed, and commanded to be adminiſtered to infants, who were, by it, admitted into the covenant of promiſe with their parents, was a ſeal of the righteouſneſs of faith.— Faith is not of works, but of grace.

Whatever ends circumciſion might be ſuppoſed to anſwer in this, or the ſucceeding diſpenſation, yet it was here a ſeal of the righteouſneſs of that faith, by which a believer is juſtified and ſaved. The apoſtle Paul referring expreſsly to this command of circumciſion, and ſpeaking of the bleſſedneſs of thoſe whoſe ſins are forgiven, ſays, Romans iv. 9, 10, 11, 12. " Cometh this
" bleſſedneſs then upon the circumciſion only,
" or upon the uncircumciſion alſo? for we ſay
" that faith was reckoned to Abraham for righ-
" teouſneſs.—How was it then reckoned? when
" he was in circumciſion, or in uncircumciſion?
" Not in circumciſion, but in uncircumciſion.—
" And he received the ſign of circumciſion, a ſeal
" of the righteouſneſs of the faith which he had

"yet being uncircumcifed: that he might be the father of all them that believe, though they be not circumcifed, that righteoufnefs might be imputed unto them alfo:—And the father of circumcifion to them who are not of the circumcifion only, but who alfo walk in the fteps of that faith of our father Abraham, which he had being yet uncircumcifed."

Having proved to you that circumcifion was a feal of the righteoufnefs of faith, and having proved, that God himfelf commanded it to be adminiftered to infants as a ftanding ordinance in his church, under the Abrahamic and Mofaic difpenfations of the covenant of promife, it, therefore, muft be evident to every impartial mind, that the true church once had this grant from heaven, and that the members of the vifible church did once, and for a long time enjoy this great, this interefting privilege. They did give up their infant offspring to God, and in token of this the feal of the righteoufnefs of faith was adminiftered to them.

Thefe are the points which were to be eftablifhed under the firft and fecond heads of this difcourfe. But before I proceed to the next head, it may be neceffary to anfwer fome objections, which have been thrown in the way of the truth, and which may ftill be lurking in fome of your minds.

It has been faid, that the law given at Sinai difannulled this covenant with Abraham; that the law was four hundred and thirty years after this; and that, fince it was an entire new difpenfation, attended with many new ceremonies, it muſt have rendered the Abrahamic difpenfation ufelefs. In confequence of this remark, fome have faid, that all arguments drawn thence are of no weight, and tend only to confufe and deceive weak minds. All this is very plaufible, indeed, and may have great weight with fome; but it is eafy to fhew every candid mind that the affertion is falfe, and that the objection has no force.

1. Though it fhould be granted that the Abrahamic difpenfation ceafed, when fucceeded by the Mofaic economy; yet it will by no means follow, that the covenant of promife was made void. Neither will it follow, that any of the bleſſings and privileges once granted to believers, were taken away. Theſe may ſtand good, and promifed bleſſings be more clearly holden up to view, and more liberally beſtowed on the church, in a new way, by the fucceeding difpenfation, agreeably to the gracious defign of God, more fully to difplay his mercy.

2. It is certain, that circumcifion, as a fign of the Abrahamic covenant, and as a feal of the righteoufnefs of faith, was continued under the Jewifh difpenfation; that the privileges granted to the church were continued—that many of the bleſſings promifed to Abraham, as the father of believers, were enjoyed by the Jewifh church, and that God beſtowed thefe bleſſings on that people, as the God of Abraham, the God of Ifaac, and the God of Jacob. It, therefore, muſt follow, that the Abrahamic covenant was not made void by the Jewifh difpenfation.

F

3. But what is more than all, we have the apostle's exprefs declaration on this head—a declaration, which, when properly confidered, muft for ever filence all fuch objectors. Gal. iii. 17. "And this I fay, that the covenant that was confirmed before of God in Chrift, the law which was four hundred and thirty years after cannot difannul, that it fhould make the promife of none effect." If the law, or Jewifh difpenfation, had made void this great promife, or privilege, it would now have been of none effect.—The bleffings could not have come upon us Gentiles.

III. It is here propofed to fhew, that the privilege once granted to Abraham, as the father of believers, that infants fhould be received into the vifible church with their parents, is confirmed under the gofpel, and is continued to believers. Here it would be eafy to fhew, that all the promifes, bleffings and privileges of the church, contained in every difpenfation, in all their true fpiritual meaning, are, under the gofpel, confirmed and continued to believers; but we are confined, by the narrow limits of our difcourfe, to only one privilege. But let it be our prefent comfort, that this is not fmall.

1. Every fpiritual privilege once granted to the church by its great King and Head, remains in full force until repealed. This may be thus illuftrated—God once granted unto Abraham, as a father in the church, the privilege of giving up himfelf in covenant. This remained in force under the Jewifh difpenfation to all his feed, and as it is not yet repealed, remains ftill in force to

all his fpiritual children. This, I believe, will hold good with refpect to all the fpiritual bleffings and privileges God has granted to his church in every age. Modes and fhadows may be changed, but the fubftance ftill remains. It has been proved, that God did grant and confirm unto his church the privilege that infants fhould be received into the vifible church with their parents, and that the feal of the righteoufnefs of faith fhould be given unto them. This, unlefs it has been repealed, moft certainly remains as an inheritance for believers, which they may enjoy as members of the vifible, church and true children of Abraham. For to ufe the apoftle's argument, believers are all one in Chrift Jefus, and if ye be Chrift's, then are ye Abraham's feed, and heirs according to the promife.

If believers have now an undoubted right, by heirfhip, to all the privileges of the covenant of promife granted to Abraham, which are not repealed under the gofpel, we may boldly affert, that if this privilege is not now repealed, the command of God is now on all true believers to give up their infants to him in covenant; and, as a token to this, ought to adminifter to them that which is now the fign of the covenant, and feal of the righteoufnefs of faith.

But we believe, and confidently affirm, that all the fpiritual bleffings and privileges formerly granted to the church are now in full force.

We have particularly proved, that this privilege alfo was once granted, it, therefore, remains confirmed under the gofpel, and continued to believers. Those who undertake to release Christians from this command of God, and deny believers the inestimable pleasure of giving up their dear infant-offspring to God in covenant through Jesus Christ, ought now solemnly to prove, that this privilege is made void by the gospel. The burden of proof now lies upon our brethren, the Baptists. Here we ought alway to put the laboring oar into their hands, and then let them labor since they will undertake it. But, alas! their task here is as difficult as it is unthankful. —Our blessed Saviour charges us not to think that he came to " destroy the law and the pro-" phets," (Matth. v. 17.) The apostle also assures us, that all the promises are yea and amen in Christ Jesus, (2 Cor. i. 20.) Agreeably to this we may be assured that Christ came to be unto his dear people all that the law typified of him —to fulfil all that the prophets foretold of him, and to bestow all the spiritual blessings promised in his word.

But let us calmly hear, and let us without prejudice examine what our brethren the Baptists say to prove that this privilege is repealed by the gospel.

1. It is said that this covenant belonged to the Jewish dispensation, which was wholly done away by Christ, and that consequently it is now of no force.

Ans. 1. But though we allow that the Jewish dispensation is now wholly done away—though we also grant that this privilege belonged to it, yet it will not follow that this, or, indeed, any of the spiritual blessings and privileges are now repealed. We must here distinguish between a dispensation, and the blessings dispensed. The former is the way in which the latter are displayed and communicated. The Jewish dispensation was only the manner which God chose, by various laws, types and shadows to display and communicate the blessings of his covenant to the Jewish church. It is easy to see, that one dispensation may entirely cease and give place to another, and yet all the covenant-blessings and privileges of the former may be continued, and, indeed, many more added and enjoyed under the latter. This, in fact, has been the case in the church through various successive dispensations, as might very easily be shewn, were it necessary.

2. But we utterly deny that the covenant of promise containing the privilege for which we contend, ever belonged to the Jewish dispensation. We assert the reverse, that the Mosaic dispensation belonged wholly to this, and was added four hundred and thirty years after, for special reasons as the apostle says.* Since therefore, the giving of the law did not disannul the covenant of promise, the taking of it away, certainly could not destroy the privilege for which we contend. Neither could it make void the solemn command by which it was enjoined, nor hinder the blessing of Abraham, in this respect, from coming on the Gentiles. This is most evidently the true state of the matter. When the Jewish dispensation was taken away, the covenant command and promise, with all the spiritual privileges and blessings, came under the gos-

* Gal. iii. 17, 18.

pel difpenfation confirmed to true believers, the fpiritual feed of Abraham, the true heirs according to the promife. Thus it is eafy to fee, how the bleffing of Abraham is now come on us Gentiles.

To this it is objected that the promife of the land of Canaan is done away. Though this objection is not fo very evident in every refpect; Yet grant it, and then the heavenly Canaan remains to the Church, which was the fpiritual meaning of the original promife. That circumcifion is abolifhed by the gofpel, is another objection. But notwithftanding this, the fpiritual bleffings fignified by circumcifion, remain under the gofpel; and Jefus Chrift fulfils it to his people by circumcifing their hearts. Chrift, under the gofpel difpenfation, has alfo inftituted baptifm, to be the fign of the covenant, and the feal of the righteoufnefs of faith. This, therefore, is called by the apoftle the circumcifion of Chrift. Col. ii. 11, 12. "In whom alfo ye are circum-
" cifed with the circumcifion made without hands,
" in putting off the body of the fins of the flefh,
" by the circumcifion of Chrift, buried with him
" in baptifm," &c.

Baptifm now remains under the gofpel an initiating ordinance into the church. It is now the fign of the covenant of promife, and the true feal of the righteoufnefs of faith. From this there is not the leaft evidence that the command is repealed, and the granted privilege taken away; but, on the contrary, it clearly fhews, that they are in full force on believers under the gofpel.

Though the Jewish dispensation be abolished—though circumcision be done away, yet the grant is not repealed—the privilege remains to believers—the command is in full force, and since baptism is the circumcision of Christ, and a seal of the righteousness of faith, through the administration of this, the blessing of Abraham may now come upon the Gentiles. Some, to prove that this privilege is now repealed, and that infants are cut off from the church by the gospel, bring Matth. iii. 8, 9. " Bring forth, therefore, " fruits meet for repentance: And think not to " say within yourselves, We have Abraham to our " father: for I say unto you, That God is able " of these stones to raise up children unto Abra-" ham." Upon this I would make the following observations.

1. The infants of believers are here either intended, or not intended. If infants are not spoken of in this place, it is nothing to the purpose, for which it is cited. But should any say, that the infants of believers are here intended, and are by this cut off from the church as well as others, it will also as certainly follow, according to verses 10—12. " That since they cannot bring forth " fruit, they will also be hewn down, and cast in-" to unquenchable fire."

2. The truth is this, adult persons only are intended by John in this address. They are trees full grown, which must bring forth good fruit, or be excluded the church by the gospel, and be hewn down, and cast into unquenchable fire.— The Pharisees and Sadducees presumed that they had a good right to baptism, merely because they

were the natural feed of Abraham. But John shewed them, that under the gofpel this would be of no avail to any adults, who do not bring forth good fruit. This implies what we contend for, that all who bring forth fruit meet for repentance, fhould, under the gofpel, inherit the covenant-bleffing of Father Abraham.

Others think that, what the apoftle fays, in his epiftle to the Hebrews,* refpecting God's making a new covenant and deftroying the old, fully repeals the grant, command and promife for which we contend. But it will be evident to any one, at leaft to every impartial mind, who attentively reads this and the following chapter, that the apoftle here refers only to the law given at Sinai, or the Jewifh difpenfation. This, we have proved, may be abolifhed, and the privileges which God had before granted his church, with the command by which they were enforced, remain unaffected. Whatever, in the Jewifh difpenfation, was defigned by the old covenant, which was taken away, it could not difannul the covenant which was before confirmed in Chrift, it could not fo difannul it, as to make void any of the fpiritual privileges and bleffings. For thefe were before confirmed in Chrift to believers.— (Gal. iii. 17.

It alfo appears from this whole epiftle, that the apoftle was laboring to convince the Jews, that God's defign in the abolition of the Sinaic economy, containing many coftly, carnal, and bloody ordinances, and a worldly fanctuary, was to make way for the gofpel difpenfation, a dif-

* Hebrews viii. 7, 8, 9.

penfation which, inftead of contracting the bleſſings and privileges of his dear people, ſhould eſtabliſh them on a better foundation, with great additions, and ſhould increaſe their ſpiritual bleſſings in heavenly places in Chriſt Jeſus. Here certainly can be nothing like a repeal of the grant made to Abraham. It is worthy of particular notice, that in giving a view of the new covenant, the apoſtle makes uſe of the ſame expreſſion which God uſed with Abraham. By this he doubtleſs intended to ſhew, that the privileges granted to Abraham are confirmed and continued to believers under the goſpel.

But if the Abrahamic bleſſing reſpecting infants is confirmed and continued to believers under the goſpel, it is moſt certain that the command alſo comes clothed with all the weight of the vaſtly ſuperior light and grace which diſtinguiſh the goſpel diſpenſation. We may, with much greater propriety, inſiſt, that the Baptiſts ſhould point out a repeal of this command—that they ſhould point out an expreſs prohibition of infant-baptiſm in the New Teſtament, with much greater propriety, I ſay, than they can demand of us a new command for a privilege once granted to the church, a privilege always enjoyed before, and a privilege ſo clearly eſtabliſhed and continued to believers under the goſpel. We cannot, we dare not give up this privilege of believers without ſome expreſs warrant from God. An expreſs command from him is as neceſſary to nullify, as to eſtabliſh a poſitive inſtitution, to revoke as to grant a privilege to the church.— The Chriſtian church thus underſtood it, and both circumcifion and baptifm were at firft adminiftered together even to the Gentiles, till circumcifion was exprefsly prohibited by infpiration, and baptifm alone eftablifhed in the church, as the fign of the covenant, and feal of the righteoufnefs of faith. But there is no prohibition of the privilege granted to the church, refpecting their infant feed; it, therefore, remains to believers under the fanction of the divine command, and is fealed to them for their children in the ordinance of baptifm. We have no neceffity of a new command, fince baptifm is now the feal of the righteoufnefs of that faith by which we become the feed of Abraham, and heirs according to the promife. We might, with the greateft propriety, reft the controverfy here, for the Baptifts cannot fhew any prohibition of this privilege in the facred fcriptures—believe and be baptized refpects adult perfons in the firft inftance, and their offspring through them, as is proved. If the grant is no where repealed, it is moft certainly continued to believers under the gofpel difpenfation. But in addition to this, we think it is eafy to fhew, that this privilege is confirmed to believers in many places in the New Teftament. We have fhewn from fcripture, that God did grant this privilege unto Abraham as the father of believers, and that he did command that infants fhould be received into the vifible church with their parents, and enjoined, that the feal of the righteoufnefs of faith be adminiftered to them. When, therefore, we find the apoftle declaring, that they who are of the faith are the children of Abraham,* that they are bleffed with faithful Abraham,† that the bleff-

---

* Gal. iii. 7.   † Verfe 9.

ing of Abraham is come on the Gentiles through Jesus Christ, (Gal. iii. 14.) and then declaring, in our text, that if ye be Christ's then are ye Abraham's feed, and heirs according to the promise; we must firmly believe that this Abrahamic privilege or blessing, as well as others, is confirmed to believers under the gospel dispensation.

The apostle, in his epistle to the Romans, affirms very clearly, by a striking similitude, that the Gentile believers were to enjoy, at least, the spiritual privileges and blessings granted to the Jewish church, Romans xi. 16, 17. " For if the " first fruit be holy, the lump is also holy: and if " the root be holy, so are the branches.—And " if some of the branches be broken off, and thou, " being a wild olive-tree, wert graffed in among " them, and with them partakest of the root and " fatness of the olive-tree." For whether by the root is meant Jesus Christ, or Abraham, and by the olive-tree is understood the church, or the covenant, yet being grafted in by faith they partook of the root and fatness of the olive-tree.— This cannot be understood of the enjoyment of any thing short of the same spiritual privileges and blessings, of which the Jews were deprived. But the Jews once enjoyed this Abrahamic privilege respecting infants, and are now deprived of it by their unbelief. If Gentile believers, under the gospel, are cut off from the privilege of having their infant-offspring admitted with them into the visible church by baptism, then though they partake of the root, yet are they cut off from the fatness of the olive-tree—a consequence which is both unnatural and absurd. It is evidently contrary to the apostle's design; and it greatly weakens, if not wholly deſtroys the force of his reaſoning in this place. Our bleſſed Saviour very ſeverely reproved thoſe diſciples who forbad that little children ſhould be brought to him, that they might receive his bleſſing. On that occaſion, he gave them a command, which may be conſidered as binding upon all his diſciples. He replied, "ſuffer little children to "come unto me, and forbid them not; for, ſaid "he, of ſuch is the kingdom of God:" Or, in other words, ſuch as are brought to me by faith for my bleſſing, belong to my church, or kingdom on earth. The order which immediately follows reſpecting the admiſſion of adult members into this kingdom, ſeems to favor this ſenſe of the words, (Mark x. 14, 15.) This command alſo ſeems to be a plain confirmation of the former privilege granted to his people. Thus the apoſtle learned of Chriſt, and taught the Corinthians, (1 Cor. vii. 14. and onward) that if either parent was a believer, the children were, by God's appointment, ſet apart for him, or conſecrated, as the word, tranſlated holy, often ſignifies in the ſacred oracles.

To bring the matter to a point—That the infant children of believers are to be baptized, is a neceſſary conſequence of the propoſitions which have been already eſtabliſhed. In whatever light we take them, either together or ſeparately, it will clearly follow, that the infant children of believers are to be baptized. God granted unto Abraham, as the father of believers, that infants ſhould be received into the viſible church with their parents; and he alſo commanded that the ſeal of the righteouſneſs of faith ſhould be adminiftered unto them. But we have proved that this great privilege is, under the gofpel, confirmed and continued to believers, confequently the infants of believers, under the gofpel, are to be received into the vifible church with their parents, and, by the command of God, muft have the feal of the righteoufnefs of faith given to them, which is the Chriftian circumcifion or baptifm.

1. God did grant unto Abraham, as the father of believers, that infants fhould be received into the vifible church with their parents. All true believers, under the gofpel, are Abraham's feed, and as his children they are the true heirs, in Chrift, of this privilege, therefore, by the divine appointment, their infant children muft be received into the vifible church with them, and are to be circumcifed with the circumcifion of Chrift; or, in other words, they muft be baptized.

2. God commanded that the feal of the righteoufnefs of faith fhould be adminiftered to infants, who are received into the church with their parents. Circumcifion was once this feal in the church, but, under the gofpel, baptifm is the feal of the righteoufnefs of faith; therefore, by divine appointment, baptifm muft be adminiftered to thofe infants, who are admitted into the church with their parents under the gofpel difpenfation.

3. The great privilege, that infant children fhould be received into the church with their parents, and have the fign of the covenant, the feal of the righteoufnefs of faith, adminiftered to them, is, under the gofpel, confirmed and con-

tinued to believers. Hence it clearly follows, since baptism is the seal of the righteousness of faith, that when adult persons, upon their repentance and faith, are admitted into the gospel church, their infant children are to be received with them, and to be baptized. Thus the apostle Peter, on the day of Pentecost, in the application of that most successful sermon, applies the promise exactly to this purpose. He enforces on his affected audience the gospel call to repentance, faith and Christian baptism, by this inestimable privilege. (Acts iii. 19.) "Repent " ye, therefore, and be converted, that your sins " may be blotted out, when the times of refresh- " ing shall come from the presence of the Lord." It may not be improper here to take notice of some other passages of the sacred scriptures, which may be considered as direct proofs of infant baptism. The commission of our blessed Saviour on this point, claims our first attention, (Matt. xxviii. 19.) Though it is brought by the Baptists as an objection; yet, properly considered, I think it is so far from being in their favor, that it will afford a convincing proof of our doctrine to any person free from prepossessions.

1. The apostles were commanded to go out into all the world. Till then they had been confined to the Jews, and both circumcision and baptism were administered to those who embraced the gospel, and to their infants. There was not the least hint antecedent to this, that infants were to be excluded, but much to the contrary, as has been shewn. The apostles themselves did not know that it would be lawful for them to go out to the Gentiles; much less that infants, as

the Baptists assert, were to be cut off from this privilege in the gospel church. They were here commanded to teach all nations, and preach the gospel to every creature. It is probable that even the baptists do not imagine, that this immediately respects infants, as to the external teaching and preaching of the word, they being wholly incapable of this. But it certainly does some way respect them. The words are plain—The command is express—Go teach all nations—Go preach the gospel to every creature. Surely our Saviour, who so tenderly took the dear little ones into his gracious arms, who so affectionately blessed them, I say surely he did not forget them on this most interesting occasion—Surely he was not ignorant of the tender feelings—Surely he was not a stranger to the pious breathings of the parental heart of his dear people in ages past. On this occasion, when the life of a thousand poor Ishmaelites was at stake, he had not forgotten the burst of Abraham's fatherly heart, "Oh, that Ishmael might live before thee!" (Gen. xvii. 18.) Nor was the compassionate Saviour insensible to those pious parental desires of true believers towards their infant offspring through all future ages. Much less can any suppose, that he excludes them from the race of intelligent creatures, to whom the apostles were to preach the gospel. We must either deny that they are part of all nations—we must also either deny that they are rational creatures, or we must suppose that they are some how included in the apostles mission.

2. The apostles are hereby commanded, to teach (*mathetcusate*) to disciple all nations, and

preach the gospel to every creature. Since then it is certain, that the teaching and preaching of the gospel does some way respect infants, I confess, upon the Baptist's plan, I am utterly at a loss how to understand it, unless it be wholly to exclude them from Christian baptism, from the church, and from heaven; and either to strike them out of existence all together, or to plunge them headlong into eternal damnation. But if we understand the commission in the plain and natural sense, according to the circumstances in which it was spoken, as an honest, pious Jew would take it, and as it is clear the apostles understood it, the whole matter is plain. The teaching and preaching of the gospel, were to disciple infants by baptism with their believing parents, as had been a common known custom among the Jews, when they proselyted a heathen to the true religion.

The commission was express—It was very easy to be understood by those to whom it was given—Since they were well acquainted with the command by which infants were to be received into the church with their parents—since they knew this had always been the practice—and since they had never heard any thing to the contrary drop from the blessed lips of their divine master, but much in favor of such little ones, was it possible for them to understand it in such a manner, as to exclude the infants of believers from the church and from baptism?

Upon the whole, it is with me beyond all doubt that the apostles so understood their blessed master, as fully to warrant and oblige them to receive infants into the vifible church with their believing parents, and baptize them. Agreeably to this they practifed, when it is faid that Lydia and her houfhold were baptized—when the jailor and all his were baptized, and when Paul baptized the houfe of Stephanus, &c. It thus continued, no doubt, through the apoftolic age; and from the beft account we have in hiftory infant-baptifm was generally, if not univerfally, practifed in the church more than twelve hundred years, though much corrupted. Notwithftanding fome have fince called it in queftion, yet, through all this long fpace of time, there was no church or fociety of Chriftians which denied infant-baptifm, except thofe who denied all baptifm with water. We have a particular authentic hiftory, both of the firft rife and progrefs of this fect that denied infant-baptifm. It firft appeared in Germany at the place called Munfter, foon after the reformation from Popery.

If we grant, as the Baptifts affert, that infant-baptifm was neither allowed nor practifed by the church in the apoftolic age, it is utterly impoffible that it fhould have been introduced in any fubfequent period of the church. They, therefore, might as well affert that it never has been practifed.

Let us now candidly examine this matter.—Some confidently affirm, that this practice was firft introduced into the church in the dark days of Popery. This cannot poffibly be true. It is eafy to fhew from the moft authentic writers in thofe times, that it was practifed in the church

H

long before; and, if I miſtake not, ſome of the Baptiſt writers themſelves allow that it was practiſed in the African church before the *dark period of Popery*. But be this as it may, it was not then firſt introduced into the church. If it was not the practice in the apoſtles' day, it muſt have begun in ſome of the ſucceeding ages before Popery.— It is generally allowed that it commonly prevailed through all the churches after the fourth century. Mr. Tombs, on the part of the Baptiſts,* expreſsly ſays, that St. Auſtin's authority carried it in the following ages almoſt without control; but St. Auſtin moſt ſolemnly profeſſes, that he never heard of any in his time that oppoſed infant-baptiſm. We have only the four firſt centuries to examine. We are certain that the practice was firſt begun in one of them. Let us, therefore, go back and ſee if we can poſſibly find when it was firſt introduced into the church.— Our brethren, the Baptiſts, are, with us, equally intereſted in this inquiry. St. Auſtin, who lived in the fourth century, ſpeaks of it as prevailing in his day; and that it was not decreed by any council, but had been ever in uſe. The ſame author, in his diſpute with the Pelagians about original ſin, brings infant-baptiſm as an unanſwerable proof of original corruption. This was about A. D. 390. We alſo have a number of writers through the whole of this century, who ſpeak of infant-baptiſm, but ſay nothing of its introduction. As Siricius, A. D. 384, St. Ambroſe 374, Greg. Nazianzen 360, Optatus 306, the Council of Elibrius 305, and many others, mention infant-baptiſm as a thing in common

* Part I, Section 3.

ufe in the church. Thus, we fee, it was not firſt introduced in the fourth century.*

In the third Century, there are feveral remarkable teſtimonies concerning infant-baptiſm, which make it very evident that it was not firſt introduced in that day. About the middle of this century Cyprian called a council of fixty-fix miniſters or biſhops on this queſtion, "Whether "infants might be baptized before they were "eight days old?" This council unanimouſly agreed, there was no neceſſity for fuch a delay. In confequence of this, a letter, which was figned by Cyprian, was written to the churches, to notify to them the refult of their deliberation.

Origen, who was born lefs than an hundred years after the apoſtles, and flouriſhed in the beginning of this century, fpeaks often of infant-baptifm in his Homilies on Original Sin, as an eſtabliſhed practice in the church. In one place he exprefsly fays, that the church had a traditional order from the apoſtles to give baptifm to infants. This clearly ſhews, that infant-baptifm was then an uſage in the church. Tertullian alfo, who lived about the fame time, mentions infant-baptifm as no novelty in his day. He pleads for the delaying of the baptiſm of infants on account only of the danger which might attend the introduction of fponfors. This can properly apply only in thofe cafes, where parents were unbelievers, or were fick. Jacob Pamelius obferves, in his Annotations on this place, that Ter-

---

* Hiftory of Infant Baptifm, part 1, chap. 7, 8, to the 2ᵈ. Dr. Forbafius Hift. Theology.

tullian had reference to such.* From these observations, it is clear that infant-baptism was not first introduced either in the third or fourth century. It certainly was not introduced in the fourth, because we find it in the third—neither in the third, because it is there spoken of as a common undisputed practice. Our inquiry is now reduced to the limits only of two centuries, and it is clear to me, that infant-baptism must have been introduced into the Christian church in one or the other. Let us now carefully examine the matter with respect to the second century, the age that immediately followed the apostles and first ministers of Jesus Christ.

All the immediate successors of the apostles must personally know, what was the practice of the apostles themselves. The churches also must know whether their infants were baptized or not. If the ministers and churches knew that infant-baptism had never been practized by the apostles, it is utterly impossible that it should then have been introduced into the church without making great disturbance. It must have met with the greatest opposition, both from the ministers and churches, of primitive zeal and purity. Were that fact, is it credible that we should not have heard something of it, when some of the writings of those Fathers have come down to us?— Two of them are frequently mentioned on this subject, but not a word that there was any controversy in the church respecting infant-baptism. Ireneus, who flourished about the middle of this century, was acquainted with Polycarp, St. John's

* Dr. Forbesius' Hist. Theology.

disciple, and also saw and conversed with those who had seen Jesus Christ. He mentioned infant-baptism as no matter of dispute. Reckoning up several sorts of persons who were born again unto God, he expresly mentioned infants among them. It is naturally supposed that he there must mean their being born of the water, or baptized, as many of the Fathers used the word in this sense, as infants could give evidence of no other regeneration.

Justin Martyr, who is supposed to have been born about thirty years after the death of our blessed Saviour, in his Apology, written in the year 140, mentions persons who were discipled to Christ in infancy. He also speaks of baptism's being to us instead of circumcision. Ignatius lived in the end of the first century. He conversed with the apostles, and suffered martyrdom under Trajan, A. D. 107.* But from none of these have we a word respecting the first rise of infant-baptism in their day. Since we have now pursued our inquiry back to the first century without success, I would just make one remark here on the whole. If infant-baptism is such a gross error and corruption—if its introduction destroys the very being of the church, it is utterly incredible, if not impossible, that the practice of it could have obtained, either in the second, third, or fourth centuries, without its rise and progress being mentioned, or even that there were ever such heretics in the world. This remark obtains great weight when we consider that St. Austin, in the close of the fourth centu-

* Dr. Forbesius' Hist. Theology.

ry, wrote a book, giving a particular account of all fects that were, or ever had been in the church —(he enumerates eighty-eight with their feveral tenets.)—And when we find, in the writings of the Fathers, an account of all the particular errors, and fmalleft departures from the faith and practice once eftablifhed in the church, we are reduced to this dilemma, either that infant-baptifm was introduced into the church in the firft century by the apoftles themfelves, or that it never has been practifed in any age of the world.— The latter is contrary to known fact. The former is the truth, and it is the very doctrine propofed to be illuftrated and eftablifhed by this difcourfe. I fhall now conclude with a few remarks.

1. We have both fcripture command and example, for receiving infants of believers into the vifible church with their parents, and for adminiftering to them the feal of the righteoufnefs of faith. This command and this example from Abraham the father of the faithful, evidently run through the whole of the Old and New-Teftaments. When Chrift came and fulfilled the law and the prophets, he confirmed the covenant of promife, he enlarged it with greater privileges, and he continued it to believers under the glorious gofpel, as examples of infant-baptifm. We alfo have the evident practice of all the churches of Chrift in ages of the greateft zeal and purity. Thofe who deny that there is either command or example for this practice, ought firft to point out from authentic hiftory, a church or fociety of Chriftians, within twelve hundred years of the apoftles, who did not practife infant-baptifm.

2. Those who deny infant-baptism have no just ground for breaking off from all the churches of Christ on this account; and much less for esteeming themselves the only true church in the world. For though they hold this to be an error, yet it is not such as to subvert the foundation, nor indeed has it always been their sentiments, as appears by a confession of the faith of a hundred churches of their communion.* Awful have been the consequences of this separation, and, perhaps, nothing tarnished the glory of the reformation from Popery more than the conduct of its first founders. Those, therefore, who, in the present day would break off from other churches of Christ and join this separate communion, ought first well to consider the nature of the action, lest they be involved in the awful guilt of many generations. On the whole, it is high time that all party-zeal was banished from the church of Christ, and that all denominations were united in the common cause. The day of the Lord is at hand. In the mean time, let us give up ourselves and all ours to God and to his disposal—Let us take hold of the covenant through Jesus Christ, and thankfully enjoy the privileges—Let us plead the promises for ourselves and our children—and finally, let us wait patiently for his coming and kingdom, who will then reveal his righteous judgment, and reward every man according to his works.

* Printed in London, 1693.

SERMON IV.

BELIEVERS AND THEIR OFFSPRING IN COVENANT WITH GOD.

Acts ii. 39.
For the promise is unto you, and to your children, and to all that are afar off, even as many as the Lord our God shall call.

IN the former part of this chapter, we have an account of that wonderful out-pouring of the Holy Ghost upon the apostles on the day of Pentecost. In the context we have Peter's folemn addrefs to the mixed multitude, collected together on that occafion, in which the apoftle proves to them that Jefus Chrift, whom they had taken, and by wicked hands crucified and flain, was the Son of God, the true Meffiah and Saviour of the world. And he folemnly teftifies that God had raifed him from the dead, and had exalted him at his right hand, whofe blood they had impioufly imprecated on themfelves, and on their children. Under a fenfe of this guilt they were pricked to the heart, and, under awful apprehenfions of the divine wrath, in agonies of diftrefs they cried out, men, brethren, what *shall* we do? The apoftle then called them to repent of their fins—to embrace the gofpel, and to be baptized in the name of Jefus Chrift, as the only way to escape the divine wrath, which was coming on that wicked generation, and as the only way to enjoy the blessings and privileges of the gospel-dispensation. This call they enforced by the weighty argument in our text. " For the promise " is unto you, and to your children, and to all " that are afar off, even as many as the Lord our " God shall call."

It is generally supposed that this declaration respects both Jews and Gentiles. The promise is to you, and to your children. This respects those who were of the Jewish religion. The promise is to them who are afar off, when God shall call them, and to their children. This is supposed to have reference to the Gentiles, who should also be gathered into the church by the gospel, and should then enjoy the blessings and privileges of the covenant of promise with God's people.

We have seen in the preceding discourse, that all who believe are Abraham's seed, and heirs according to the promise; and that, by divine appointment, the infant children of such are to be received with their parents, and to be baptized. But it has been asked, what advantage is this to parents, or to their children? To give an answer to this question shall be the subject of my present discourse. I shall, therefore, now endeavor, by divine assistance, to shew,

I. What the covenant of promise contains for believing parents with respect to themselves.

I

II. What it contains for them with respect to their children.

III. Shew how parents may have an interest in this covenant, and enjoy its peculiar blessings and privileges for themselves, and for their children.

1. Under this head I do not propose to speak of those blessings which are common to believers in general, but only of those which are peculiar to them as parents. It is highly reasonable to suppose, that as they have a peculiar trust and charge, they also should have special assistance, and particular blessings and privileges. The apostle says, they are blessed with faithful Abraham. Believing parents being heirs of God and joint-heirs with Jesus Christ, have not only their sins forgiven; they have not only God for their God, for their father and portion—they have not only Jesus Christ for their Saviour, the Holy Spirit for their Sanctifier; but, in the first place, they also have the great privilege, that their infant children should be considered as in covenant with them. That this is a great privilege, every parental feeling is ready to acknowledge. It was before proved and illustrated, that under every dispensation of the covenant, this has been granted to believing parents, as God said to Abraham, the father of believers, " I will be a God to thee " and to thy seed after thee."

It must certainly be considered as a great favor to the parent, that the great and good God should thus graciously mention their infant-offspring in the covenant with them. By this he doubtlefs intended to fhew his condefcending grace and mercy to his people, that they might be encouraged in the faithful difcharge of their important truft.

2. The covenant of promife, as has been proved in the former difcourfe, contains, for believing parents, the privilege of giving up their children to God in baptifm, through Jefus Chrift.— This is a great favor in every refpect, but efpecially, that by faith believers may thus bring their infants to the compaffionate Saviour for his bleffing—the Saviour who is ever prefent in his ordinances. When thus given to him, they may always with freedom, in their prayers, bring them to the throne of free covenant-grace and mercy; they may, with hope, commit them to God's fatherly care; and they may, by faith, take hold of the covenant of his own appointment, and plead its bleffings for them, as for their own fouls.

3. Another privilege this promife contains for parents is, that their children, in their infant and moft helplefs ftate, may be, with them, members of the church. They may here confider them, in a peculiar fenfe, not their own, but the children of the houfhold of faith. They may confider them the Lord's property, and that they are to be brought up for him. Thefe reflections will not only ftrengthen all their obligations, but alfo greatly fweeten all their care and labor. They afford, to believing parents, a fovereign balm for all their wounds, and a fweet cordial for all their fears refpecting their dear infant-children. How wonderful are the condefcending grace and good-

nefs of God to his dear people! But how vile the ingratitude and unbelief of the human heart!

4. This promife contains, for believing parents, all needed wifdom and grace to bring their offspring up for God, while he continues them under their care. How often do parents find their ftrength fail in trying circumftances refpecting them even in their infant-ftate? But what a blefling have they in the covenant! Here is ftrength and affiftance; and, indeed, they never fail of obtaining a recruit when they come here by faith. In the riper years of their children how often do they find that they lack both wifdom and grace to give them inftruction, to reftrain them from evil practices, and to bring them up for God? But here is both grace and wifdom in ftore. Here they may come freely by faith, and obtain mercy, wifdom and grace to help in every time of need. God fays, in the covenant of promife, I will be a God to thee, O believing parent! The promife is to thee in the character of a parent, and contains every blefling and grace neceffary for the education of your children, who are devoted to his fervice. Thefe bleffings are treafured up in Chrift to be communicated to all thofe parents, who come to God for them by faith—by that faith which takes hold of the covenant—which works by love, and is productive of new obedience. Ignorant and unbelieving parents may think lightly of all thefe bleffings, but they muft certainly be exceeding precious to him, who has been made fenfible what it is to be without God in the world—to him who is fenfible what it is to have a covenant-God and father through Jefus Chrift, and to him who knows what

it is by faith to plead the precious promifes for his own foul.—How fupporting to the tender, faithful, parental heart, when ready to fink under a view of the many evils which are thickly fcattered in the vale of tears, through which their dear child muft pafs! How fupporting, I fay, are thefe covenant-bleffings, efpecially when parents can take hold of the covenant, and, by faith, obtain grace to inftruct, warn, and guard their children, and thus chearfully commit them to the holy keeping and difpofal of a heavenly father.

5. In this promife there is abundant mercy to make their prayers, inftructions and corrections effectual. Here is not only grace to make them faithful, but mercy to render them fuccefsful.— Pious parents, when they confider the total depravity of the human heart—when they fee that the imagination of the thoughts of the heart is evil, and only evil continually, and when, upon a fmall trial, they perceive the obftinacy of their children, then they are exceedingly apt to be difcouraged. But the promife contains grace fovereign and powerful enough to fubdue the moft ftubborn will, and to break the hardeft heart.— Here is mercy fufficient to make the weak, but faithful and perfevering endeavors of pious parents fuccefsful, on the moft finifhed piece of human corruption.—God fays, " I know Abraham, " that he will command his children, and his houf- " hold after him, and they *shall* keep the way of the " Lord—Gen. xviii. 19. Train up a child in the " way he fhould go, and when he is old he *will* " not depart from it"—Prov. xxii. 6. The Lord

himself answers for the event. To this source fainting believers ought always to look. Faithful parents, who have given their children to God in covenant, may undoubtedly depend on the all-sufficient mercy of a covenant-keeping God. Is this no advantage to parents? Is there no peculiar blessing for them who have given up themselves and their children to God in covenant? Is there no suitable encouragement—no particular assistance for them in this covenant, which is so well ordered in all things and sure?—But here let me observe, that as these covenant-blessings are spiritual—the spiritual person only can enjoy them. They are so little attended to and understood, and so little believed even by pious people in the present day, that we need not wonder they have so little apparent effect; and especially when so few parents take hold of the covenant truly by faith, and are active and diligent in the use of all those means by which God communicates the covenanted-blessings to his people.

Sixthly, and lastly—Should it please God to take away the infants of believers by death, the promise gives them full liberty, by faith, to commit, through Jesus Christ, their infants, as their own souls, into their heavenly Father's hands.—To this great privilege they are undoubted heirs, as children of Abraham. No favor, perhaps, could be more grateful to the feelings, no blessing more suitable to the desires, and no privilege could more exactly correspond, than this, with the wishes of a pious parent, in such an affecting situation. O parent! behold the grace and condescending goodness of a covenant-God and Father.

II. I am to shew, what are the promises and blessings contained in this covenant, for believing parents, respecting their children.

First—In their infant and most helpless state, they are admitted into Christ's family on earth—This is no small privilege. How great would you think the favor to your children, to be taken into the family of an earthly king? But the church is the houshold of faith, the family of the king of kings. Here are the richest promises, and greatest blessings, and here is a foundation for the most sanguine expectations. In this situation they are interested in all the public prayers for the welfare of the church, and they ought to be always remembered in the private and secret petitions of all God's people.

Secondly—The God of Abraham is their God—The promise is to believing parents, and to their children. "I will be a God to thee and to " thy seed." This is certainly an inestimable blessing of the covenant, which believers have for their infants. God, therefore, will preserve them through the dangers of their infant-state, or will take them to himself. All this is doubtless implied in his being their God. For if believers are, by the divine command, to give their infants to God, and they in obedience, do give them up to him as he hath appointed, will he not accept them? He certainly will, and through Jesus Christ, he doubtless becomes their God in life, agreeably to the tenor of the gracious covenant. But to such as die in an infant-state, he is forever a God and portion. Thus only can this be an everlasting covenant respecting such, and in this view alone his mercy to them endureth forever. Those, therefore, who believe that the promise contains any thing respecting the infants of believers, who die in their infant state, can hardly doubt of its securing to them the saving blessings of the covenant in the eternal world. What blessings are here for the dying infants of believers? Blessings infinitely rich—infinitely free!— This is not a new sentiment—It was holden, and firmly believed by the most zealous and pious ancient fathers in the church.

Should these infants, on the contrary, live and advance to the state of childhood, there are still great blessings for them in this gracious covenant.

First—That grace, promised to believing parents to make them faithful, has some special reference to children in this state. If believing parents have grace to be faithful, this is a great blessing, not to parents only, but also in a very special manner to their children: It gives them the advantage of their faithful pious instruction.

Secondly—Believing parents, respecting their children in this state, have the promise of the blessing to attend faithful instruction and discipline. Prov. xxii. 6—xxiii. 13, 14—xx. 7. " Train up a
" child in the way he should go, and when he is
" old he *will not* depart from it—Withhold not
" correction from the child; for if thou beatest him
" with a rod, he *shall not* die—Thou shalt beat him
" with the rod, and *shall deliver* his soul from hell

" The juſt man walketh in his integrity; *his children*
" *are bleſſed* after him." What precious promiſes!
What unſpeakable bleſſings for their children!
If God gracneuſly grants his bleſſing to attend
the faithful care of pious parents, this will certainly make it effectual, and lay a glorious foundation for their children's *uſefulneſs* here, and for
their eternal felicity in the world to come. This
has often been the caſe, and it is more than probable always will be the caſe, where parents take
hold of the covenant, and are perſeveringly faithful in their inſtruction and diſcipline towards
their children, agreeably to the following paſ-
ſages of ſacred ſcripture.—" And I will eſtabliſh
" my covenant between me and thee, and thy
" ſeed after thee, in their generations for an e-
" verlaſting covenant, to be a God unto thee,
" and to thy ſeed after thee. For I know him,
" that he will command his children, and his
" houſhold after him, and they *ſhall* keep the
" way of the Lord, to do juſtice and judgment,
" *that* the Lord *may bring* upon Abraham that
" which he hath ſpoken of him"—Gen. xvii. 7.
and xviii. 19. " So then they which be of faith
" are bleſſed with faithful Abraham. That the
" bleſſing of Abraham might come on the Gen-
" tiles through Jeſus Chriſt, that we might re-
" ceive the promiſe of the ſpirit through faith"—
Gal. iii. 9—14. " For I the Lord love judgment,
" I hate robbery for burnt-offering; and *I will*
" direct their work in truth, and *I will* make an
" everlaſting covenant with them; and *their ſeed*
" *ſhall be known* among the Gentiles, and *their*
" *offspring* among the people: all that ſee *them*
" *ſhall* acknowledge *them*, that *they are* the *ſeed*
K

" *which the Lord hath bleſſed. They ſhall not labor*
" *in vain*, nor bring forth for trouble: for *they are*
" the feed of the bleſſed of the Lord, and *their off-*
"*ſpring with them.*" Iſaiah lxi. 8, 9. and lxv. 23.

Thirdly—In this ſtate the children of believers, in covenant, are alſo under the care, watch, and diſcipline of the church. This alſo is no ſmall privilege. And where the church is faithful, it moſt certainly is a very great bleſſing; not only as a powerful incitement to faithfulneſs in parents, but alſo as it adds great weight to their parental inſtruction and diſcipline.

In this age, human nature is capable of the moſt deep and laſting impreſſions. The foundation of a future life of virtue or vice, and conſequenlty of happineſs or miſery, is much oftener laid in childhood than is generally imagined.—In this age, therefore, to have our children under the care, watch, and diſcipline of the church —under the faithful inſtruction of pious parents, attended with divine aſſiſtance and bleſſing, muſt be conſidered, by every ſerious and enlightened mind, as advantages unſpeakably great—as privileges moſt important and precious.

Fourthly—In childhood alſo they have a ſpecial intereſt in the prayers of the church and people of God. As members with their parents, they are included in all the prayers which are made for the church throughout the whole world. How great an advantage this may be none can tell. When we conſider, that God is pleaſed to beſtow the greateſt bleſſings in anſwer to the prayers of his dear people; and when we conſider, that the effectual fervent prayer of the righteous availeth much, (James v. 16.) we muſt conſider this is no ſmall privilege.

In adult age there are ſtill peculiar privileges and bleſſings for the children of believers, unleſs they have cut themſelves off by their wickedneſs, or have been excluded by the diſcipline of the church.

Though the ax is now laid at the root of the tree, and every tree that bringeth not forth good fruit muſt finally be hewn down; and though ſomething more is required of them, as adults, that they may enjoy all the privileges of the church, yet they are ſtill under the care and diſcipline of the church. This is undoubtedly a great privilege, and if properly and faithfully exerciſed over ſuch by the church, may actually be to them, under divine influence, one of the greateſt bleſſings. They are under the bonds of the covenant—the ſacred ties are ſtill upon them to be the Lord's—the way of ſin is more hedged up from ſuch, and the way to final deſtruction more barred. Theſe are no ſmall advantages.— Such ſtill have a ſpecial intereſt in the prayers of the church and people of God, which may, and will prevail, unleſs obſtinately rejected and deſpiſed. They muſt be under great advantages for eternal life. Thus lifted up to heaven, in point of privilege, if they periſh, they muſt diſſolve every ſacred tie—break through every barrier; they muſt burſt aſunder every band, and obſtinately plunge themſelves headlong into remedileſs deſtruction. Theſe, my brethren, are ſome of the ineſtimable bleſſings and privileges of the covenant of promiſe, in which believing parents, for themselves, and for their children, are interested. Surely they cannot be considered either few, or small, by any serious mind; on the contrary, I am perſuaded that, what advantage is the covenant of promiſe? and what profit is their in baptiſm? would never have been queſtions had miniſters always been faithful in diſpenſing the privilege, and had parents and churches diſcharged their reſpective obligations.

It is, indeed, a melancholy truth, that in the preſent day, the viſibility of the peculiar bleſſings of the covenant of promiſe have almoſt diſappeared. To this, perhaps, more than to any thing elſe, it may be attributed, that ſo many parents, who hold to the covenant, are ſo eaſy in the neglect of baptiſm for their children; and alſo, that ſo many wholly deny infant-baptiſm. Had the adminiſtration of infant-baptiſm never been corrupted—had the church kept up the primitive diſcipline over both parents and children; and eſpecially, had parents always been faithful to their children, according to the covenant, we have the greateſt aſſurance, that all the peculiar covenant-bleſſings would have been enjoyed by believers and their children. The world would then have known that theſe are the ſeed of the bleſſed of the Lord, and their offspring with them.

III. I am now to ſhew how parents may be intereſted in the covenant of promiſe, and enjoy the peculiar bleſſings and privileges of it, for themſelves, and their children.

Two things here are the ſubject of inquiry—
1. How parents may be intereſted in the co-

venant of promise. 2. How they may enjoy the peculiar blessings and privileges of the covenant respecting themselves and their children, under the gospel dispensation.

With respect to the first, it is clear from what has been said, that parents must be true believers in order to be interested in the covenant; or in scripture language, they must be Christ's, and consequently Abraham's seed, to be heirs according to the promise. The apostle says expresly, " if any man have not the spirit of Christ he is " none of his." Romans viii. 9.—Therefore he is not interested in the covenant of promise, and can have no right to its privileges.

But how parents, under the gospel, may enjoy all the peculiar blessings and privileges of such, for themselves, and for their children, must now have a more particular discussion.

Some, through ignorance and unbelief, reject and despise them. Many acknowledge the covenant, and have their children baptized, and yet do not appear to enjoy any of its spiritual blessings: And some, who are interested in the covenant, and appear really to give up their children to God in baptism, yet seem to lose the parental blessing. Parents need all these promises and blessings—they are treasured up in Christ for them —they are clearly proposed, and freely offered to them, in the covenant of promise. But O how affecting! How distressing must it be to miss of them, whatever may be the cause!

To illustrate this matter, I would suggest a few things.—Parents, I beseech you, give your most serious attention—look to God for his blessing, and may the Father of light give you understanding. To give yourselves and your children to God, and to his church, in covenant, through Jesus Christ, is necessary, in order to have an interest in the covenant.—Covenant-blessings are given in a covenant way.

First—To insure the enjoyment of these blessings, parents must believe, and take hold of the covenant. Not to believe is, perhaps, in God's view, to reject the covenant—Not to take hold of it, and depend upon it, is probably to slight the covenant with all its blessings. This, perhaps, may be the very reason, why so few parents enjoy these peculiar parental blessings. It is highly reasonable, and it is agreeable to the analogy of faith, to suppose, that when God makes gracious proposals to parents, and they believe them, take hold and depend upon them, as proposed, that the blessings are sure, and the enjoyment certain.

Secondly—Let parents go to God as to a father, through Christ, and ask these covenant-blessings—let this be a continual fervent prayer. It is reasonable, and, in some respects, it seems necessary to the very enjoyment of them, that parents should ask these blessings of their heavenly Father. "Ask," says the blessed Saviour, "and ye shall receive". The apostle James says, "If any of you lack wisdom, let him ask of God, that giveth to all men liberally, and upbraideth not, and it shall be given him. But let him ask in faith, nothing wavering."—If parents, therefore, are so ignorant of the covenant, and so faithless respecting its blessings, that they do not ask for them, it is no wonder that they fail of their enjoyment.

Thirdly—Let parents be faithful to the covenant respecting their children, in training them up in the way they should go, and in bringing them up for God, agreeably to his will. This is of the last importance, and seems to be a condition of the enjoyment of covenant-blessings respecting their children. Parents, who are not faithful in this, do break the covenant. They make light of the promise, and thus lose the blessing. But, on the other hand, those parents, who are faithful, and bring up their children for God, agreeably to the tenor of the covenant, may depend on the enjoyment of the blessings in their fullest extent, with regard both to themselves and their children, and with regard to time and eternity. Should any say, that this is carrying the matter too far, and that, by proving too much, we overset the whole, and prove nothing. Should any say, that the faithfulness necessary to obtain this, is wholly unattainable in this imperfect state. I answer, that the objection is very plausible, and probably, with some, has more weight than merit. But let us try its weight in a similar case. According to scripture the Christian must be faithful in order to enjoy the covenant-blessing for his own soul. For the unfaithful will doubtless be shut out.—But how is this? Can a believer in this imperfect state be so faithful with respect to the covenant, as to ensure for himself the promised blessings for time and eternity? And why not in the case before us? efpecially as we have no reafon to fuppofe, that here a greater perfection of faithfulnefs is required.

IMPROVEMENT.—1. We learn the duty of parents, under the gofpel, refpecting their children. This is, in general, to fecure the covenant-bleffings for them, by giving them to God in baptifm, and bringing them up for him in the gofpel-way. To this, parents, the gofpel invites you in our text: "For the promife is unto you and "to your children, and to all that are afar off, "even as many as the Lord our God fhall call." The church fays come—Minifters call upon you to become heirs according to the covenant of promife—to be faithful, and infure the peculiar, parental bleffings for yourfelves and for your dear offspring. But to be more particular—It is your duty, when your children are thus given up to God, to confider them his, and to take the moft tender care of them for him in their infant ftate. You ought to pray for them, and particularly by faith to take hold of the covenant, and afk for them, and for yourfelves, the peculiar parental bleffings. When they are capable of inftruction, you are bound, by the moft folemn ties, carefully and perfeveringly to teach them the will of God, their heavenly Father. You are to continue in prayer both with, and for them.—It is your duty conftantly to fet before them good examples in all godlinefs and holinefs. It is your duty, as parents, to reftrain them from wicked ways—from wicked company, and from all dangerous and corrupting practices, however fafhionable.—When neceffary, you ought to ufe the rod of paternal correction, always remembering that there is in it a promifed bleffing. It is alfo your duty to call, if neceſſary, upon the church for aſſiſtance to reſtrain and govern your children according to the ſcriptures. In all things you muſt look to God for his bleſſing.

2. The duty of children, eſpecially of thoſe who are given up to God—It is their duty to be the Lord's. But to be more particular—It is your duty, O ye little ones! the dear lambs of the flock—it is your duty to obey your parents in the Lord. God has put you under their care, and given them authority over you. You are bound to receive their inſtruction—to hearken to their counſel—to yield to their reſtraints, and obey their commands agreeably to his will. You are to be obedient to the calls and inſtructions of your miniſter—of your Chriſtian friends, and of the church, always remembering your ſolemn obligations. It is your duty to renounce all the ſinful pleaſures and vanities of this world—the luſt of the fleſh, and the cauſe of the devil. You are under the moſt ſacred obligations to give up yourſelves to God, through Jeſus Chriſt, to join the cauſe and people of God, and to devote yourſelves to his intereſt and ſervice for ever and ever.

I ſhall now conclude with a ſhort addreſs to parents and to children.

Firſt—Let me ſpeak a few words to thoſe profeſſing parents, who deny the covenant, and infant-baptiſm.—Let me, my brethren, moſt ſolemnly beſeech you impartially and candidly to examine the ſacred ſcriptures on this ſubject.—

L

With all meekness let me entreat you to attend, without prejudice, to what has been now offered to your confideration. You may be affured it comes from a friendly heart—a heart that ardently wifhes well to you, and to your dear children, that you may have a large fhare in the peculiar parental bleffings of the covenant of promife. Confider, if you err in this matter, what an affecting lofs you muft fuftain, both as to yourfelves and your dear offspring. Confider what encouragement, affiftance and comfort you are deprived of as parents—what covenant-privileges and bleffings for your dear little ones are loft for ever!—Thefe you, as parents, ought to have received by faith, according to the covenant of promife, and fecured to them for time and eternity. Be cordially willing to receive the truth, and may the Lord give you underftanding, and to his name be all the glory.

Secondly—Let me addrefs thofe who have given up themfelves and their children to God in covenant. You, my dear brethren, are interefted in this gracious covenant—here are treafures of good things—here are precious promifes for you, and for your children. But can you be fatisfied with the bare right without the enjoyment of the bleffings? If you can, you are doubtlefs of thofe who have a name to live but are dead.— Ye drowfy parents, let me befeech you to awake! Confider what a price is put into your hands, and confider how much depends on your faithfulnefs! Do your dear little ones look to you for temporal bleffings under God? Does your daily labor fupply their wants?—In the covenant of promife God has made more ample provifion for their precious fouls. He has given you much greater encouragement to labor, that you may obtain for them the meat which endureth to eternal life. The unfaithful parent is, in this respect, cruel like the oftrich.—But I would hope better things of you: Be faithful to the fouls of your dear children, that you and they may enjoy the peculiar bleffings of the covenant of promife, and be truly the feed of the bleffed of the Lord.

Thirdly—To parents who have not given up themfelves to God, nor their children in baptifm.—You have heard of the covenant of promife, propofed to you freely, through Jefus Chrift, with all its bleffings; yet, alas! you neglect to comply. Can you be eafy in this fituation? Here are parental bleffings—but where are your parental feelings? Tremble left your children perifh with you. It is true, they are not beyond the reach of uncovenanted mercy. But what will become of you, a faithlefs parent?— Never, never be eafy in this awful fituation— " Repent and believe on the Lord Jefus Chrift; " for the promife is unto you, and to your chil- " dren, and to all that are afar off, even as many " as the Lord our God fhall call."

Fourthly—To thofe children who have, from their infancy, been given up to God in baptifm. —You, my dear children, have been fet apart, in a peculiar manner, for God, who has been pleafed to diftinguifh you from others in the covenant of promife. He has put you under great advantages to know, to love, to ferve him, and to be happy for ever: He has gracioufly hedged up from you the path of vice, and barred the broad way to deſtruction—and he has opened before you the path of virtue, and ſmoothed for you the narrow way of life and eternal happineſs. My dear children, I now beſeech you, know the God of your fathers: He is the beſt of beings—he is a good God—his favor is life, and bleſſed are they whom he bleſſeth: Let it be your firſt thing to ſeek the Lord—You have the greateſt encouragement. If you ſeek him early, you ſhall find him. Remember you are under the ſtrongeſt obligations to be his. Receive, I beſeech you, the inſtructions and admonitions of thoſe who are over you in the Lord—of thoſe who earneſtly pray for, and ſteadily ſeek your everlaſting welfare:—Chearfully obey your parents in the Lord;—you know not how often they bend their knees at the throne of grace, in agonies of prayer, for you. Remember—oh! do remember, as you grow up, that the ax is laid at the root of the tree. If, therefore, you do not bring forth good fruit you muſt certainly be cut down, and caſt into everlaſting fire. *But* if, after all, you grow up in wickedneſs, how great muſt be your guilt, and how aggravated all your ſins?— Should any of you thus go on in ſin with the wicked, and finally periſh, certainly, in the day of judgment, it will be more tolerable for the children of Sodom and Gomorrah than for you.

Laſtly—One word to thoſe children who are not given up to God in covenant by baptiſm.— Though your parents have not given up themſelves, nor you, to God in covenant, and though you have no ſpecial intereſt in covenant-bleſſings and privileges, yet you are in a goſpel land, and have many advantages for eternal life. You have the calls—the offers and invitation of the gofpel. You are called to give up yourfelves to God through Jefus Chrift. There is provifion enough in the uncovenanted mercy of God. The door of mercy is open. If you repent and come to Chrift he will receive you, while he rejects thofe wicked children who, though they are baptized, yet ftill go on in fin, and defpife the God of their fathers. Be perfuaded to feek the Lord—be not difcouraged, for though you are now afar off, you may yet be brought nigh by the blood of Chrift. The gofpel is come to you. Now is the accepted time—now is the day of falvation. The time is fhort—The day of grace may be foon over, and the day of wrath may quickly be at hand. Awake—fly from the wrath to come.— Lay hold on the bleffed hope now fet before you. Youth is a good time—It often is the only time, and it always is the beft time to make your peace with God through Jefus Chrift.—Come then—O now come! for all things are ready. The Spirit and the Bride fay come: Let him that heareth fay come—and whofoever will, let him take of the water of life freely.—May the God of mercy blefs his own word, and to his name be all the glory for ever and ever—AMEN.

F I N I S.

ERRATA.—Page 1, line 2d from bottom, for *imformed*, read *informed*.—P. 6, l. 4, for *teach*, read *preach*—8 and 9 l. same p. for *disciplined*, read *discipled*—P. 31, l. 2, for *there*, read *those*.

ERRORS OF COPY.—Page 13, line 14 from bottom, for *improbable*, read *probable*.—P. 17, l. 14 from bottom, read, *the sinner is overwhelmed*.—P. 54, l. 12, read *Acts* ii. 38, 39, for *Acts* iii. 19.—P. 58, l. 2 from bottom, for *Eliberius*, read *Elibrius*.

A Fair and Rational

VINDICATION

OF THE

Right of INFANTS

To the Ordinance of

BAPTISM:

BEING THE

Substance of several DISCOURSES from
Acts ii. 39.

CONTAINING

I. The Scripture Ground, on which the Right of Infants to Baptism is founded.

II. The Evidence by which it is supported. And,

III. A Solution of the most material Objections.

By *DAVID BOSTWICK*, A. M.
Late Minister of the Presbyterian Church, in the City of
NEW-YORK.

That the Blessing of Abraham *might come on the* Gentiles, *thro'*
Jesus Christ. Gal. iii. 14.

NEW-YORK Printed:
London, Re-printed for Edward and Charles Dilly, in the
Poultry, near the *Mansion-House.*
MDCCLXV.

PREFACE.

THE *Reverend* and *pious Author* of the following Treatife, compofed it for the *Pulpit*, and delivered it in fundry *Sermons*, but a few Weeks before his Deceafe: which being found to have a very happy Effect, in the Confirmation and Eftablifhment of fome wavering Minds among his own People, he was urged to tranfcribe his Notes for the Prefs; but foon after he had begun this Work, he was (as to the particular Time of it) unexpectedly called to his fuperior Station *in God's Temple above*. Yet by a *kind Providence*, a few Days before his laft Illnefs, a *young Minifter*, in the Neighbourhood of this City, who had a Defire to improve himfelf by Mr. *Boftwick*'s Notes, which were written in a kind of Short-Hand of his own Invention, applied to him, and at his Requeft Mr. *Boftwick* fpent feveral Hours in teaching him in fome Degree to underftand them; and by *his* Means, the Copy now printed, was recovered from Oblivion, and tranfcribed fince Mr. *Boftwick*'s Death.

Under this View, it is hoped, the candid Reader will difpenfe with a Stile a little too diffufe for a printed Argumentation, and pardon any Inaccuracy, that would probably have been avoided, if the Work had paffed under it's *Author's laft Hand*.

Thofe that were acquainted with Mr. *Boftwick*'s mild and pacific Temper, and knew the general Courfe

PREFACE.

discerning therein an admirable *Display* of the infinite Perfections of the DEITY, with a perfect Accommodation to the various States of *Man*. He considered it not only as a SYSTEM of *Divine Knowledge*, but as revealing a practical and experimental *Discipline*; and felt it's *vital Energy*, and had. it's *Truth* sealed on his *Heart*, with that Kind of Evidence as would doubtless have stood the Fire upon the severest Trial.

AFTER THIS, I scarce need add, that he was a DIVINE OF THE OLD STAMP, and could well defend his *System* against all *Gainsayers*. In these Things he was a Scribe well instructed, and with great *Sagacity* and *Penetration* could discern the *Spirit of Error* in it's most distant Approaches. He knew it's *Connections*, and *Tendencies* (ever aiming at *God*'s Dishonour or *Man*'s Ruin) and therefore as a faithful *Watchman* always gave the speediest Warning of the *Danger*.

He had those Gifts which rendered him a very popular PREACHER. With a strong commanding *Voice*, his *Pronunciation* was clear, distinct, and deliberate; His *Speech* and *Gesture* decent and natural, without any Affectation; His *Language* elegant and pure, but with studied Plainness, never below the Dignity of the Pulpit, nor above the Capacity of the meanest of his Auditory. The Strength of his *Memory*, and the Flow of his *Elocution*, enabled him to preach without Notes, but seldom or never extempore: He furnished the *Lamps of the Sanctuary with beaten Oil*, and the *Matter* and *Method* of his *Sermons* were well studied.

In treating *divine Subjects*, he manifested an *habitual Reverence* for the MAJESTY OF HEAVEN, a deep Sense of the *Worth of Souls*, an intimate *Knowledge* of the *human Heart*, and it's various Workings in it's two-fold State of *Nature* and *Grace*. He dealt

faithfully

faithfully with his *Hearers, declaring to them the whole Counsel of God,* shewing them their Danger and Remedy. And none will *perish* from under his *Ministry,* but their *Blood* must lie *upon their own Heads.* He always spake from a *deep Sense* of the Truths he delivered, and declared those Things, *which he had seen and which he had heard, and his Hands had handled of the Word of Life*; and delivered nothing to his *Auditory,* but with a Solemnity that discovered it's IMPORTANCE.

His *Mind* had a *poetic* Turn. His *Stile* was copious and florid. He sometimes soared, when his Subject would admit of it, with an elevated *Wing*; and his *Imagination* enabled him to paint his SCENE, *whatever it was,* in very strong and lively *Colours.* Few *Men* could describe the *hideous Deformity* of Sin, the *Misery* of Men's Apostacy from GOD, the *Wonders* of *redeeming* Love, the *Glory* and *Riches* of divine *Grace,* in stronger Lines, and more affecting Strains than he.

In the *Conduct* of *Life,* he was remarkably *gentle towards all Men,* vastly *prudent* and *cautious,* and always behaved *with the Meekness of Wisdom,* and filled up every *Relation* in *Life,* with it's proper *Duty,* and was a living Example of the Truth of that Religion, which he taught to others. *He preached not himself, but Christ Jesus his Lord.* In this View his *Eye* was *single,* and he regarded no other *Object.* He knew in *whose* Place he stood, and feared no Man. He dared to flash the *Terrors* of the *Law* in the Face of the stoutest *Transgressor,* with the same *Freedom* as he display'd the amiable Beauties and Glories of the Gospel for the *Comfort* and *Refreshment* of the penitent Believer.

As he highly honoured his divine *Master* he was highly favoured by *him,* of which take one Instance.

In a *former Illness*, from which it was thought he could not recover, which happened some *Months* before he died, he was greatly distressed by a *deep Concern* for his *Widow* and his *great Family*, on the Event of his Death. But GOD was pleased in a Time of great *Extremity*, to grant him a *glorious* and *astonishing View* of his *Power, Wisdom*, and *Goodness*, and the *Riches of his Grace*, with a particular *Appropriation* to *himself* and *his*. Such as dispelled every Fear, and at that Time, rendered him impatient to live, but at length on his Recovery, which commenced immediately on the Removal of this Distress, his *Mind* settled into a *divine Calm*; he perceived himself equally willing *to live* or *die* as GOD pleased. In which *Temper* he continued to his last *Moment*, when placidly he resigned his *Soul* and all his *mortal Interests*, into the Hands of HIS SAVIOUR and HIS GOD! Such Intercourse sometimes passes between the Father of Spirits and the human Spirit, and such Honour have they that fear God!

Thus lived, and *thus* died, in the midst of his Days and Usefulness, *this excellent Minister of Jesus Christ*, to the unspeakable Loss of the *World*, the *Church*, and his *Family*. He departed this *Life* on the 12th Day of *November, in the Year of our Lord One Thousand Seven Hundred and Sixty-Three*, and in the *Forty-fourth* Year of his *Age*, leaving his *Widow* and *Ten Children* to the Care of *Providence*, and his Remains lie buried in the Front Isle of the Presbyterian Church in this City.

Dated at New-York *April the Ninth, One Thousand Seven Hundred and Sixty-Four.*

A FAIR and RATIONAL

VINDICATION, &c.

ACTS II. 39.

For the Promise is unto you, and to your Children, and to all that are afar off; even as many as the Lord our God shall call.

YOU are very sensible, my Brethren, that it has not been my usual Practice to fill your Minds with litigious Disputes, or to introduce Matters of needless Controversy into the sacred Desk; much less to throw out occasional Reflections, or fix opprobrious Epithets on those of different Denominations.—This, I ever esteemed a mean, unmanly Way of opposing Error, or advancing the Cause of Truth.—I have rather in general considered my Hearers, as transient, itinerant Mortals bound to an eternal World; and thefore have made it my principal Business, to inculcate upon them, those plain, practical, and important Truths, that have the nearest Connection with, and are of the greatest Consequence to their eternal Interest.

Convinced, however, of my indispensable Duty, by several concurring Circumstances; I shall now attempt to illustrate, what I suppose a precious Gospel-Truth; and vindicate a valuable Privilege, of which the Church of Christ has been in Possession from its first Institution, though by some made a Matter of Dispute; and that is, *the Right of Infant-Children,*

Children, descending from con-fœderate, or covenanted Parents, to that Ordinance of Baptism, which is the eternal Seal of the Gospel-Covenant.—And as this is known to be my Principle, from my constant Practice; surely none can take it amiss, or think it strange, that I stand forth in its Vindication; especially as I design no unchristian Reflection, no acrimonious Expressions, or uncharitable Censures, on those of contrary Sentiments and Practice; but only a fair and rational Vindication of my own; having principally in View, the Satisfaction of a Number of my Hearers, who have expressed their Desire of being further instructed in the scriptural Grounds and Reasons of our constant Practice.—And though on the one Hand, I will not place this Point, of Infant-Baptism, among the Things that are absolutely essential to Salvation; yet on the other, I am far from supposing it to be a Matter of trifling Indifference, or of little or no Consequence.—For if the Baptism of Infants is not agreeable to divine Institution, or warranted by the sacred Word, then not only we, but the *Protestant* Churches in general must be in a very unhappy Situation——having no regular Gospel-Ordinances of any Kind whatsoever.—Nay, if Infant-Baptism be a meer Nullity, as some pretend, then we, with the Generality of the *Protestant* Churches, are in fact, a Company of unbaptised *Heathens*; who have neither Churches, Ministers, or Ordinances, according to the Institution of Jesus Christ: Our Ministers themselves, being unbaptised, can have no regular Authority to baptise others; and we being all unbaptised, cannot, without the greatest Impropriety, approach the sacred Ordinance of the Lord's Supper.

Having

Having therefore, on this Suppofition, no regular Ordinances among us, we, with our numerous *Proteſtant* Brethren of various Denominations, muſt want the very Eſſence of a regular Goſpel-Church, and in this Reſpect be reduced to a State of abſolute *Heatheniſm.*—I do not adduce this, as a Proof, that Infant-Baptiſm is a divine Inſtitution; that, I truſt, will be proved by more direct and poſitive Evidences; I only mention it to ſhew that the Controverſy is no Trifle, but of ſufficient Importance to demand our Attention, and engage our impartial Inquiry, whether we are right, or whether we are wrong? And can our Opponents, whoſe Principles and Conduct neceſſarily unchurch the whole *Proteſtant* World, except themſelves,—can they, I ſay, think themſelves offended, that we do not ſilently ſubmit to their uncharitable Cenſures? will they be diſpleaſed, that we aſſert and vindicate our ſtanding in the viſible Kingdom of Chriſt, and that we are a Goſpel-Church as well as they? Surely, thoſe that are Men of Conſcience among them will not; or if they ſhould, yet theſe are Matters too intereſting to be given up, out of meer Complaiſance, to any Society of Men in the Univerſe.——Let us then aim at the Truth, without any Regard to the Pleaſure or Diſpleaſure of Mortals; and if our Infant-Baptiſm can be vindicated, for Conſcience ſake let it be done.—If not, if the Truth is not for us, but againſt us, let us honeſtly give it up, and no more practiſe what the ſacred Word will not defend.

Having thus hinted the Importance of the Controverſy, as a ſufficient Warrant for my preſent Attempt, I ſhall now conſider the Occaſion, and the proper Meaning of the Words before us,—*For the Promiſe is to you and to your Children,* &c.

In the preceding Context, we have an Account of that remarkable divine Energy, which attended the firſt Goſpel-Sermon after the miraculous Effuſion of the Holy Ghoſt, awakening in the Hearers that moſt anxious and important Inquiry, *Men and Bretben, what ſhall we do?*

We have alſo the Apoſtle's Anſwer to this momentous and intereſting Inquiry, *Repent and be baptiſed every one of you, in the Name of Jeſus Chriſt, for the Remiſſion of Sins, and ye ſhall receive the Gift of the Holy Ghoſt*; i. e. "Return unfeignedly from Sin to God, through Jeſus Chriſt; ſubmit to the Grace and Government of this divine Redeemer; and make a ſolemn public Profeſſion of this Submiſſion, by being baptiſed in the Name of Jeſus Chriſt, and your Baptiſm ſhall be an external Sign of the Remiſſion of Sins, and of the renewing and ſanctifying Influences of the Holy Ghoſt."

This Exhortation plainly conſiſts of two Branches, each of which is urged with a diſtinct Motive. The firſt is *Repentance*, or a Turning to God through Jeſus Chriſt. This is urged with the encouraging Motive, that they ſhall receive the Forgiveneſs of Sins, and the ordinary ſanctifying Influences of the Holy Ghoſt. The ſecond Branch of the Exhortation, is a *Submiſſion* to this new Diſpenſation of the Goſpel-Covenant, by being baptiſed in the Name of Jeſus Chriſt. This is urged with the Motive in the Text, *For the Promiſe is unto you and to your Children,* &c. q. d. "The Promiſe which encourages you to enter into this new Covenant, by Baptiſm, is *primarily* to you, and your Children, as the Deſcendents of *Abraham*; and *ſecondarily* to *as many* of the *Gentiles*, who are yet *afar off*, (and, including their Children alſo) as by the Miniſtry of the Word, *the Lord our God*

ſhall

shall call." It is plain then, that this Promise, whatever is intended by it, is urged as a Reason why they ought to submit to this new Institution of the Gospel, and *be baptised in the Name of the Lord Jesus.* This Reason then must hold good with Respect to *all* to whom the Promise is made; but the Promise is made equally to *them,* and their *Children*; it is therefore an equal Reason why *they,* and *their Children* should be baptised; *i. e.* If the Promise being made to them was any Reason why they ought to be baptised, as the Apostle expresly declares, then the same Promise extending to their Children, must be an equal Reason why Baptism should be administered to them; nor can I possibly see how the Apostle's Argument can have any more Force with respect to the Parents, than it has with respect to the Children.—The Sum of the Argument is plainly this: The Promise is to you, therefore be baptised in the Name of Jesus Christ.— But the Promise is to your Children also; therefore let your Children be baptised would seem a necessary Consequence.—And indeed to suppose their Children excluded from Baptism, must render the Apostle's Argument very confused and inconclusive; for then it must stand thus: *The Promise is to you,* therefore be baptised in the Name of the Lord Jesus; the same Promise is equally to your Children—yet let not your Children be baptised; for they are not the proper Subjects of such an Ordinance.—And what an Absurdity is this? How easily might the *Jews* object and say: If the Promise to our Children is no Reason why they should be baptised, then neither is the Promise to us any Ground or Reason why we would submit to this new Institution, and therefore to say the least, there is just nothing at all in the Argument.

The

The *Jews*, to whom the Apostle is speaking, knew very well, that under the ancient Dispensation of the Covenant their Children were always included with the covenanted Parents, and that the Promise of *Abraham*'s Covenant had always run in that Tenor, including Parents and Children.—When therefore the Apostle is persuading them to come under this new Dispensation of the Covenant, he assures them that their Children are still to continue in Possession of their ancient Privilege; for that very Promise, which included them under the Law, equally includes them now under the Gospel.—For observe, he does not say, the Promise *was* to you and your Children, but it *is still*; otherwise they might naturally be supposed to object, that their Children were like to be in a worse Condition under the Gospel, than they were under the Law; which must greatly strengthen their Prejudices against the evangelical Dispensation. The Apostle therefore precludes any such Objection, by informing them, that they can lose nothing by submitting to this new Dispensation of the Covenant; for the Privileges of the Gospel should by no Means be more confined and limited than those of the Law; but on the contrary more enlarged: for under the Law the Promise was only to them and their Children, as Descendants of *Abraham*; but now it shall extend to all among the *Gentiles*, and their Children also, *whom the Lord our God shall call*.

All that is further necessary to shew this Text an unanswerable Argument for the Right of Infants to Baptism, is only to prove these two Points.

1. That by the *Promise* here, must be understood the Covenant-Promise made to *Abraham*, which

which gave his Infant-Children a Right to the Ordinance of Circumcifion.

2. That the Word *Children* in the Text does not intend their adult Defcendants, as fome pretend,' but their Infant-Offspring.

If thefe two Things are proved, the Argument ftands thus: The Covenant-Promife made to *Abraham*, which gave his Infant-Children a Right to Circumcifion under the Law, is now to you and your Infant-Children under the Gofpel.—And this Promife being urged as a Reafon why the Parents fhould be baptifed, muft necefsarily carry an equal Reafon for the Baptifm of their Children; and muft be fo underftood both by the Apoftle and his Jewifh Hearers.

The firft Queftion then is, whether by the *Promife*, in the Text, the Apoftle means that Covenant-Promife made to *Abraham*, which entitled his Infant-Children to Circumcifion? This fome deny, and fuppofe that by this Promife the Apoftle only intends that of *Joel*'s Prophecy, which he had quoted in the preceding Sermon, from the 16th to the 22d Verfe; but let any one read that Prophecy of *Joel*, as quoted by the Apoftle, in thofe Verfes, and he muft be immediately convinced, that the extraordinary and miraculous Gifts of the Holy Ghoft are there intended; confequently that the Promife, contained in this Prophecy, could never *here* be urged, as a Ground or Motive to Baptifm; for extraordinary and miraculous Gifts, were neither required, as the Ground of Baptifm, or numbered among the Blefsings that ufualiy attend or flow from it. Nor is there the leaft Intimation given in this Hiftory, that the 3000 here baptifed, did receive thefe miraculous Gifts.—If therefore *this* was the Promife the Apoftle fpeaks of to them and their

Children,

Children, it will follow that the Promise was not made good; for neither they nor their Children, (that we read of) were ever possessed of these extraordinary Gifts. Besides, the Promise in *Joel* had already its Accomplishment, in that extraordinary Effusion of the Holy Ghost upon the Apostles. This St. *Peter* declares, and quotes the Promise on purpose to prove his Declaration. It is plain then, he can have no Reference to this, in the *Promise* here mentioned; nor can it with the least Propriety, be understood of any thing else but that very PROMISE which God made to *Abraham*, when he took him, and his Infant-Children, into Covenant.—This Covenant was so eminent, and so well known, that it was often emphatically called THE PROMISE, without any other Characteristic or Note of Distinction.—Thus the spiritual Seed of *Abraham* are said to be Heirs according to THE PROMISE. And in many other Places too numerous to mention.—But to conclude this Point, the Apostle himself has plainly informed us, in another Place, what he here intends by the Promise, see *Acts* iii. 25. where urging much the same Exhortation upon his Jewish Hearers, as he does here, he enforces it with this Argument: *Ye are the Children of the Covenant, which God made with our Fathers, saying unto* Abraham, *and in thy Seed shall all the Kindreds of the Earth be blessed; unto you first God hath raised up his Son Jesus, and sent him to bless you,* &c. And as the *Promise* is here propounded as a Motive and Obligation to Baptism, nothing could be more natural than for the *Jews* to understand it of the Promise of *Abraham*'s Covenant, on which was grounded the Ordinance of Circumcision.

Allowing then (for indeed it cannot with any Consistency be disputed) that the Promise of *Abraham*'s *ham*'s Covenant is the Thing to which the Apoſtle refers. The ſecond Queſtion is, *who* are intended by their *Children*, to whom this Promiſe is ſaid to belong? Some ſuppoſe their adult Deſcendants, and not their Infant Offspring are the Children here intended; but of this there is not the leaſt Intimation in the Text, nor does it at all agree with the Scope of the Apoſtle's Argument; nay, ſuch a Conſtruction would ſeem to make him ſpeak Nonſenſe; for then he muſt be underſtood thus, " The Promiſe is unto you and to your Children, but not to them as your Children, or as ſuſtaining any Relation to you; but when they ſhall advance to an adult Age, and be called by the Miniſtry of the Word; then the Promiſe ſhall be to *them* as well as to you." Which is no more than might be ſaid of the Children of an *Ethiopian.* Why then is their Relation to their Parents mentioned at all, and why are they joined with them, as the Subjects of the Promiſe, if after all they are to ſtand on their own Footing, as Adults, as much as the Children of *Heathens?* Nor does this Conſtruction conſiſt with the plain grammatical Senſe of the Words, for the Apoſtle does not ſay the Promiſe is now to you, and ſhall be to your Children when grown and called by the Word, but the Promiſe is now to you and your Children: by which he very plainly intends the preſent Privilege the Jewiſh Children enjoy, above the preſent unconverted *Gentiles*, who are ſaid to be afar off, and to whom he ſays the Promiſe ſhall belong when called into a Church-State, and to their Children alſo.

Having thus proved that by the PROMISE here the Apoſtle means the Covenant made with *Abraham*, and by CHILDREN, their *Infant* Offspring, the Concluſion is plain, that if the Promiſe is propoſed,

posed as a Reason why the Parents should be baptised, as the Text plainly asserts, it is then an equal Reason, why Baptism should be administered to their Children; for the Promise is equally to *both*.

Having thus explained the Text, I shall endeavour to illustrate and establish this Proposition.

That the Infant Children of con-federate, or covenanted Parents have a Right to the Seal of the Covenant, under the Gospel, as much as they had under the Law, and therefore ought to be baptised. To set this in a proper Light I shall attempt to shew,

I. The Scripture Ground on which the Right of Infants to Baptism is founded.

II. The Evidence we have both from Scripture and History that the Baptism of Infants was the common Practice both of the Apostles and the primitive Church. And,

III. I shall attempt a Solution of the most material and common Objections raised against the Doctrine.

I. We begin with the Scripture-Ground on which the Right of Infants to Baptism is founded. And this Ground is the Covenant that God made with *Abraham* and his Seed,—the Institution of Circumcision as a Seal of that Covenant,—and the Administration of that Seal, by God's Appointment, to his Infant-Children,—whence this Conclusion is natural, *(viz.)* that the Infant-Children of covenanted Parents had, by God's Appointment, a Right to the external Seal of the Covenant

venant under the Law, and therefore, as the fame Covenant continues, they have doubtlefs the fame Right under the Gofpel.

To bring out this Conclufion, *that they have the fame Right under the Gofpel,* I fhall endeavour to prove thefe three Things.

i. *That the Covenant made with Abraham was a Covenant of Grace, and the fame for Subftance that is now in Force under the Gofpel.*

ii. *That Circumcifion was the external Seal of this Covenant, and was by God's Appointment adminiftered to Infant-Children.*

iii. *That Baptifm is now a Seal of the fame Covenant, inftituted in the Room of Circumcifion, and therefore ought to be adminiftered to the fame Subjects,* viz. *to the Infant-Children of covenanted Parents.*

i. *The Covenant made with* Abraham *was a Covenant of Grace, and the fame for Subftance that is now in Force under the Gofpel.* This I look upon to be the grand turning Point on which the Iffue of the Controverfy very much depends; for if *Abraham*'s Covenant, which included his Infant-Children, and gave them a Right to Circumcifion, was not the Covenant of Grace, then I freely confefs that the main Ground on which we affert the Right of Infants to Baptifm is taken away; and confequently the principal Arguments in fupport of the Doctrine are overturned.

But on the other Hand, if this Covenant, which included *Abraham*'s Children, and gave them a Right to Circumcifion, was the fame Covenant of Grace, under which the fpiritual Seed of *Abraham* now are; then, I think, the Covenant-Relation of Believer's Children, and confequently their Right to the Seal of the Covenant, under the Gofpel, as well as under the Law, is indifputable.

C 2 And

And that *Abraham*'s Covenant was the same Covenant of Grace, that now subsists under the Gospel, I shall prove from the following Arguments.

1. The Nature of the Covenant *itself*, and the Tenor of the *Promise* it contains, are the same with the Covenant of Grace, see GEN. xvii. 7. *And I will establish my Covenant between me and thee, and thy Seed after thee, in their Generations, for an everlasting Covenant*; TO BE A GOD TO THEE AND THY SEED AFTER THEE. Now this is the constant Stile of the Covenant of Grace. I WILL BE A GOD TO THEE, &c. God never was, or ever will be a God to any Man, since the Fall, in the Sense of that Phrase, but through Christ, and by a Covenant of Grace. Hence the Apostle mentions this, as the express Tenor of the Covenant of Grace, and the grand Sum of all the Promises it contains, see HEB. viii. 10. *I will be to them a God, and they shall be to me a People*. A greater Good than this cannot be promised; for it is the Sum of eternal Life. Hence it is said, REV. xxi. 7. *He that overcometh, shall inherit all Things, and* I WILL BE HIS GOD. As therefore *Abraham*'s Covenant promised the greatest Blessing that can be promised, even the very same, in express Words, as is promised in the Covenant of Grace, sure it must be the same Covenant, or else there must be two Covenants promising the same thing, and in the same Words, which is absurd.

2. The Apostle testifies that Believers under the Gospel are the spiritual Seed of *Abraham*, and consequently Heirs of the Promise of *Abraham*'s Covenant, and if so, then surely his Covenant must have been the Covenant of Grace, since it was the same which Believers are under *now*, and will be to the End of the World, see GAL. iii. 29.

And if ye be Chrift's, then are ye Abraham's *Seed, and Heirs according to the Promife.* What Promife? why the Promife of *Abraham's* Covenant; *that he would be a God to him, and his Seed after him.* It is plain then that the Covenant that promifeth this, and of which all Believers, under the Gofpel, are Heirs, muft be the Covenant of Grace.

3. The Apoftle tells us, that the Covenant made with *Abraham was confirmed of God in Chrift*, GAL. iii. 17. but no Covenant made with Man, was ever *confirmed of God in Chrift*, but the Covenant of Grace; for there was no Mediator in any other Covenant; therefore *Abraham's* Covenant was a Covenant of Grace.

4. We are abundantly affured, that *Abraham* was juftified by Faith, as all Believers are under the Gofpel, ROM. iv. 3, 23. But no Covenant in the Univerfe ever did, or can admit of Juftification by Faith, except the Covenant of Grace; therefore as all Believers have Communion with *Abraham*, in this grand Covenant-Privilege of Juftification, and are juftified on the fame Terms with *him*; it certainly muft follow, that if Believers are *now* under the Covenant of Grace, fo was *Abraham* alfo. Let me add to this, that the Scripture affures us, in plain Terms, that *the Gofpel was preached unto* Abraham, in that Article of his Covenant, *in thee fhall all Nations be bleffed.* Therefore if the Gofpel contains the Covenant of Grace, I hope the Point will admit of no further Difpute. From the Whole I think I may now fairly draw this Conclufion; that the Covenant made with *Abraham*, including his Infant-Children, was the fame for Subftance, with that which is now in Force with Believers under the Gofpel, and differed only in the external Mode of

Adminiftra_

Administration: For (1) the Matter of the Covenant is the *same*—*I will be your God, and the God of your Seed, and ye shall be my People.* (2) The Term, or Condition of the Covenant is the *same*; for in both Justification is by Faith, without Works. (3) The Mediator of the Covenant is the *same*, *Jesus Christ the same, Yesterday, To-day, and forever.* (4) The Sacraments under each Administration, (though consisting of different Rites) had the *same* spiritual Use and Meaning. Hence the Apostle asserts, that the Church of *Israel*, under *Abraham*'s Covenant, by Incidents and Actions which had a typical Reference to the Sacraments, did *eat the* SAME *spiritual Meat, and drink the* SAME *spiritual Drink*, with Believers, under the Gospel, *for they drank of the Rock that followed them, and that Rock was Christ.*

Thus I think it appears, beyond Contradiction, that the Covenant, made with *Abraham* and his Seed, was the Covenant of Grace; and the *same* of which the spiritual Seed of *Abraham* are Heirs under the Gospel. And it is no Objection to the above mentioned Conclusion, that the Promise of the Land of *Canaan* was included in that Covenant; for temporal Blessings are included in the Covenant of Grace. *Godliness is profitable unto all Things, having the* PROMISE *of the Life, that now is, as well as for that which is to come,* 1 Tim. iv. 8.

ii. *Circumcision was a Seal of this Covenant of Grace, and was, by God's Appointment, administered to Infant-Children.* That it was the Token, or Seal of *Abraham*'s Covenant, you see in the very Institution, GEN. xvii. 11. *Ye shall be circumcised, and it shall be a Token of the Covenant between me and you.* And again, *this is my Covenant, which ye shall keep between me and you, every Man Child among you*

you shall be circumcised. And the Apostle tells us expresly, ROM. iii. 11. That *Abraham received the Sign of Circumcision, a Seal of the Righteousness of Faith*: and that the Promise of his Covenant was not *to Abraham, and his Seed, through the Law, but through the Righteousness of Faith*; i. e. the Covenant of Grace; for what has Faith to do with a legal Covenant of Works? And that this Seal of the Covenant was, by God's Appointment, administered to the Infant-Children of *Abraham*'s Posterity, in all their succeeding Generations, will not be denied by *any*, who have read the History of the Old Testament.

Now from these two Propositions, that the Covenant with *Abraham* was the Covenant of Grace, and that Circumcision was the Seal of that Covenant, and administered to Infant-Children by God's Appointment, it follows, as plain as any Consequence can follow, that the Children of confœderate Parents, were once included, together with their Parents, in the Covenant of Grace.

That this was the Case of *Abraham*'s Children has been undeniably proved, and that this was the Case of the *Israelites*, under the *Mosaick* Dispensation, is evident from the express Word, DEUT. xxix. 10. and onward; where we have a Renewal of the *same* Covenant.

Ye stand this Day, all of you, before the Lord your God; your Captains of your Tribes, your Elders, and your Officers, with all the Men of Israel; *your Little-ones, your Wives, and the Stranger that is in thy Camp; from the Hewer of thy Wood, unto the Drawer of thy Water; that thou shouldst enter into Covenant with the Lord thy God, and into his Oath, which the Lord thy God maketh with thee this Day; that he may establish thee to Day for a People unto himself, and*
tha

that he may be to thee a God. &c. Obferve how their LITTLE-ONES are Partakers in this folemn Tranfaction. He then who denies that Children were taken into this Covenant, may as well deny this to be the Word of God. Nay, it is evident, from the conftant Practice of circumcifing Infants, that they were *always* confidered as included with the con-fœderate Parents; and on this Footing, *that Seal* of the Covenant was adminiftered. Since then the Children of con-fœderate Parents were, by God himfelf, admitted into Covenant, they muft ftill be acknowleged by God as Parties in the new Covenant, or *rather* new Adminiftration of the Covenant; and ought to be *fo* acknowleged by us, unlefs there is good Ground for their Exclufion, for a Privilege, once granted to the Church, muft continue through all Ages, unlefs the Donor is pleafed to revoke it; and that the Covenant-Intereft of Children is a Privilege, the Apoftle plainly proves, in his Anfwer to the Queftion, *What Advantage hath the* Jew, *and what Profit is there in Circumcifion? Much every Way.* David acknowledged it a Privilege, and pleaded it before God. *I am thy Servant, and the Son of thy Hand-Maid,* Pfal. cxvi. 16. Now if this be a Privilege, and God has *once* granted it to his Church, when has he ever revoked it? It is certain he did receive Children into his Church, with their Parents, and granted them the Seal; this is undeniable Fact. Now, has he given the leaft Intimation, that it was his Defign ever to exclude them? There is not a fingle Text in the Bible, that teaches *either exprefsly* or by *Confequence* that they ought to be cut off from that *antient* Privilege. Neither has Jefus Chrift, by any Doctrine, or Inftitution, debared them from their Covenant-Intereft, but rather

rather confirmed it, as I shall shew in the Sequel.

There is nothing in the Nature, or Constitution of the Gospel-Covenant that excludes them; nor can any Reason be suggested for it from their Incapacity; for they are as capable now of Blessings, and of the Seal of the Covenant, as they were under the Law. Therefore, since it is undeniable, that God has of old received Infants into Covenant, and has never since, either directly, or consequentially debarred, or cut them off from this Privilege; and since no Reason can be assigned, why they ought to be excluded; I must, I am constrained to believe that it is still his Will that they should be reckoned as Parties in his Covenant, and entitled to the external Seal.

iii. I now proceed to the third Thing that was proposed under the first general Head, *(viz.) That Baptism is a Seal of the same Covenant, made with Abraham, instituted in the Room of Circumcision, and therefore ought to be administered to the Children of professed Believers.*

1*st*, If the Covenant made with *Abraham* was a Covenant of Grace, and an everlasting Covenant, as has been proved, then Baptism must be a Seal of the *same* Covenant, and must have been instituted in the Room of Circumcision, just as the Lord's-Supper is instituted in the Room of the ancient Passover; and this the Apostle plainly asserts to be the Case, *Col.* ii. 11. *In whom also ye are circumcised with the Circumcision made without Hands, in putting off the Body of the Sins of the Flesh, by the Circumcision of Christ; buried with him in Baptism.* Here it is necessary to observe, that the *Colossians* were perplexed with *Judaizing* Teachers, urging the Necessity of Circumcision. The Apostle tells

D   them

them they need it not but are complete in Chrift without that Jewifh Rite, fince they had been baptifed in the Name of the Lord Jefus; which he calls the Circumcifion of Chrift, or, as it might be rendered, the Chriftian Circumcifion, which exactly anfwers the fpiritual Ufe and Defign of that Jewifh Inftitution. What then can be meant by the Circumcifion of Chrift, but Baptifm? It cannot be the Circumcifion that Chrift received when an Infant; for that was the Jewifh Rite the Apoftle was arguing againft. It cannot be the fpiritual Circumcifion of the Heart; for this is mentioned in the foregoing Claufe, and called a Circumcifion without Hands. And to underftand this Circumcifion of Chrift to be the *fame*, would make an unreafonable Tautology; as if he had faid, ye are circumcifed with the fpiritual Circumcifion by the fpiritual Circumcifion, which would have been Nonfenfe. But the Apoftle has put it out of all Doubt; for he explains the Circumcifion of Chrift, to mean, their being buried with him in Baptifm. The plain Senfe then is, Ye have the myftical Intention of that Jewifh Rite in the Circumcifion of Chrift, which is a being baptized in the Name of the Lord. But,

2*dly*, Baptifm fignifies the fame Thing with Circumcifion, and may we not therefore conclude that Baptifm was inftituted in its Room? Did the Blood of Circumcifion point to the Blood of Jefus Chrift, as that whereby Guilt is removed? fo does the Water of Baptifm. Did Circumcifion fignify our natural Corruption, and our Need of Regeneration and Sanctification by the Spirit? fo does Baptifm. Was Circumcifion the Sacrament of Admiffion into that Church of *Ifrael*? fo is Baptifm into the Chriftian Church. Was Circumcifion a

Badge

Badge of Relation to the God of *Ifrael*? fo is Baptifm of Relation to Chrift. And was Circumcifion a Sign and Seal of the Covenant of Grace, and of the Righteoufnefs of Faith? fo is Baptifm. The Analogy in *thefe*, and in many other Particulars, that might be mentioned, plainly fhews, that Baptifm was inftituted in the Room of Circumcifion.

Again, 3*dly*, If Baptifm does not come in the Room of Circumcifion, then we have no Ordinance anfwering to that Jewifh Rite, and confequently the Chriftian Church, by the Coming of Chrift, has been deprived of a Sacrament, which was reckoned of fingular Advantage in the Jewifh Difpenfation; for the *Profit of Circumcifion*, the Apoftle afferts, *was much every Way*. And if fo, the Chriftian Church has loft much every Way, by having nothing appointed in its Stead. We find that other Inftitutions, under the Old-Teftament, are fupplied by fomething anfwerable in the New. Inftead of the Paffover, we have the Lord's-Supper. Inftead of the Jewifh-Priefts, Gofpel-Minifters. Inftead of the meeting of the Tribes at the Temple, our Chriftian Affemblies. Inftead of the Seventh-Day Sabbath, we have the firft Day of the Week. And does nothing fucceed Circumcifion? Is a divine Ordinance totally loft? Surely fuch a Suppofition is abfurd. And if any thing does fucceed Circumcifion, Baptifm certainly ftands the faireft for its Succeffor, as it has the fame Ufe and Meaning, and is a Sign of the fame Covenant.

Now if Baptifm fucceeds Circumcifion, as a Seal of the fame Covenant, is it not an undeniable Inference, that it ought to be adminiftered to the fame Subjects as Circumcision was, that is to the Infants of con-fœderate Parents.

Could that Circumcision of Christ, which the Apostle calls Baptism, satisfy his Jewish Hearers, if it was not to extend to their Children, as well as the Circumcision of *Abraham*? They were enraged at *Paul*, we are told, when they heard that he taught the *Jews*, who were among the *Gentiles*, that they ought not to circumcise their Children, *Acts* xxi. 21. Therefore, his telling them that Baptism was the Circumcision of Christ, and took Place instead of the antient Rite, would have been no Satisfaction to them, had it been only for Adults, and not for their Infant-Children. The Apostle therefore must have intended it for both, or else he had given no satifactory Answer to the Plea of the *Jews* for retaining Circumcision.

Thus I have shewn, that the Covenant with *Abraham*, was a Covenant of Grace—that Circumcision was a Seal of that Covenant, and by God's Appointment administered to his Infant-Children,—that Baptism is a Seal of the *same* Covenant, and therefore ought to be administered to the *same* Subjects; *i. e.* the Infant-Children of con-fœderate and believing Parents; because their antient Right to this Seal has never been disannulled.

II. I now proceed to shew the Evidences we have, both from Scripture and History, that the Baptism of Infants was the common Practice, both of the Apostles and the primitive Churches. Now the Evidence we have, that this was the Practice of the Apostles, is of two Kinds.

1*st*,

1*st*, Their acknowledging the Covenant-Relation of Children, under the Gospel, as well as under the Law. And,

2*dly*, The strong Probability we have that there were Infant-Children among those whom they baptized.

1*st*, Then it is indisputably evident that the Apostle did allow the Covenant-Interest of Children, under the Gospel, as well as under the Law. I have already shewn, that the Text itself plainly asserts, that the Promise of *Abraham*'s Covenant was to Believers and their Infant-Children; and to this, I would add that Passage, *Rom.* xi. 16. *For if the Root be holy, so are the Branches: and if some of the Branches be broken off, and thou being a wild Olive-Tree, wert grafted in amongst them, and with them partakest of the Root and Fatness of the Olive-Tree*, &c. Now by the Root here, the Apostle intends *Abraham*, and by the Branches his Posterity, who partook in the same Privileges with him, by Virtue of their Interest in the same Covenant, till they were broken off. Here then is plainly asserted the fœderal Holiness, or Covenant-Interest of the Children of con-fœderate Parents. If the Root be holy, so are the Branches. God has said it, and who dare unsay it? And as this is not spoken of real Holiness, or truly gracious Habits, (for no Parent can convey real Holiness to his Children) it must then mean a fœderal or Covenant-Holiness, such as denominated the *Jews* in general, a holy Nation; not that they were all truly gracious, but visibly dedicated to God, and Members of his visible Church; and in consequence of this, had his Ordinances administered to them. This is the Holiness we plead, for the Children of Believers, or con-
fœderate

fœderate Parents. Now it is here afferted, that the believing *Gentiles*, are fo ingrafted into this Stock, and fo united to *Abraham*, by Covenant-Relation, as to partake of the fame Privileges that *Abraham*'s Children once did, and from which they were now broken off. For obferve, the *Grafted in*, anfwers exactly to the *Broken off*. The *Broken off* of the *Jews*, was from the vifible Church, fo is the *Grafted in*, of the *Gentiles*, into the vifible Church alfo.

The *Broken off* reached Parents and Children, and fo muft the *Grafted in*. And if the believing *Gentiles* partook of the Fatnefs of the *fame* Olive, *i. e.* of the *fame* Privileges of which the *Jews* did, then their Children certainly muft be included in the Covenant, and entitled to the external Seal; for that the Jewifh Children *were* is plain Fact; and if *Gentile* Children are excluded, and not taken into Covenant, by Baptifm, as the others were by Circumcifion, then they do not partake of the *fame* Privileges with the *Jews*, who are broken off, and confequently the Apoftle's Affertion muft be falfe, and his Argument inconclufive.

Another Text which proves the Covenant-Intereft of the Infants of believing Parents, in the Judgment of the Apoftle is, 1 *Cor.* vii. 14. *For the unbelieving Hufband is fanctified by the Wife, and the unbelieving Wife is fanctified by the Hufband, elfe were your Children unclean, but now are they holy.* The Queftion propofed was this; *Whether it was lawful for a believing Hufband or Wife, to live with their unbelieving Companion?* This the Apoftle anfwers in the Affirmative, for which he gives this Reafon, the Unbeliever is fanctified by the Believer, whofe Duty it is to confecrate his All to God, as he actually does, elfe were your Children unclean,

unclean, but now are they holy. This is a plain Intimation, that it would not be confiftent with the Chriftian Character, to continue in a Marriage-Relation with an Infidel, if their Children would, in fuch Cafe, be unclean. Here *unclean*, and *holy*, are fet in direct Oppofition. Now to be unclean in the Stile of Scripture, as oppofed to holy, is to be out of the vifible Church, or without any vifible Intereft in, or Covenant-Relation to God, fee *Acts* x. 14. where *Peter* ufes the Word unclean, with reference to *Cornelius*, becaufe he was not vifibly in Covenant, being a *Gentile*. And on the other Hand, to be holy, muft fignify to have a vifible Intereft in the Covenant, or vifibly to belong to God. So that the Covenant-Relation of the Children of believing Parents is here plainly afferted. What elfe can be meant by their being holy? It cannot mean Legitimacy, as fome pretend; for the Legitimacy of Children has no Dependence on the relative Character, or Profeffion of their Parents, but only on a lawful Marriage; which is no peculiar Privilege of the Church, but of Mankind in general. It cannot mean a real internal Holinefs; for this is not at all derived from the mofteminent believing Parents. But it is plain, the Apoftle here means fome Kind of Holinefs that depends on one of the Parents being a Believer, and without which they would be unclean. If this then is not a fœderal Holinefs, or a vifible Covenant-Relation, let any Man, if he can, tell what it is. If it is a fœderal Holinefs, or Covenant-Relation, then here is a plain Proof, that the Apoftle looked upon the Children of con-fœderate Parents, as having the fame Intereft in the Covenant, under the Gofpel, as they had under the Law; and if they had the fame Intereft in the

Covenant,

Covenant, they had the same Right to the external Seal: for a Right to Baptism is acknowledged, by all, to be founded on a visible Interest in the Covenant of Grace. This gave *Abraham* and his Children a Right to Circumcision under the Law; and this it is that gives both Parents and Children a Right to Baptism under the Gospel. Now if the Apostle looked on the Children of believing Parents, as having an Interest in the Covenant of Grace, as has been proved, and if they esteemed a visible Covenant-Interest to be the Ground of Admission to Baptism, which none will deny, then we have undeniable Evidence, that they did in Fact baptize the Children of all Professing Believers; and that they understood their Commission, as authorizing them so to do, when they were bid to *go and teach all Nations, baptizing them in the Name of the Father, of the Son, and of the Holy Ghost*. The Word *teach*, is, in the Original, to make Disciples, or learn; and Children are capable in this Sense of being made Disciples; nay, the Children of believing Parents under the Gospel, are called Disciples expresly, *Acts* xv. 10. *Now therefore, why tempt ye God to put a Yoke upon the Neck of the Disciples*, &c.

The Yoke here mentioned was Circumcision, which was appointed to be administered to Infant-Children, as you see in the Context; therefore Children are called Disciples, and as they are capable of being admitted, as Learners, in the School of Christ, and have that Interest in the Covenant, on which that Right of Baptism is founded; they must be included in the Words, *all Nations*, mentioned in the Commission. And, besides this clear Evidence, that they understood their Commission to include Believers' Infants, we have also, from Scripture

Scripture-Accounts, the higheſt Probability that their general Practice was accordingly; for we read that they baptized whole Houſholds. For inſtance, *Lydia*, and her Houſhold, the Jailor, and all that were *his*, and the Houſhold of *Stephanas*. And is it probable that there were no Infant-Children in any of theſe Families? We read, when God ſmote the Firſt-born of *Egypt*, there was not an Houſe, in which there was not *one* dead; conſequently not an Houſe in *Egypt*, in which there was not a Child. And is it probable, or credible to an unprejudiced Mind, that in all the Houſholds baptized, there was not *one* Child? Suppoſe it had been ſaid of one proſelyted to the Jewiſh Religion, that he, and his Houſhold, or that he, and all his, were circumciſed; would any doubt whether his Infant-Children were circumciſed? I believe not: for this was a known Practice, ever ſince *Abraham*'s Covenant, to receive the Children with the Parents into a Covenant-Relation. And I have ſhewn that the ſame Reaſons hold for their Admiſſion under the Goſpel. It would ſeem then, as it had always been the Practice of the Church, to adminiſter the Seal of the Covenant to the Infants of con-fœderate Parents, that there would have been ſome Diſapprobation of it, or ſome expreſs Declaration againſt it, if it is not to be continued. So great a Change as that of caſting Infants out of the viſible Church, who had been admitted for ſo many hundred Years, by a divine Appointment, can hardly be ſuppoſed, without an expreſs Declaration forbidding them.

Would the Apoſtles have refuſed them *that* Chriſtian-Memberſhip, and the Seal of the Covenant, which they had ſo long enjoyed, without any expreſs Command for that Purpoſe? And if they

they had received such 'a Command, and in consequence, made so great a Change in the Constitution of the Church, should we have had no Account of it? would it not have made a Noise and Stir among the believing *Jews*, or at least, have been a Matter of Record? Since therefore Infants were admitted to the Seal of the Covenant of Grace till the Apostles' Day, and since we have no Account that they ever rejected them, or cut them off from that Privilege: and *especially* since they baptized whole Housholds, upon the Conversion of the Parents, or Heads of the Family, we have, I think, sufficient Evidence, that it was their common Practice to baptize them.

I now pass on to consider the Evidence which we have, that the Baptism of Children was the constant Practice of the primitive Church from the Apostles' Time; which will still confirm the Evidence that it was their Practice also. For it cannot be supposed but that those, who lived so near the Apostles, as the first, second, and third Centuries, must have known what was the Practice of the Apostles themselves, and that they practised accordingly. For it is allowed by all, that the Church was then in its Purity, and not corrupted with Innovations, and Superstitions: and the Writers of those Times are not only Witnesses, that Infant-Baptism was the Practice in their Day, but expresly declare, some of them, that it was the Practice of the Apostles themselves, and of the Church from their Time.

The *1st* Evidence I would produce is *Irenus*, who, by the best Accounts, was born before the Death of the Apostle *John*, and was well acquainted with *Polycarp*, who was *John*'s Disciple; and therefore could not be mistaken about the Practice

tice of the Church down to his Time. It is true, he mentions Infant Baptifm only tranfiently; for it had not then been a Matter of Difpute, and therefore there was no Occafion given for arguing about it.

It muft alfo be obferved, that he, and many of the Fathers, when they fpoke of Baptifm, ufed the Thing fignified for the Sign; and, as in the Old-Teftament, Circumcifion is called the Covenant, inftead of the Sign and Seal of Covenant; fo by *Irenus*, and others, Baptifm is called Regeneration, becaufe it is the outward Sign of Regeneration, and the Renewing of the Holy Ghoft. With how much Propriety he calls it fo is nothing to me, if it appears that he does call it fo, and under that Character fpeaks of it as commanded to Children and Little-ones, his Teftimony is directly to the Purpofe. And that he does ufe the Word *Regeneration* for Baptifm, is plain from his own Words: " *When Chrift, fays he, gave his Difciples the Com-* " *mand of Regenerating unto God, he faid, Go and* " *teach all Nations, baptizing them in the Name of* " *Father, and of the Son, and of the Holy Ghoft.*" Here it is plain, that by the Command of regenerating, he means the Command of baptizing; not that he fuppofes Baptifm was Regeneration; but he puts the Thing fignified for the Sign, juft as God himfelf does, when he calls Circumcifion his Covenant, which was a Sign or Token of his Covenant.

Allowing then, that he ufes Regeneration for Baptifm, as the above Quotation plainly proves, his Teftimony is plain for the Baptifm of Infants; for he adds: " *Chrift came to fave thofe, who by him* " *are regenerated unto God*; (i. e. *baptized*) *both* " *Infants and Little-ones, and young Men and elderly* " *Perfons.*"

"*Perfons.*" Here he speaks of Infants and Little ones, being regenerated unto God. And that he uses the Word Regeneration for Baptism, putting the Thing signified for the Sign, is further evident from the concurring Practice of his contemporary Writers; particularly *Justin Martyr*, who has these Words: "*They are regenerated in the same*
" *Way in which we have been regenerated, for they*
" *are washed with Water, in the Name of the Fa-*
" *ther, the Son, and the Holy Ghost.*"

If it be said there was an Impropriety in calling Regeneration Baptism, it is nothing to the present Argument, for that they did call it so, is undeniably Fact from these Quotations; and it is equally fact that they spoke of it as commanded to Infants, and Little-ones, as well as young Men, and elderly Persons.

In the Beginning of the third Century, *Origen* expresly declares Infant-Baptism to have been the constant Use of the Church. The Occasion of his mentioning it was this, he was attempting, in the eighth Homily, to prove the Doctrine of Original Sin, and that Infants were guilty as soon as born, and makes use of their Baptism as an Argument. "*The Baptism of Children, says he, is given for the*
" *Forgiveness of Sins: But why, continues he, are*
" *Infants, by the Usage of the Church, baptized,*
" *if they have nothing that wants Forgiveness? And*
" *again, he adds, It is because by the Sacrament of*
" *Baptism the Pollution of our Birth is taken away,*
" *that Infants are baptised.*" With much more to the same Purpose.

Here is as plain a Testimony as can be given, that Infant-Baptism was the standing Usage of the Church; and that it was then a Point out of all Dispute; or else he never would have thought

it

it an Argument to prove Original Sin. Nay, he not only afferts it to be the Ufage of the Church in his Time, but declares that they received it from the Apoftles; for in his Comment on the Epiftle to the *Romans*, he has thefe Words: " *The* " *Church had alfo, from the Apoftles, an Order to* " *give Baptifm to Infants; for they, to whom the* " *divine Myfteries were committed, knew that there* " *was, in all Perfons, a natural Pollution, which* " *cught to be wafhed away by Water, and the* " *Spirit.*"

Now *Origen* was born about the Year of our Lord 182, within 100 Years of the Apoftles themfelves. Both his Father and Grandfather were Chriftians. He was one of the moft learned Men of that Age, and preached the Gofpel in *Rome*, in *Greece*, in *Paleftine*, and *Syria*, and therefore could not but be acquainted with the Ufage of all the Churches. And the Manner in which he fpeaks of it makes his Evidence the *ftrongeft*, as he ufes it for an Argument to prove another Doctrine, *(viz.)* Original Sin, which he could not have done with any Propriety, if it had not been an univerfally acknowledged Truth in his Day.

Tertullian alfo, who was contemporary with *Origen*, gives us a plain Proof, that Infant-Baptifm was the conftant Practice of the Church in his Day.

It is true, he fpeaks againft it, and advifes that it fhould be delayed till grown to Years, nay, till after Marriage. The Reafon was, he had entertained a Notion, that Sins, committed after Baptifm, were next to, if not utterly unpardonable; and therefore advifed that the Baptifm of Children fhould be delayed, unlefs in Cafe of Neceffity, even till after Marriage, imagining they would
then

then be less liable to Temptation, &c. Many other odd and singular Opinions are found in his Writings, and therefore it may be remembered, that I neither quote *him*, or any *other* of the Fathers, with a View to be determined, by their Opinions, whether Infants ought to be baptized, or not, but only to prove what was Matter of Fact, that the Baptism of Children was the Practice of the Church, whether right or wrong; and *Tertullian* speaking against it, (for the Reasons above-mentioned) is as plain a Proof of the Fact as any of the rest. For if it was not the Custom to baptise Children why should he speak against it? Surely he would not fight with his own Shadow, or oppose a Practice, or Custom, that had no Existence. And besides, he allows it in Cases of Necessity, *i. e.* when in Danger of Death; so that he was only against it for the absurd Reason he mentions, left they should fall into more aggravated Sin. And therefore he would not have it administered in common Cases till after Marriage.

The next Evidence, I would produce, is the blessed Martyr *Cyprian*, who was made Overseer of the Churches at *Carthage*, about 248 Years after the Birth of Christ. A Question was started in his Time, whether Infants might be baptized, before they were eight Days old? because that was the Day in which Circumcision was to be administered. On this he calls a Council of Ministers, no less than 66 in Number, who all unanimously agreed, that Baptism ought not to be delayed till the eighth Day, at least, that there was no Necessity of such a Delay. A large Letter was wrote to this Purpose to satisfy all who were in Doubt about this

Question,

Queftion, and figned by *Cyprian* in the Name of the reft.

Now obferve, the Queftion was not, whether Infants were to be baptized, this was allowed by all, but the only Queftion was, whether, like Circumcifion, it muft be limited to the eighth Day from the Birth?

And this they determined in the Negative, and fay, it may with equal Propriety be adminiftered fooner.

St. *Ambrofe*, who wrote about 274 Years from the Apoftles, declares exprefsly, that the Baptifm of Infants has been the Practice of the Apoftles themfelves, and of the Church till that Time. And this he mentions only tranfiently, when fpeaking on another Subject, which plainly proves it was not a Subject of Debate. It would weary your Patience to cite all the Authors that might be produced to this Purpofe. I fhall therefore conclude with the Teftimony of St. *Auftin*, who wrote his Piece againft the *Donatifts*, about 300 Years after the Apoftles, in which he has thefe very Words:

" *If any afk for divine Authority in the Matter of In-*
" *fants being baptized, though that which the whole*
" *Church practifes, and which has not been inftitu-*
" *ted by Council, but was ever in Ufe, is very rea-*
" *fonably believed to be no other than a Thing de-*
" *livered by the Authority of the Apoftles, yet, fays*
" *he, we may take a true Eftimate how much Baptifm*
" *avails Infants, by the Circumcifion which God's*
" *former People received.*"

The fame Thing he urges in his Controverfy with *Pelagius*, which was about the Year 410. Now *Pelagius* had taught, that Infants were born free from any finful Defilements. St. *Auftin* writes againft him, and infifts on the Baptifm of Infants, which

which was the known and standing Practife of the Church, as an Argument of their natural Defilement. In this Plea he has thefe Words: "*That Infants are by all Chriſtians acknowledged to ſtand in Need of Baptiſm, which muſt be in them for Original Sin, ſince they have no other.*" Again, ſays he, "*If they have no Sin, why are they accepted to the Uſage of the Church-Baptiſm? Why are they waſhed with the Laver of Regeneration, if they have no Defilement?*"

Pelagius was extremely puzzled with this Argument, as he could not pretend to deny Infant-Baptiſm. Nay, when ſome charged him with denying it (as the neceſſary Conſequence of this Doctrine) he tries to refute the Charge, and has theſe remarkable Words:

"*Men ſlander me,* ſays he, *as if I denied Baptiſm to Infants.*" This he calls a Slander, and ſays that he never heard of any, no not the worſt of Hereticks, that would ſay ſuch a Thing of Infants.

This Confeſſion is the ſtrongeſt Demonſtration, that Infant-Baptiſm was univerſally practiſed, Time out of Mind; or elſe he, whoſe Intereſt it was to deny it, to anſwer the Arguments of his Adverſary, would certainly have done it. But ſo far is he from that, though his Cauſe required it, that he expreſsly declares, he does not deny it, nor ever heard of any that did. Now *Pelagius* was a great Scholar, and a great Traveller. He had been to *Rome, Africa, Egypt,* and *Jeruſalem,* where he ſpent much Time; and therefore muſt be acquainted with the Rites of the Fathers, and Cuſtoms of the Churches in all thoſe Parts; and yet he declares that he had never heard of any that had denied Baptiſm to Infants. It is as plain then as

Hiſtory

Hiftory can make it, that there had been then no Difpute about the Point, and that there was not, neither had been any Sect of People profeffing Chriftianity, that denied it, from the Apoftles' Time to that Day. Nor is there the leaft Evidence, that it was ever oppofed by any Man, or Society of Men, for fix or feven hundred Years from that Time. And now, what is the Confequence? You fee, that the baptizing Infants was the Practice of Churches, derived from the Apoftles' Time, and fo on for eleven or twelve hundred Years, which is as plain a Fact as Hiftory, and the Writings of thofe Times can make it. The Confequence is, that if Infant-Baptifm is a Nullity, and not agreeable to the Inftitution of Chrift, then the Church muft have loft an Ordinance of Chrift during all this Period. Nay, they muft have loft it in the very firft Ages, and pureft Times, and there muft have been no regular Baptifm, confequently no Chriftian Minifters, or any Ordinances, for eleven hundred Years or more. And can any Man, of an impartial Mind, believe this? What then would become of our Saviour's Promife, to be prefent in the Adminiftration of Baptifm? *Lo! I am with you always, even to the End of the World.* For that they baptized Infants you fee is Fact; and if this was not agreeable to his Inftitution, he could not be with them in the Adminiftration of that Ordinance, and therefore his Prefence muft fail, and his Church, during all that long Period, of many hundred Years, muft have had no regular Baptifm, and confequently could be no regular Gofpel-Church. And who can perfuade himfelf, or imagine, that Chrift had no Church in the World during all that Period? Befides, if Infant-Baptifm had, in any of thofe

F Periods,

Periods, been introduced by Men, and had not been the Cuſtom of the Church from the Apoſtles; how a ſtrange muſt it appear that there ſhould be no Account, no not the leaſt Hint, in all Antiquity, when it was introduced, or by whom? Had it been human Invention, would it have been ſo univerſal in the firſt 300 Years, and yet no Record left, when it was introduced, nor of any Diſpute, or Controverſy about it? This is incredible.

We have particular Accounts in Hiſtory, when the Baptiſm of Infants began to be denied and diſputed, and by whom; but no Account of any Time or Means of its Introduction: which is a plain Proof that it muſt have been handed down from the Apoſtles, and have been a ſtanding Privilege in the Church from their Time. Again, if Infant-Baptiſm is a Nullity, it is plain, from the hiſtorical Facts above-mentioned, there can *now* be no regular Baptiſm in the World, nor ever will be to the End of Time, ſince a Succeſſion of adult Baptiſms cannot ſo much as be pretended to.

Thoſe then, who firſt began to baptize Adults, were themſelves baptized in their Infancy, and therefore, being unbaptized themſelves, according to the *Anabaptiſt*'s Scheme, could never have Authority to baptize others. So that all the preſent adult Baptiſms, if traced back, muſt come originally from thoſe, who were baptized in Infancy; and conſequently, on *their* Principles, can have no Validity in them. We muſt therefore give into one of theſe three Things, either 1*ſt*, That a Succeſſion of adult *Baptiſts* can be traced from the Apoſtles; or 2*dly*, That Infant-Baptiſm is valid, and agreeable to the Inſtitution of Chriſt;

or

or elſe 3*dly*, That there neither is, nor can be, any' regular Baptiſm in the Church, to the End of the World:

The 1*ſt*, can never be done, as all muſt allow. The laſt is too ſhocking and impious to be admitted. And therefore the 2*d*. muſt be acknowledged, *viz*. that Infant-Baptiſm is valid and agreeable to the Inſtitution of Jeſus Chriſt; for a fourth Concluſion cannot be thought on.

III. But I haſten in the laſt Place, to anſwer ſome of the moſt material Objections that are made againſt the Doctrine, and by which thoſe of contrary Sentiments puzzle and confound the Minds of Men, and endeavour to render the Subject obſcure. The moſt common Objections are ſuch as theſe; 1*ſt*, We have no expreſs Command in Scripture for baptizing Infants, and therefore, it is inſinuated, we act without any Warrant from the divine Word. To this I anſwer, If there are virtual and implicit Commands for it, and if it is commanded by clear Scripture-Conſequence, it is of equal Force, as if it had been ſaid in expreſs Terms, *baptize your Infant-Children*.

A Command may be as clearly inferred, by way of Conſequence, from certain Premiſes, as if it was in expreſs Words. See an Inſtance of this in *Paul* and *Barnabas*, Acts xiii. 46. *Lo! ſay they, we turn to the* Gentiles, *for ſo hath the Lord commanded us ſaying, I have ſet thee to be a Light of the* Gentiles. Now the Command they ſpeak of, is not at all *expreſs*, but *implicit*; for what they call a *Command*, is a *Promiſe* made to Chriſt: *I have ſet thee to be a Light of the* Gentiles. This they conſtrue to be an implicit Command, directing them in the Way of Duty. *Lo! we turn to the* Gentiles, *for ſo hath the Lord commanded us.* Where had the Lord commanded them? Why *virtually* and *implicitly* in this Promise, made to his Son, *I have set thee to be a Light to the* Gentiles, &c. This then being granted, that a virtual and implicit Command, is of equal Force, as if it had been expressed; it is easy to deny the Objection, and say, we have many Commands to baptize our Infant-Children. And 1*st*. God's Command to *Abraham* to circumcise his Infant-Children, is a virtual and implicit Command to Believers to baptize *their's*; for Believers are *Abraham*'s spiritual Seed, and Heirs according to the Promise. Here you see an express Command was once given to initiate Children into the Church, by a sacramental Rite that is commanded, and has never been repealed, and therefore still remains in Force, as I have proved before. Again, Christ's commanding to suffer little Children to come unto him, and not forbid them; is a virtual, or implicit Command, that Parents ought to bring their Children to him in Baptism. For the Ground on which that Command is founded, is, *of such is the Kingdom of Heaven.* Which, to make the least that can be made of it, is, that they have a visible Interest in the Covenant, and a Right to Membership in his visible Kingdom. And we know, yea, it is acknowledged by *all*, that a visible Interest in the Covenant is the Scripture-Ground on which Baptism ought to be administered.

Again, the Command that our Saviour gave, *Go and disciple all Nations, and baptize them,* is an implicit, if not an express Command to baptize the Children of Christian Nations; for *Nations* must include Children, as you see in the Promise made to *Abraham*, in thy Seed, *i. e.* in thy Children

dren shall all Nations be blessed. Now if Children are not here included in the Words *all Nations*, then it will follow, that all that die in Infancy must perish without Exception, having no Interest in the Blessings of Christ, and if the Words *all Nations* include them here, so it must in the Commission above-mentioned, and consequently they are virtually, and implicitly commanded to be baptized. *Again*, the Exhortation to the *Jews* in the Text *to be baptized*, is an implicit, if not an express Command to baptize their Children; for the Exhortation is grounded on the Promise, and the Promise is to them and their Children.

Thus you see the Scripture abounds with implicit and virtual Commands to baptize our Children, and such Commands are looked upon sufficient to determine our Conduct in other Cases, and therefore, why not in this? For example, who doubts but it is a commanded Duty to keep the first Day of the Week for a Sabbath, and yet where is the formal express Command? It is commanded *only* virtually and implicitly.

Who doubts that public Worship is a commanded Duty? Yet, where is the express Command in so many Words? We are bid not to forsake the Assembling ourselves together, but this is a negative Precept, the Affirmative requiring us *so* to assemble, is an implicit Command. It is therefore a foolish Cavil to say, there is no express Command to baptize Infants; for this may be said of Womens' receiving the Sacrament, of keeping the first Day of the Week, and a hundred other Things, which all allow are implicitly commanded, and have the same Obligation on Mens' Consciences, as if ever so formally expressed. Besides, what Necessity could there be of an express prefs Command, for that, which had been once inftituted, and never repealed? The Children of covenanted Parents were once exprefsly command- ed to receive the Seal of the Covenant, and this Command has never been reverfed, as we have already proved, therefore the original exprefs Com- mand continuing in Force, there would be no Neceffity of another. And as it had been the conftant Practice of the Church, for many Ages, to adminifter the Seal of the Covenant to their Children, there was no Neceffity of renewing the Inftitution, in cafe it was to continue. But on the other Hand, there was an abfolute Neceffity of an exprefs Declaration againft it, if it was then to have ceafed.

Another Objection is this, that there is no ex- prefs Inftance in all the Hiftory of the New-Tefta- ment of an Infant Child's being baptized; and therefore we proceed without any Scripture-Ex- ample. Let me reply. I have told you already of whole Houfholds being baptized, on the Con- verfion of the Parent, or Head of the Family; which carries the ftrongeft Probability of the Baptifm of Infant-Children, and would be eafily underftood to include them, had the fame been faid of Circumcifion. And there is the fame Reafon for it in the one Cafe, as in the other.

But fuppofing there is no exprefs Mention made in the Hiftory of the New-Teftament, of one In- fant-Baptifm, yet no Man has any Right to con- clude from hence, that, in Fact, there was none; for if fo, we might as well conclude there were whole Churches which never were baptized. For there is no exprefs Account, in the Hiftory of the New-Teftament, that the Churches of *Antioch*, of *Iconium*, of the *Romans*, *Galatians*, *Theffaloni- ans*,

ans, and *Colloſſians*, were ever baptized. Would it be fair to conclude from hence, that they there were not? Nay, you may read the Hiſtory of the Old-Teſtament, for ſeveral Ages of the Church, and never find one Inſtance of a Child's Circumciſion. And will it do from hence to conclude, that they lived without circumciſing their Children? No, you will ſay, it may be argued by clear Conſequence; and ſo, I ſay, may the Baptiſm of Children; beſides, this Objection lies with greater Force againſt *thoſe*, who practiſe adult Baptiſm, than it does againſt *us*; for they cannot produce one Example from Scripture that warrants their Practice. That there were many adult Baptiſms, I grant, becauſe the Subjects were grown to adult Years before they profeſſed Chriſtianity. And in this we agree with them, that adult Perſons, who are converted from *Judaiſm*, or *Heatheniſm*, to Chriſtianity, ought, in their adult Years, to be baptized, and all *ſuch*, as have never been baptized before. But Scripture-Inſtances of this are nothing to the Purpoſe, for in this we all agree, and have no Controverſy. But if they would give a Scripture-Example of their own preſent Practice, they muſt give an Inſtance of a Perſon born and brought up of Chriſtian, or baptized Parents, that was baptized in adult Years. If they could do this, it would be ſome Evidence, that Infant-Baptiſm was not in Practice. If they cannot, as it is certain they cannot produce ſuch an Inſtance, let them no more pretend the Want of Scripture-Example againſt baptizing Children, or that they have Scripture-Example on their Side. And why ſhould there be no Inſtances of this Kind, if ſuch was the common Practice? For the Hiſtory of the *Acts* of the Apoſtles, continued above the Space of thirty Years from Chriſt's Aſcent to *Paul*'s Impriſonment

at

at *Rome*; and during that Time, thousands were born of Christian Parents, and grown up to the Age of twenty or thirty Years, and yet there is not one Instance in Scripture of any such Baptisms in adult Years. If therefore they were not baptized in Infancy, there is no Account of any, no not of one, of the Posterity of Christian-Parents, being baptized at all; for all the Account of adult Baptisms are only of such as in adult Years embraced the Christian Religion, having been before either *Jews* or *Heathens*.

A third Objection is, that Infants can receive no Benefit from Baptism, because of their Incapacity, and therefore ought not to be baptized.

To this I answer, the same Objection might be offered against their being circumcised under the Law; for the Capacity of Infants is doubtless as great *now*, as it was *then*. Therefore, in the first Place, Infants are capable of being entered into Covenant with God; for that the Children of the *Jews* were so, is plain Fact, not only from the Tenor of the Covenant with *Abraham*, which expresly included them, but from that solemn Renewal of it in *Deuteronomy*, where their Little-ones are expresly mentioned as Partakers in the Covenant-Transaction. Secondly, they are capable of the Seal of the Covenant, for this was by God's Appointment administred to them under the Law, at eight Days old. Thirdly, they are capable of being cleansed by the Blood of Christ, and of being regenerated by his Spirit, which are the Things signified by Baptism. He who denies this, must deny that they are capable of Salvation, and therefore, dying in Infancy, must perish, on supposition of original Guilt and Pollution. And if they are capable of deriving original Guilt and Pollution

lution from the firſt *Adam*, without their Knowledge and Conſent; they certainly are as capable of deriving Pardon, and renewing Grace from the ſecond *Adam*, without any explicit Knowledge of, or actual conſenting to his Covenant. And if they are capable of the Root, and Principle of all Sin, they are equally capable of the Habit and Principle of all ſpiritual Grace.

Again, They are as capable of being laid under Obligations of Duty to God, to be perform'd when grown up, as the Children of the *Jews* were, and the Apoſtle ſays expreſsly, *I teſtify unto every Man that is circumciſed, that he is a Debtor to the whole Law*. And why are not Children *now* as capable of the baptiſmal Obligations to the Law of Chriſt, as the circumciſed Children of the *Jews* were, of being Debtors to the Law of *Moſes*? And is it not Matter of daily Obſervation, that Infants are capable of having earthly Inheritances ſettled upon them, by Inſtruments ſigned, and ſealed, while they are ignorant of the whole Tranſaction? And what Reaſon can be given, why they ſhould not be as capable of the Bleſſings of the new Covenant, and of having them ſealed by Baptiſm, though they are ignorant of it?

To ſay that it is no Advantage to Children to adminiſter the Seal of the Covenant to them, becauſe of their Incapacity, is to reflect on an Inſtitution of Heaven, and on the Wiſdom and Goodneſs of its Author. The Apoſtle *Paul* was of another Mind; for he ſays the Profit of Circumcſion was much every Way, notwithſtanding the Incapacity of the Subjects, being but eight Days old.

G But

But a 4*th*, and most common Objection is, that Faith and Repentance, or a Profession of them, at least, are mentioned in the New-Testament, as the necessary Pre-requisites of Baptism, and therefore, as Children are incapable of these, they must be incapable of the Ordinance itself. I answer, that Children are capable of the Habits and Principles of Faith, as has been observed before, and must be allowed by all, who do not exclude them from Salvation. Now is their a greater Absurdity in allowing them to be capable of the Root and Principle of every Grace, than to allow them to be capable of the Root and Principle of every Sin? Besides, our Lord says of a little Child, whom he set before his Disciples, as a Pattern of Humility, *whosoever shall offend one of these little Ones, that believeth in me*, &c. Whence it is plain, that Little-ones may believe in him, *i. e.* they may have the Habits or Principles of Faith, though incapable of the Act; or else, as I said before, we must necessarily embrace that *uncharitable* Sentiment, that all, who die in Infancy, must perish without Remedy.

If it be said, that it is a Profession of Faith, which the Scripture mentions as a Pre-requisite to Baptism; I grant it with respect to adult Persons, who embrace Christianity in their adult Years. And this is all that can possibly be argued from it; for all must allow, that when ever these Pre-requisites are spoken of in Scripture, it is with reference to Adults, who were converted from *Judaism* or *Heathenism* to Christianity; and in all such Cases we allow, that there must be a Profession of Faith, antecedent to Baptism. In this we have no Controversy

troversy with those, who practise adult Baptism. But they then must allow, that all these Passages, which require the Profession of Faith, as necessary to Baptism, have no reference at all to Infants, but are intirely confin'd to those, who embrace Christianity in their adult Years; and therefore no Argument can be drawn from hence, against the Baptism of Children; for they are not at all the Persons spoken of. Yet we find, in fact, that when those Adults, that embraced Christianity, in the Apostles Times, professed their Faith, not only themselves, but their Housholds, and all that were theirs, were baptized. And as there is not a Word said of such a Profession being required of the Members of those Families, we must therefore conclude, either that they were young Children, and so incapable; or else, that Adults were baptized without a Profession.

So under the antient Dispensation, the professing Stranger was obliged to embrace the *Jewish* Religion instantly, in order to his Circumcision; but when this was done; and himself circumcised, the same Ordinance was always administered to his Family and Children, as you see *Exodus* xii. 48, 49.

So *here*, those Adults, who were converted to the Christian Religion, were obliged to profess their Faith, in order to their being baptized; and on this Profession, not only themselves, but their Housholds were baptized also.

This Objection then, viz. *A Profession of Faith being a Pre-requisite to Baptism*, is no more an Objection against Childrens being baptized, on the Profession of their Parents, than it was against the Childrens being circumcised, because the Parents were previously obliged to embrace the *Jewish* Religion.

Some other trivial Objections there may be raised against the Baptism of Infants, but I know of none besides *these*, of any Consequence, that have not been precluded in this Discourse; and these, I think, every one must see from what has been said, are not of the least Weight, when impartially examined, against the Foundation that has been laid of the Covenant-Relation of the Children of confœderate Parents and the Arguments that have been produced to prove their undoubted Right to Baptism, according to Christ's Institution. The Conclusion then is plain, that, as they had a Right by God's own Appointment, to the Seal of the Covenant of Grace, under the Law, and as that Right has never been repealed, either explicitly, or by Consequence, it must still remain; and that, as it was the universal Practice of the primitive Churches, for the three first Centuries, which were the purest Times, and no Account has been given of its ever having been introduced as an Innovation, it must have been the Practice of the Apostles themselves, and must have its divine Original in that Covenant-Promise, made to *Abraham*, which the Apostle declares in our Text is to believing Parents and their Children, under the Gospel, as well us under the Law. On the other Hand, to deny Infant-Baptism to be a divine Institution, is attended with many Absurdities, and much Confusion.

It is as much as to say, that the Covenant made with *Abraham*, including his Children, is not an everlasting Covenant; that therefore Believers under the Gospel are not *Abraham's* Seed;

and

and Heirs of his Promife; for his Promife was to Parents and Children: yea, that the ingrafted *Gentiles* do not partake of the fame Privileges, in the Church, from which the *Jews* were broken off. And on the Whole, that the Privileges of the Gofpel-Difpenfation are lefs than thofe of the Law; all which are flat Contradictions to Scripture.

Again, to deny the Validity of Infant-Baptifm, is as much as to fay, that there was no true Baptifm in the Church for eleven or twelve hundred Years after Chrift, and that the Generality of the prefent Profeffors of Chriftianity, are now a Company of unbaptized *Heathens*; and although it muft be allowed, that there are, and always have been, vaftly more truly religious People, who have been baptized in the Infancy, than of others; yet all who have been fo baptized, are on thefe Principles, out of the vifible Church, and the Confequence will be, that vaftly great Numbers are faved out of the Church than in it, which is very abfurd, to fay no worfe. Thefe, and many other like Confequences neceffarily follow from denying the Validity of Infant-Baptifm.

Again, if Infant-Baptifm is a divine Inftitution, and warranted by the Word of God, then they who confent to be baptifed in their adult Age, do in that Tranfaction, neceffarily renounce a divine Inftitution, and an Ordinance of Jefus Chrift; and as it were vacate the former Covenant between God and them; nay, they practically fay, there are no baptized Perfons, no regular Minifters, nor Ordinances, in all the numerous profeffing Churches, but their own: and if the Baptifm of all thofe numerous profeffing Churches is a Nullity, all the Adminiftrations of their Minifters muft be fo too,

and

and then the Promife of Chrift, to be with his Minifters, in the Adminiftration of this Ordinance, to the End of the World, muft have failed during thofe hundreds and hundreds of Years, in which Infant-Baptifm was fo univerfally practifed.

. Nay, further, as the Succeffion of adult Baptifms cannot be traced to the Apoftles' Times, fo it will follow, that if Infant-Baptifm is a Nullity, there neither is, nor ever will, or can be, any regular Baptifm hereafter to the End of the World; and confequently an Ordinance of Chrift, as to its regular Adminiftration, muft be loft; for adult Baptifm now adminiftered, if originally derived from thofe, who were baptized in Infancy, cannot be valid, if Infant-Baptifm be not valid.

I have finifhed the Subject, as far as it is a Point of our Controverfy. It was my Defign to clofe all with an Addrefs, both to Parents and Children, enforcing the Obligations upon *each*, in Confequence of their folem Tranfaction with the great God, in this Ordinance of Baptifm; but the Time will not permit. May God lead us into all neceffary Truth, for Chrift's Sake! AMEN.

F I N I S.

Books juft imported from *America*,

And fold by Edward and Charles Dilly, in the *Poultry*, near the *Manfion-Houfe*.

1. **B**Ellamy's Effay on the Nature and Glory of the Gofpel of Jefus Chrift, &c. 1 vol. Twelves.

2. Chanler's Doctrines of glorious Grace, &c. with an Appendix againft Dr. Fofter. Quarto.

3. Clarke's Defence of Infant-Baptifm; being an Anfwer to Dr. Gill, 1 vol. 8vo.

4. Moody's Gofpel-Way, 1 vol. 12mo.

5. Clarke's Scripture-Doctrine of Original Sin.

6. Hobby on Self-Examination.

7. Hopkin's Hiftorical Memoirs, relating to the Indians.

8. The Laws of New-England, 1 vol. Folio.

In the Prefs, and fpeedily will be Publifhed,

Neatly printed in one Volume Duodecimo.

(Recommended by the Rev. Dr. Colman, Mr. Sewall, Prince, Le Mercier, and Webb, of Bofton, New-England)

THE Doctrine of PREDESTINATION unto LIFE, explained and vindicated. By the Rev. WILLIAM COOPER, of Bofton.

NEW BOOKS, in Divinity, Publifhed this Day,
By *Edward* and *Charles Dilly*, in the *Poultry*, near the *Manfion-Houfe*.
(Recommended by the Rev. Dr. John Gill, Dr. Walker, Dr. King, Mr. Hall, Mr. Brine, Mr. Gibbons, and by the late Rev. Mr. James Hervey, in his Theron and Afpafio, Vol. II. *p.* 366.)

1. THE OECONOMY of the COVENANTS between GOD and MAN: Comprehending a Complete BODY of DIVINITY. By HERMAN WITSIUS, D. D. Profeffor of Divinity in the Univerfities of *Leyden*, &c. Faithfully tranflated from the *Latin*, and carefully revifed by WILLIAM CROOKSHANK, D. D. In three Volumes Octavo, Price bound 15s.

Extract of a Letter from a Clergyman in the Country to the Publifher.

———" The Sale of *Witfius's Oeconomy of the Covenants* in-
" creafes among my Friends. The Tranflation is very juft;
" and the Excellency of the Work merits a Place in every
" Chriftian's Library. .I fhall do my utmoft to recommend it
" at all Times, and upon all proper Occafions. No pious
" Perfon on Earth can read this Book without Wonder,
" Rapture, and Devotion; it exceeds all Commendation.
" *Hervey* might well fay, *I would not fcruple to rifk all my*
" *Reputation upon the Merits of this Performance*. For my own Part,
" I am not afhamed nor afraid of any Scorn and Ridicule that
" may be poured on me from any Quarter, whilft I conftantly
" aver, that the Work has not its Equal in the World.".

2. ESSAYS on IMPORTANT SUBJECTS: Intended to eftablifh the *Doctrine of Salvation by Grace*, and to point out its Influence on Holinefs of Life. By JOHN WITHERSPOON, D. D.

To which are added by the Publifhers,

Ecclefiaftical Characteriftics; or, The Arcana of Church-Policy; with a ferious Apology, which have been generally afcribed to the fame Author, neatly printed in three Volumes. Price bound 9s.

†‡† The third Volume, containing a practical Treatife on Regeneration, may be had alone. Price bound 3s.

3. THEOLOGICAL DISSERTATIONS. By *John Erfkine*, M. A. one of the Minifters of *Edinburgh*, neatly printed in one Volume. Price bound 3s.

4. IMPORTANT CASES of CONSCIENCE anfwered at the Cafuiftical Lecture in *Little St. Helen's*. By S. *Pike* and S. *Hayward*. A new Edition. To which is now added, Four Cafes never before printed, by the late Rev. Mr. S. *Hayward*, neatly printed in two Volumes. Price bound 6s.

The Depravity of human Nature Illustrated.

A

S E R M O N

DELIVERED AT

R O W L E Y,

JULY 5, 1789,

BY EBENEZER BRADFORD, A. M.

PASTOR OF THE FIRST CHURCH OF CHRIST IN

R O W L E Y.

Published by Desire.

NEWBURYPORT.
PRINTED AND SOLD BY JOHN MYCALL.   MDCCXCI.

A SERMON, &c.

ROMANS III. 12.

THEY ARE ALL GONE OUT OF THE WAY, THEY ARE TOGETHER BECOME UNPROFITABLE: THERE IS NONE THAT DOETH GOOD, NO, NOT ONE.

THE words of our text are applicable *only* to men in the state of nature—for they are not true, with respect to men in the state of grace—who sometimes do, in some degree, that which is good in the sight of God.

By nature we are all children of wrath, because we are children of disobedience.—In this state we are so far removed from the rules of righteousness, that all we do, of a moral kind, is a violation of the law of God, consequently we are together become unprofitable—there is
none

none in this state that doth good, no, not one. Melancholy picture! And yet as true as the word of truth.

DOCTRINE.

ALL men, in the state of nature, are totally depraved.

FIRST, We will endeavour to explain the Doctrine:

SECONDLY, Offer several arguments to prove its truth——Then close the subject, with an improvement.

BY the *state of nature*, we are to understand the moral situation in which all men are born into the world—and, in which they live, till God, by his grace, changes their hearts. This state is entirely different from the state of Adam in innocency; and exactly like that of Adam immediately upon his fall—Moreover, it is different from a state of grace and a state of glory.—In a state of grace, men have some degrees of holiness—in a state of nature, they have none: In a state of glory, they are perfectly holy—in a state of nature, they are totally sinful.

By the depravity of human nature, we are not to understand, as some have erroneously thought, the destruction of our natural powers and faculties, which constitute us intelligent creatures, for GOD says unto wicked men, *Come, let us reason together*; which he would no more have done, than he would have addressed the

trees

trees of the foreſt in this manner, if they had loſt their natural powers and faculties by the fall; yea, the whole courſe of the divine conduct towards fallen men, loudly proclaims againſt this idea of human depravity.

NEITHER does the depravity of man conſiſt in the deſtruction of his moral agency, ſo that whatever ruin is involved in the depravity of man, this makes no part of it.—For it is an inconteſtible fact, that thoſe beings who invariably chooſe to do wrong, are as really moral agents, as thoſe who invariably chooſe to do right.

HE who is not a moral agent cannot be accountable to GOD for any of his actions—he cannot be a ſubject of moral law and government, is not capable of moral good or evil—is not capable of the happineſs of heaven, or the puniſhment of hell: But fallen men are accountable to GOD for all their actions; the capable of moral good and evil, are capable of enjoying the pleaſures of heaven, or enduring the miſeries of hell—and therefore their depravity cannot conſiſt in the deſtruction of this moral agency.

NOR is human depravity of ſuch a nature, as is utterly inconſiſtent with our doing any thing, which in a courſe of providence may promote the declarative glory of God, and the good of mankind—many ſuch things may, and often are done by men in a ſtate of nature, when nothing is aimed at, but their own private ſelfiſh intereſt.

THUS,

THUS, from selfish motives only, wicked men sometimes pay their just debts, and so promote the good of society: They expend their money in building houses for public worship—in supporting the preachers of the gospel—they will spend their strength and treasure, yea their lives, for the support of civil government; and in these, and many other respects, the earth helps the woman—the wicked world helps the church of Christ; and so these actions, in a course of providence, tend to promote the declarative glory of God, and the good of mankind.

A MAN entirely depraved, may put on the whole external appearance of a good man; and as men have no infallible knowledge of the hearts of one another, this may, in the view of men, promote the declarative glory of God—though *no* such thing is designed by the vile wretch himself: *His* highest motive is self—he goes into this course of conduct to hide the wickedness of his heart, and insensibly forms the character of the hypocrite.

THIS was the nature of Ahab's humility—Amaziah's righteousness in the sight of the Lord; Jehu's zeal for the Lord of Hosts; Jehoahaz' prayer, and the praises, that the ungodly Israelites sang at the red sea. This too, was the nature of all that following after Christ, for the sake of the loaves, spoken of in the new testament—of all those religious exercises and actions of men in the state of nature, down from the days of Cain to the present moment—they are nothing but selfishness covered over with the garb of religion. NOR

NOR does human depravity confist in being indifferent to pain and pleasure—for the most depraved among men have as great an appetite for happinefs, and as great a dread of misery as SAINTS or ANGELS.

Once more——Human depravity does not necessarily imply the abfence of natural affection, fympathy and gratitude—these men may have, as animals, and yet be entirely depraved; we find them all in the beasts that perish, who are incapable of the depravity, of which men are the subjects.

IF, then, human depravity does not consist in the destruction of our natural powers and faculties, nor in the destruction of our moral agency, nor in being bound down to such a scene of conduct, that none of our external actions, in a course of providence, should ever promote the declarative glory of God, and good of mankind: Nor in an indifferency to pain and pleasure—nor in the absence of those animal exercises, called natural gratitude, affection and fympathy: If it confifts in none of these things, what do men mean by depravity? and in what does it consist?

WE answer—By human depravity, we mean those moral exercises which are a violation of the law of God, and nothing else. Our text informs us, that mankind have gone out of the way; by which we are doubtlefs to understand that their depravity confifts in those voluntary exercises which are a transgreffion of the law of God.

WHEN

When we say man is totally depraved, we would be underſtood to mean, that all his moral exerciſes are tranſgreſſions of the law :— Hence it is ſaid, there is none that doth good, no, not one. If man, in the ſtate of nature, is the ſubject of one moral exerciſe, which is not a violation of the law of God, he is not totally or entirely depraved or corrupt.

The man that is depraved totally, has entirely loſt the moral image of God, which conſiſted in moral exerciſes correſponding with his holy law—and contracted a temper or diſpoſition of heart, which is total and poſitive enmity againſt God, and in no reſpect ſubject to the law of God.—Such an heart is, in all reſpects, ſelfiſh, for there is no other moral affection that is entire oppoſition to the law of God.

We now paſs to the

Second general head of this diſcourſe—which was, to offer ſeveral arguments, to prove that all mankind, in the ſtate of nature, are totally depraved—or in other words, that all their moral exerciſes, are a violation of God's holy law.— That this in fact is the caſe, will appear,

1. From the conſideration of the impoſſibility of accounting for the wickedneſs of mankind upon any other principle.

When we make proper allowance for thoſe reſtraints laid upon men in the ſtate of nature ; when we admit, that they may, and often do many things which, in a courſe of providence, may promote the declarative glory of God, and the good of mankind, from principles of ſelfiſhneſs,

fishness, we are, notwithstanding, unable to account for the wickedness that appears in their lives, upon any other supposition than that they are totally depraved. How can we account for the wickedness of children universally; yea, of men in all periods of their life, who are destitute of grace, but by admitting this humiliating idea of human nature.

THEY who have read the histories of mankind, and marked their moral characters with any great degree of accuracy, have found them to be one continued scene of wickedness.

AFTER making allowance for the happy effects of divine grace upon a very few persons, what is the history of the *old world*, but an history of such wickedness, that the Judge of all the earth, who will do right, saw fit to destroy every man, woman and child, by an awful flood? And what is the history of Sodom and Gomorrha, but an history of such wickedness as deserved to be punished with fire and brimstone from heaven, yea, to be punished with the vengeance of eternal fire?

WHAT is the history of the ancient, learned and polite Egyptians, Chaldeans, Grecians, Romans; yea, all the civilized nations of the earth, but an history of wickedness!

IF there were a nation, a family, or a single person, to be found upon the face of the earth, out of Christ, that could be proved to possess a single holy exercise, our mouths would be stopped, and we should be obliged to give up the doctrine of total and universal depravity; but the wickedness of mankind, from the days of Adam to the present moment, has been such, as utterly to exclude this fond idea of human nature; therefore, we conclude that mankind universally are naturally and totally depraved.

2. If mankind were not totally depraved, the means of knowledge and reformation, which God makes use of to reclaim them from their wicked ways, would have a more desirable effect.

IT is exceedingly evident from the scriptures of divine truth, that Noah, a preacher of righteousness, labored with the old world an hundred and twenty years, and failed of persuading one, out of his own family, to forsake the ways of sin, and walk in the paths of righteousness, which could not have happened, if mankind had not been totally depraved.

RIGHTEOUS Lot, whose soul was vexed with the filthy conversation of Sodom, could not persuade his sons in law, nor any of the inhabitants of that ungodly city, to walk in the paths of righteousness, though they were exposed to suffer the vengeance of eternal fire.

THE Lord Jesus Christ, who had given unto his people, the Jews, the lively oracles of truth, and sent unto them the prophets, and done many mighty works before their eyes, challenges them to say what he could have done more for his vineyard, than he had not done for it; and yet declares, that when he looked that it should bring forth grapes, it brought forth wild grapes; that is, nothing but wickedness.

AND,

AND, in what pathetic strains does he bewail the situation of Jerusalem; saying, O Jerusalem, Jerusalem ! thou that killest the Prophets, and stonest them which are sent unto thee, how often would I have gathered thy children together, even as a hen gathereth her chickens under her wings, and ye would not : Plainly manifesting, that all the arguments and motives, which infinite wisdom could set before their minds, would not prevail upon them to leave their sinful ways, and walk in the paths of righteousness ; which is an incontestible evidence, that they were totally depraved.

BUT, why need we go to the old world, to Sodom, to God's ancient people, the Jews, for instances, to prove that means will not reform men ? Have we not many striking instances of this truth in this assembly ; are there not many here, who have lived under the clearest light of the gospel to old age, and are not, even to this day, persuaded to walk in the ways of holiness ?

3. If mankind are not totally depraved, the *experiences* of the best of men are a delusion.

IT is the united testimony of the best of men in all ages, that they have seen themselves wholly corrupt ; that by nature they are entirely sinful. And, indeed, all conviction of sin, short of this, leaves a man ignorant of his own character.--- David viewed himself in this point of light, and said, Behold ! *I was shapen in iniquity.* And Paul viewed himself in the same situation by nature, and says, there is no good thing dwelleth in me, that is, in my flesh. All who have

had

had the same religious experience, have seen themselves in the same totally depraved situation.

ONE of the five points, held by Calvin, and all his genuine followers, was the total depravity of mankind, as is evident to every one who looks into the history of his sentiments. Hence the Assembly of Divines, who closed their last session in the year 1649, in their confession of faith---chap. 6, solemnly affirm that our first parents, by their sin, "*fell from their original righteousness and communion with God, and so became dead in sin, and wholly defiled in all the faculties and parts of soul and body.*" They further observe, That *from this original corruption, whereby we are utterly indisposed, disabled, and made opposite to all good, and wholly inclined to all evil, do proceed all actual transgressions.* They moreover take notice, That "*every sin, both original and actual, being a transgression of the righteous law of God, and contrary thereunto, doth in its own nature, bring guilt upon the sinner, whereby he is bound over to the wrath of God, and curse of the law, and so made subject to death, with all miseries, spiritual, temporal and eternal.*"

THIS same sentiment is contained in the articles of faith espoused by the church of England, and in all the confessions of faith made by all the reformed churches, except those who have publicly espoused the sentiments of Arminians, who openly deny the doctrine of total depravity.

4. IF

4. If mankind are not totally depraved, the bible-diſtinction between ſaints and ſinners is not true. We are not told in the bible, that ſinners have a little holineſs---but ſaints have more. The bible divides mankind into two claſſes only; and theſe are denominated by the terms righteous, and unrighteous, holy and unholy, ſaints and ſinners, pure and impure, clean and unclean, he that ſerveth God, and he that ſerveth him not, godly, and ungodly, good and bad, believer and unbeliever, friends and enemies, penitents and impenitents, children of God, and children of the devil, juſtified and condemned, bleſſed and curſed.

Now it is exceedingly evident, that the firſt claſs of terms in this catalogue, as they are applicable to men in this world, cannot be underſtood as deſcriptive of a ſinleſs character; for there is no ſuch character among the children of men; they muſt therefore be uſed to point out a character that has ſome degree of holineſs, and as applicable to the character that has the leaſt degree of holineſs in it. And it is likewiſe as evident, that the ſecond claſs of terms, in the above catalogue, are uſed, in their application to men here, to point out a character entirely deſtitute of holineſs.---For if this be not the caſe, there is no other difference between the holy and unholy, but what conſiſts in the degrees of holineſs; and the truth is, that the unholy man has ſome holineſs; and the holy man differs from the unholy man, only in this reſpect, that he has a little more holineſs

ness, which is absurd, for this makes the distinction between saints and sinners, to be the same as that which is between saints and saints; there are little saints and great saints, and consequently destroys the bible-distinction between saints and sinners altogether; but the goodness of saints is the effect of grace, and the bible-distinction between saints and sinners must stand: Therefore, we conclude, that mankind are by nature, *totally depraved*.

5. If mankind are not totally depraved, while in a state of nature, sinners will have some good deed for which they will be rewarded at the day of judgment, and, in this respect, be just like saints; but as there are only two characters of men in this world, so there will be only two characters of men in the day of judgment, doers of good and doers of evil; and these shall be rewarded according to their deeds, whether they be good or evil. The character of him who shall be condemned at the great day, is *worker* of iniquity, and not worker of righteousness. The works of righteousness, for which men will be rewarded at that day, are the effects of grace: Therefore, we conclude, that all men are by nature totally depraved. Rom. v. 11.

6. If mankind are not totally depraved, they will all inevitably be saved. The promises of the gospel are made to the least degree of holy affection. But if we are not totally depraved, we have some degree of holiness, as we are by nature, and the promise of salvation is made to us as we are by nature, and we must be saved.

But

But all men will not be saved, as is evident from the scriptures: Therefore, we conclude, that mankind are totally depraved.

7. ANOTHER argument to prove the doctrine under consideration is, that mankind, in their natural state, have no goodness whereof they may boast.

IF men were not totally depraved, they would be in possession of some degree of holiness, which they had not received as an act of grace, and consequently might say, that they had not received all their goodness as an act of free sovereign grace through the Redeemer: But the Apostle has proved, that boasting is excluded, not by the law of works, but by the law of faith or grace: Therefore, we conclude, that all men are by nature totally depraved.

8. If men are not totally depraved, those who die in a state of nature, cannot be compleatly miserable. For the Judge of all the earth will do right, and therefore it is impossible, in the nature of things, but that the person who has some holiness, should be the subject of some degree of happiness. God will render *to every man according to his deeds*; and, according to this rule, he will render *glory, honor and peace, to every man that worketh righteousness*; and, therefore, it will be impossible, if men are not totally depraved, for any of the human race, though in hell, to be entirely excluded from happiness, and made compleatly miserable, if happiness implies *glory*, honor and peace.---
But hell, the proper home of every depraved creature,

creature, is a place or state of complete misery. Therefore we are necessitated to conclude that mankind by nature are totally depraved.

9. THE doctrine under consideration, is evident from several scripture-declarations.

THE first text we would present to your minds, for this purpose, is recorded in Gen. vi. chapter, at the 5th verse. *And God saw that the wickedness of man was great in the earth, and that every imagination of the thoughts of his heart was only evil continually.*

THIS text is descriptive of the whole human race, as they are by nature. The word man, used here, is not confined in its signification, to a single person, nor to any considerable number of persons only, but extends to the whole human race, and signifies the same as the word *mankind.* And God saw that the wickedness of mankind was great in the earth! How great? Answer, so great, that every imagination of the thoughts of their hearts, was only evil continually. This is not true with respect to mankind, in the state of grace, and therefore is true, only with respect to men in the state of nature. Here let it be observed, that if this text does not prove that *man* is totally depraved, it is impossible to prove any thing by the scriptures.

IF human depravity consists in those moral exercises which are a violation of God's law---And if every imagination of the thoughts of the heart of man, in the state of nature, be only evil continually, then this text proves, beyond all contradiction, that man is totally depraved.

WE

We beg leave to prefent you with another text, which we think proves the doctrine under confideration. It is in Eph. ii. 1. *And you hath he quickened, who were dead in trefpaffes and fins.* The Ephefians here fpoken of were, previoufly to the quickening influences of the fpirit of God, dead in trefpaffes and fins.---This death confifted in trefpaffes and fins; and plainly imports, that they who are dead in this fenfe, are the fubjects of no moral exercifes, but fuch as are a violation of God's law. Natural death fignifies an abfence of life, and fpiritual death muft mean an abfence of holinefs; and this fpiritual death, confifts in trefpaffes and fins— in voluntary exercifes. If a perfon is the fubject of one holy exercife, he is then alive---if alive, not dead; but if all his exercifes are finful, then dead, totally dead or depraved. This was the cafe not with the Ephefians only, but all others, by nature: Therefore the Apoftle faid, And you hath he quickened, who were dead in trefpaffes and fins; wherein, in time paft, ye walked according to the courfe of this world, according to the prince of the power of the air, the fpirit that now worketh in the children of difobedience. Among whom alfo we all had our converfation in times paft, in the lufts of our flefh, fulfilling the defires of the flefh and the mind; and were, *by nature*, the children of wrath, even as others. Again,

The heart of the fons of men, is fully fet in them to do evil. Ecclef. viii. 11.

This text affords us an ample proof of the total depravity of human nature.

The heart, which is the seat of all moral exercises.---The heart of the sons of men, that is, of all the children of men, by nature, is fully set in them to do evil; fully inclined or disposed to do evil.

God's testimony concerning his ancient people, while in a state of nature, is full to our purpose. See Jer. iv. 22. *My people is foolish, they have not known me; they are sottish children, and they have none understanding; they are wise to do evil, but to do good, they have no knowledge*: Consequently they do no good, and so are entirely depraved.

Behold, I was shapen in iniquity, said David; *so then, they that are in the flesh cannot please God*, said Paul. Now to be in the flesh, is to be in that moral situation, in which David was, in his first existence; and it is affirmed, that, while we are in this situation, we cannot please God; the natural consequence is, that every moral exercise, of which we are the subjects in this state, is a violation of the law of God; and consequently, that we are entirely depraved.

Of mankind, in the state of nature, there is no *difference*.---*For all have sinned, and come short of the glory of God.* All are such sinners, as to do nothing to the glory of God; consequently totally depraved.

In the third chapter of Rom. the Apostle represents, Jews and Gentiles, by nature, altogether corrupt.

There

There is none righteous, no, not one; there is none that understandeth; there is none that seeketh after God. They are all gone out of the way; they are together become unprofitable; there is none that doeth good, no, not one; there is no fear of God before their eyes.

THIS description is applicable to none, but those who are in the state of nature; for those who are in the state of grace, do fear God---do seek after God---do understand the love and favor of God. Again,

If ye know that he is righteous, ye know that every one that doth righteousness is born of God. 1. Epistle of John, ii. 29.

Now to be born of God, is a change from a state of nature to a state of grace. And if every one that doth righteousness is born of God, then every one that is not born of God, doth not righteousness, and consequently is totally depraved: All he doth, is a violation of God's holy law; these texts, and many others, plainly prove the doctrine of total depravity.

BUT it is time we should make some improvement of this subject.

I. IF mankind are totally depraved, we may learn what full and genuine conviction means: It is nothing short of being convinced of our true characters as we are by nature. Men, under conviction, who are pained under the sense of some great crimes only, and view not all their moral exercises as a violation of the law of God, are under a delusion with respect to themselves, and have not thorough conviction.

IT

It is no uncommon thing, for sinners, to confess that they are sinners, that is, that they have done some things which are wrong; but to see and feel that all our moral exercises, while in a state of nature, are a violation of the divine law, is what never takes place without the commandments coming, sin reviving, and the creature dying.

II. If mankind are totally depraved, we may learn the reason why sinners behave as they do, under conviction. While their imaginary goodness takes her flight, and their hopes of justification, by the deeds of the law die, their hearts rise in dreadful opposition, against the method of salvation through the Redeemer; they refuse to repent of their known iniquities---they refuse to believe on the Lord Jesus Christ, under the clearest conviction, that *unbelief* is a soul-damning sin; and, with all their heart, under the full blaze of genuine conviction, they refuse to do any *thing*, as God hath required in the law and in the gospel---which conduct of the sinner, under these circumstances, can be accounted for, only by the entire depravity of his nature. He fights against his reason---his conscience---his bible, and his God.

III. From what hath been said, we may learn the reason why means, without the spirit of God, will not reform sinners.---It is because they are entirely depraved. Were sinners not entirely depraved, they would be, in some measure, disposed to do right; and then there would be nothing in their way of performing their duty, ty, but their want of knowledge, and the means of knowledge would supply this want; and they of consequence would be reformed; but being totally depraved, all the means of knowledge, without the influence of the spirit of God, fail of producing the least reformation of heart, the least degree of holiness. Without the influence of the spirit of God, bibles may be worn out in reading; ministers worn out in preaching, and the lives of sinners consumed in attending on means; and after all, their souls lost.

IV. IN the light of this subject, we may see why sinners, under genuine conviction, are so exceedingly distressed.

WHO does not see, that the sinner, who views himself the subject of no moral exercise, but what is a violation of God's law; who considers himself as possessed of a carnal mind, which is enmity against God, and not subject to his law, nor indeed can be? Who views himself righteously condemned by a just God, and consequently exposed, every moment, to drop into hell, and suffer the vengeance of eternal fire? Who, I say, does not see that such a man must be exceedingly distressed? What, this side of hell, can fill the mind of a selfish creature, with greater distress, than a full view of his own sinfulness, and his constant exposedness to endure the just punishment thereof: In this situation, do not the pains of hell get hold of the creature, and wreck and torture his mind?— Does he not feel that he has kindled a fire in the divine anger, which may burn to the lowest

est hell? With horror inexpressible, will he not cry out, Who can dwell with devouring fire?— Who can dwell with everlasting burnings? Is not tophet ordained of old? Is it not made deep and large? Is not the pile thereof fire and much wood---such fuel as I am; and doth not the breath of the Lord, like a stream of brimstone, kindle it? Wo, wo, is me, for I have *sinned!* and come *short* of the glory of God. I have done nothing but what is to his dishonor; and now it must be rendered to me according to my deeds. I am afraid; fearfulness seizes my soul, and the keenest horrors pierce my heart! Men and brethren, what shall I do?

V. ARE mankind totally depraved, then it is a matter of great importance, that the ministers of the gospel preach this doctrine to their hearers. If this be the true character of men in the state of nature, it is necessary that they should know it; and it is the business of the preacher, to furnish the hearer with the means of knowledge. The priests' lips should preserve knowledge; they should not daub with untempered mortar; they should not flatter the pride of their hearers, by withholding from them their true characters by nature, and so deceive and delude them.

IT is impossible for a man to feel aright towards himself, while he is ignorant of himself; and therefore, if he be entirely depraved, & know it not, it is impossible for him to feel towards himself as he ought to do. But every man should feel toward himself, according to his true

character;

character; therefore, it is a matter of great importance, that this humiliating doctrine be founded in the ears of a world that lieth in wickedness.

How odious in the sight of God, and all good men, is that minister, who employs his learning, talents and influence, in preaching and publishing against the doctrine of total depravity! If what has been said upon this subject be true, they are opposing the God of truth; promoting ignorance and delusion, rather than knowledge and religion; the cause of the devil, rather than the cause of God in the world.

VI. FROM what we have heard, we may learn, why wicked men hate to hear this doctrine preached, and why wicked ministers hate to preach it. It is because it sets their true characters in the most odious point of light.---Wicked men love darkness rather than light, because their deeds are evil; for every one that doth evil, hateth the light, neither cometh to the light, lest his deeds should be reproved.---And the light of God's word, respecting the true characters of men in the state of nature, is as really an object of their hatred, as the light of the word of God, respecting any other thing, is an object of their hatred: And, therefore, the wicked murmur and complain, when their true characters are painted before their eyes.

VII. IN the light of this subject, we may see the *necessity* of the gracious influences of the spirit of God, to prepare men for the enjoyment of him in heaven. If men be so disposed as to

do

do nothing but what is a violation of God's law, that all the motives that infinite wifdom can fet before them will fail of perfuading them to do the leaft thing as God has commanded, we may eafily fee the neceffity of that influence, which will take away the heart of ftone, and give an heart of flefh. Except a man be born by the fpirit and by water, he cannot fee the kingdom of God ; he cannot have fellowfhip with God here, nor hereafter.

VIII. To conclude this difcourfe.———From what we have heard, we may learn, that mankind finners deferve that dreadful damnation with which they are threatened by a juft and holy God. If there be any fuch thing as deferved punifhment, thofe muft deferve it, all of whofe moral exercifes are a violation of the law of God. If fallen angels deferve to be punifhed becaufe all their moral exercifes are wrong, are fin, fallen men muft deferve to be banifhed into everlafting fire, prepared for the devil and his angels ; becaufe all their moral exercifes are wrong, are fin.

O my dear hearers, in the view of this dreadful, this eternal punifhment, let the wicked forfake his way, and the unrighteous man his thoughts, and let him return *immediately* unto the Lord, and he will have mercy upon him, and to our God, for he will abundantly pardon.

A M E N.

FAMILY RELIGION

RECOMMENDED.

A

SERMON

PREACHED FROM

JOSHUA xxiv. 15.

By WILLIAM ARTHUR.

PHILADELPHIA:
Printed by STEWART & COCHRAN, No. 34, South Second-street.
M,DCC,XCIV.

THE *following Sermon was delivered, a few weeks ago, in the Rev. Mr. Robert Annan's church, Philadelphia, and, since, in the Rev. Mr. John M. Mason's, New-York. The Author does not pretend to be able to say any thing new on the subject; or to clothe his ideas with superior elegance of diction. His aim, in all his pulpit-performances, is to express himself with perspecuity and ease. He has contemplated, with grief, the total neglect of the worship of God in some families, and the carelessness, the formality attending it in other. If the following plain discourse be the means of doing good to any, his end is gained.*

PHILADELPHIA, March 13th, 1794.

FAMILY RELIGION

RECOMMENDED, &c.

JOSHUA xxiv. 15.

—*As for me, and my houſe, we will ſerve the Lord.*

MY BRETHREN,

THE mournful neglect of Family Religion is, I believe, one of the principal grounds of Jehovah's controverſy with us in this *day of trouble, of blaſphemy, and of rebuke.* To recommend it to your attention is the deſign of this diſcourſe. I wiſh to remind you of a few obvious conſiderations, which could not fail to recur to yourſelves, were you to think ſeriouſly upon the ſubject. Religion has every thing to recommend it to us. It is its own reward. *Them, that honour me,* ſays the gracious Redeemer, *I will honour; and they that deſpiſe me ſhall be lightly eſteemed.*

The

The words of a dear friend, efpecially his *laſt* words, make a deep, a permanent impreſſion upon our minds. We remember them with care. We meditate often upon them. The words of my text appear to have been part of Joſhua's farewell addreſs to Iſrael. He ſaw the day of his diſſolution drawing nigh; when he was to receive the celeſtial reward of his ſervices. We are told in the twenty-ninth verſe of this chapter, that *he died, being an hundred and ten years old.* How impartial is death! The grim meſſenger knows no diſtinctions. The braveſt champions of war fall promiſcuouſly with the ſons of cowardice. Like many, very many parents and governors, the Hebrew General was not unconcerned what courſe his family and followers purſued, after death removed him from them. No. Prompted by the duties of a wiſe commander, and impelled by the feelings of a pious father, he gathered the choſen tribes to Shechem; reminded them of the memorable appearances, which the God of Abram had made for them; and ſolemnly charged them to walk in his ways. How exemplary is his reſolution in my text! As if he had ſaid, " Children! Hearken unto Joſhua your father. Ere long you ſhall ſee me no more in this world.

world. With all the tendernefs, which the immediate profpect of our feparation infpires, I wifh to put you in mind of your duty. Remember, I befeech you, *the one thing needful.* There is a neceffity for you to make, if you have not already made, a choice in religion. How deteſtable is the idolatry of your fathers, who ferved ſtrange Gods! Renouncing this, *fear* the God of Ifrael, *and ferve him in fincerity and in truth.—As for me and my houfe,* if I be able to influence their choice, *we will ferve the Lord.* I am a veteran in his fervice. But, inftead of wifhing to recant, inftead of repenting my choice, I would make it a thoufand times, were it practicable; and may my authority and example continue to fpeak to you, when I am fleeping in the duſt!"

To excite you, my friends, to ſtudy a humble imitation, if not a holy emulation, of Jofhua's pious example, I will call your attention to the following confiderations. And

FIRST, It belongs to God himfelf to unite and to diffolve families.

Says the Pfalmiſt, he *maketh him families like a flock.* How confpicuous is divine wifdom wisdom in the arrangement of human affairs! Jehovah, sitting in his holy habitation, at the helm of the universe, does all things wisely and well. No change, which takes place in either the world or the church, is to be attributed to the caprice of contingency; for, strictly speaking, there is no *chance*. Is not society, whatever form it assumes, under the superintendence of heaven? Is the conjunction of such and such persons in a domestic relation accidental? No. The sovereign Ruler among the nations determined that they should be born at a particular period; in a particular part of the world, and be connected as members of one houshold. Is it by chance that a master has such a servant, or a servant such a master? No. However inconsiderable and frivolous these things may appear to us, as if we presumed to think them unworthy Jehovah's attention, they were minutely marked out by his express fore-ordination. A hair cannot fall to the ground; or any creature from the serpent, that licks the dust, up to the exalted seraph before the celestial throne, move his body unobserved by him, whose eyes are like a flame of fire. Hence, if you are comfortably connected with pious relations, or, if otherwise, the dispensation

is

is of your *Father in heaven*, who is a God of righteous judgment, as well as tender mercy, and had the wifest reasons for ordering it so! How affecting the consideration, that persons, however nearly and intimately related in one family, are soon to be separated! Such relations must, in the nature of things, be short-lived. If not suspended by some providential incidents, which separate the sons of a father, ordering the lot of one, in one place, of another, in another place, death shall, ere long, dissolve them; and then is the servant eternally free from his master. How useful is it to read often and carefully in the volume of divine providence! *Whoso is wise, and will observe these things, even they shall understand the loving kindness of the Lord.* How transient is the present state of things? Where are many families, on which the sun of prosperity once shone with meridian effulgence? Wherefore should the prosperous, in a worldly view, be elated? Wherefore should the afflicted be despondent? Has not this consideration a tendency to enforce domestic religion; for, as you are soon to be separated, should not this induce you to be cordial and active in the service of God?

SECOND,

SECOND, We will not, either as individuals, or as families, serve God aright, till he, by his Spirit and grace, incline and difpofe us for our duty.

Where is the fociety, all the members of which worfhip him in fpirit, and in truth ? In how many houfes is the Bible never read but to be turned into burlefque? Is it unlawful for a Mahometan to touch his alcoran with unwafhen hands? Is *their* veneration for that fyftem of lies, invented by the eaftern impoftor, fuch ? Blufh, Chriftians! blufh and be afhamed. In how many houfes are all the fecret and focial duties of religion totally neglected? Alas! the natural part of the human heart is *evil, only evil,* and that *continually.* How many are there, who, if fomeafflictive difpenfation of divine providence, on account of which their animal fpirits are depreffed, does not force them to their duty, lie down, in the evening, and rife, in the morning, as though their knees were jointlefs and their finews brafs ? What is the reafon that we can receive our ftated meals without fo much as acknowledging our bounteous benefactor? Or what is the reafon that we implore a heavenly bleffing on one meal, not on another? Are not all
equally

equally the gift of God? Why are many families not more regular, especially on the first day of the week? Is it lawful to give, or to receive visits from our irreligious acquaintance and friends on that day? In the 12th chap. of Zechariah, we read of every family mourning for their sins apart, the family of David, the family of Nathan, the family of Levi, the family of Shemei, *each apart;* and, if it be proper to fast in a solitary way, why not sequestrate ourselves on the first day of the week? Why is our conversation not more spiritual; not more in heaven, *whence we look for the great God, and our Saviour Jesus Christ?* Whether have political news, and foreign intelligence, respecting the nations of this world; or whether have the good news, the gladsome tidings of salvation a greater tendency to sanctify the Sabbath? How were the disciples, going to Emmaus, employed on the first day of the week? Did they not talk together of all things, relating to the Redeemer, which had taken place at Jerusalem? And, testifying his approbation of their exercises, did he not draw nigh to them? After he left them, they said, *Did not our heart burn within us, while he talked with us by the way, and while he opened to us the Scriptures?*

B THIRD,

THIRD, The duties of family religion are of the *stated*, not of the *occasional* kind.

Fasting, under the New Testament, is an occasional duty to be observed just as circumstances require. The duties, of which I am speaking, are rather stated and ordinary. There are, no doubt, seasons, in which especially, there is a loud call to them. Such is the season of adversity; for, says God, *I will go and return to my place till they acknowledge their offences, and seek my face; in their affliction they will seek me early.* But is not *the voice of thanksgiving heard* statedly *in the tabernacles of the righteous?* How good is it *to show forth his loving kindness in the morning, and his faithfulness every night;* presenting on the altar of a willing heart a gratulatory sacrifice to the gracious hearer of prayer! When we read of the daily sacrifice, which was offered by the pious Jews, why is the time, at which it was offered, mentioned in the New Testament, if not to show that it was divinely intended to be a pattern to individuals, and to families in all succeeding ages? It is called *the hour* of prayer. *Peter and John*, we are informed in the third of the Acts, *went up together into the temple at the hour of prayer, being*
the

the ninth hour. If we divide the day into twelve hours, beginning at fix in the morning, the ninth hour anfwers to three in the afternoon; the time when the evening facrifice was offered, and the pious Jews went to the temple to be engaged in devotional exercifes. Should not the Chriftian's habitation be a *Bethel*, a houfe of God, a little church, in which the head of the family prefides as the prieft? Before the commencement of the Levitical priefthood in the perfon of Aaron, fathers, elder brothers, princes, or every man for himfelf offered facrifice; which is evident in the cafe of Abel, of Noah, of Abram, Ifaac, Job, and other. In the New Teftament, in which the name, *church*, is to be varioufly underftood, we frequently read of a church in a particular houfe. One reafon is, the regularity, the order obferved in it. The church is called, *the houfe of prayer.* In her the Head has appointed a beautiful order, which is not to be changed. It is our duty to *walk about Zion, and go round about her; to tell the towers thereof; to mark her bulwarks;* to *confider her palaces.* In a manner equally exprefs, he has required the families of Ifrael to worfhip him. Confidering this, *I befeech you, brethren, by the mercies of God that ye prefent*

your

your bodies, a living sacrifice, holy, acceptable unto God, which is your reasonable service.

FOURTH, As families, we have many mercies to acknowledge, and many sins to confess.

Do not mistake me. I do not mean that domestic religion supersedes personal devotion. No. Each of us has many personal mercies to acknowledge. There is not a hair on our heads that we can call our own. Each has many personal sins to confess. It is recorded of a famous minister of the gospel, that he never saw a criminal going to the place of execution, but he smote upon his breast, and exclaimed, *the same evil is here!* Why should we not, in a social manner, acknowledge our divine benefactor as the giver of all good? Commendable was the conduct of Jacob. Testifying his gratitude to his divine deliverer, he made an altar, in Bethel, unto God, who *answered* him *in the day of his distress, and was with him in the way, which he went.* He commanded his houshold to *put away strange Gods* that were among them; to *change their garments;* to *be clean;* and to concur with him in expressions of gratitude. How readily did they comply! *They gave*

gave unto Jacob all the strange gods that were in their hand, and all their ear-rings, which were in their ears, and Jacob hid them under the oak which was by Shechem. What, my brethren, *shall* we *render unto the Lord for all his benefits towards us?* Man is a social creature. He was originally intended for society, and fitted for it. Various are the views, in which reciprocal advantages result from social connections. Society is a chain of many links. With tender care, the parents rear up the children; and the children, when pious example and education are blessed, as the means of softening, and forming their hearts, are a comfort to the parents. The servant cannot be without the master, more than the master can be without the servant. Ah! how many family sins have we to confess! How often have the members of those little societies offended against each other? Are not husbands and wives, parents and children, masters and servants culpable, very culpable for neglecting the duties of their respective stations? In very expressive terms, did holy David lament both the irreligion and the adversity of his family. *Although my house be not so with God; yet he hath made with me an everlasting covenant, ordered in all things and sure; for this is all*

my

my salvation, and all my desire, although he make it not to grow.

FIFTH, Family religion comes recommended to us by the example of the most eminent believers, who lived in both earlier and later times.

Are we not commanded to be followers of them, who have gone before us, and now inherit the promises; to walk in the good old path, in which our pious fathers walked? Says the Redeemer to the church, *If thou knowest not, O thou fairest among women, go thy way forth by the footsteps of the flock, and feed thy kids beside the shepherds tents.* When Joshua said, *as for me and my house, we will serve the Lord*, was he the only person who ever formed this resolution? By no means. A luminous cloud of witnesses presents itself to our view. Let me remind you of Abram, the father of the faithful, and the friend of God, whose faith and obedience are famous in every age; for he has exhibited to mankind a noble pattern of heavenly graces, and virtues. Said the Searcher of hearts concerning him, *I know him, that he will command his children, and his household after him; and they shall keep the way of the Lord, to do justice and judgment; that*

the

the Lord may bring upon Abraham that which he hath spoken of him. This honorable testimony was given by One, who cannot be deceived by any specious appearance, or crafty affectation of zeal. I call it an *honorable* testimony. " I know Abram, that his respect for my authority; and his love to my laws, will induce him to command his houshold to serve me; not only the stated members of his family, but also every sojourner under his roof." How praiseworthy is David's resolution; who said, *I will walk within my house with a perfect heart!* A holy life is emphatically expressed by walking with God. Enoch, who was translated that he should not see death, walked with him. The phrase bespeaks a holy familiary betwixt God and his people, which words are inadequate to express. As if the man according to God's own heart had said, " In the strength of grace, which is made perfect in our weakness, I resolve to set a proper example before my family by my pious conduct, conscientiously performing the duties, which are incumbent upon me as the head of it." But, say you, " These are Old Testament examples. What examples are there in the New?" The most illustrious instance that could be mentioned is Jesus him-

himself, who has left us an example that we should follow his steps. He was a father to his disciples, praying with them like a pious father with his children. We read of a Cornelius, who feared God with all his house; that is, I suppose, his family joined cordially in Jehovah's worship, with the devout centurion at their head. Says the Apostle, in the last chapter of his first epistle to the Corinthians, *Aquila and Priscilla salute you much in the Lord*, WITH THE CHURCH THAT IS IN THEIR HOUSE; in the last chapter of his epistle to the Colossians, *Salute the brethren, which are in Laodicea, and Nymphas*, and THE CHURCH, WHICH IS IN HIS HOUSE; and, in the second verse of his epistle to Philemon, *to our beloved Apphia, and Archippus, our fellow-soldier*, AND TO THE CHURCH IN THY HOUSE. It has, indeed, been queried what is to be understood by a church in a particular house; whether the assembling of the church, which, in those troublous times, might meet for public worship in it; or a private society of Christians, joining together in the duties of social prayer, and spiritual conversation; or the members of the family uniting in the exercises of domestic devotion. This last interpretation is adopted by not a few judicious expositors, and seems the most probable. To the honour of the jailor, who was made to exclaim, *What shall I do to be saved?* it is recorded, that he *rejoiced, believing in God with all his house.*

SIXTH, Family worship is one of the means, by which our Father in heaven is pleased to manifest himself to his people.

This consideration endears it to the saints, who, with joy unspeakable, *draw water out of the wells of salvation.* What are the ordinances in general, but meeting-places, as it were, betwixt God and his people? If we wish to find him, we must go into the *Galilees,* where he has appointed to meet with us. Why should we not embrace every opportunity of holding communion with our God? The church tells us, she *sought her beloved, but found him not.* Did she, after the first disappointment, relinquish the pursuit? No. Perseverance was necessary. Not having found her beloved in the streets, and in the broad ways of the city, she applied to the watchmen, saying, *saw ye him whom my soul loveth?* They, it appears, gave her no satisfaction. But, adds she, *It was but a little that I passed from them, but*

I found him whom my soul loveth: I held him, and would not let him go, until I had brought him into my mother's house, and into the chambers of her that conceived me. This plainly teaches that God's people, sometimes, find him in secret and private, after their expectations of meeting with him, in public, have been disappointed. We read of an impotent man, lying at the pool, called *Bethesda, who had an infirmity thirty and eight years;* and, after all, was made whole. Presumption and despondency are dangerous extremes.

SEVENTH, Families are encouraged to worship God from the consideration that many promises are suited to their case.

Has he not promised his gracious presence in *the dwellings of Jacob,* as well as in *the gates of Zion;* though he loves the one more than the other? Our blessed Lord's words have been justly accommodated to the situation of a family beginning to perform social worship, when he says, *If two of you shall agree, as touching any thing that they shall ask, it shall be done for them of my Father, who is in heaven. For where two or three are gathered together in my name, there am I in the midst of them.* How animating is the following promise;
which

which has, I suppose, a primary view to the return of the Jews from their Babylonian captivity; but has a running applicability, and a continued accomplishment, especially in the New Testament times! *At the same time saith the Lord, will I be the God of all the families of Israel, and they shall be my people.* Says he, in another part of scripture, *In all places, where I record my name, I will come unto thee, and I will bless thee;* and is not his name recorded in our habitations?

FINALLY, The neglect of family religion is awfully threatened in the word of God.

What an alarming imprecation is the prophet's! *Pour out thy fury upon the Heathen that know thee not*, AND UPON THE FAMILIES THAT CALL NOT UPON THY NAME. In scripture the name, *family*, is, I know, ambiguous, and differently understood. But, admitting this, the prohet's words apply, in their full force, to the subject under review. Families, which neglect the worship of Jehovah, and Heathens are properly joined together, for, though the former be *professedly* Christian, they are *practically* Heathen families. Hence they are objects of the divine

divine difpleafure. The word, *fury*, befpeaks an awful degree of difpleafure, even indignation; the phrafe, *pour out*, the tremendous manner in which it is executed. What aggravates their fin, and heightens their mifery is their knowledge of their duty, while they do not perform it; for, when it is faid, *the Heathen that know thee not*, it evidently implies that thofe families knew their duty, yet did not worfhip the God of their fathers. Sinners! ftand aghaft! Does any hear of the wrath of Almighty God, and his ears not tingle? What! does a family profefs to be Chriftian, in which there is not a veftige of the Chriftian religion? Tell it not in Gath. Publifh it not in Afkelon; left the uncircumcifed Philiftines triumph.

To CONCLUDE,

FIRST, Does not reafon, not to mention revalation, teach the obligation, the importance, and the utility of family religion. Does not reafon teach us to repay a generous benefactor with gratitude? Is not a grateful return of Jehovah's mercies all the return we can make for them; all the return he requires? and why not *render him the calves of our lips?*

SECOND,

SECOND, The non-performance of the duties of religion is inconfiftent with a gracious ftate; and they, who neglect them, muft unqueftionably be in the gall of bitternefs, and bond of iniquity. A gracelefs man *may*, but a gracious perfon *muft* perform thefe duties; for is not prayer the breath of the new creature? and can we live without breathing? *Behold he*, that is, the new creature, as foon as he begins to live, *prayeth!* Confider alfo that one of the views, by which our fanctification is defcribed, is by writing the law on the heart. *This is the covenant that I will make with the houfe of Ifrael after thofe days, faith the Lord: I will put my laws into their mind, and write them in their hearts; and I will be to them a God, and they fhall be to me a people.* Hence, if the divine law be engraved on a man's heart, will he not ftudy to tranfcribe it in his life, and converfation? If perfons be in a gracious ftate, are not faith in the Redeemer for affiftance, and for the acceptance of both their perfons, and their fervices, and love to him, as a Sovereign, as well as a Saviour, powerful principles impelling them to perform thefe duties, by which they fhew their refpect for the divine authority. The authority of Jefus commands,

his

his love sweetly constrains us to walk in his ways.

THIRD, Is Joshua's *your* resolution? Be not ashamed, brethren, of being religious; or, if your religion is yet to begin, be persuaded now to leave the path, in which destroyers go. *Come with us*, said Moses to Hobab, *and we will do thee good; for the Lord hath spoken good concerning Israel.* We are accountabe creatures; and the day of our death, when we must answer for all the deeds done in the body, is approaching, with rapid, though silent steps. MASTERS! You have a solemn charge of the souls of your servants; such a charge as a minister has of his people. What an eternal disgrace is it to the Christian name for the head of a family to overlook the morals, and religious instruction of any under his roof? What! have not persons, in inferior stations of life, souls to be saved or damned, to be happy or miserable for ever? It matters not whether they be *black*, or *white* men; for, *as men*, the posterity of Ham, are on a perfect equality with other descriptions of the human race. It was Cain, that primeval monument of fratricide! who said, *Am I my brother's keeper?* Nor a few, who now surround

round the celestial throne, have for a ground of thankfulness, and a note, in their ecstatical song, that the God, who saved them, ordered their lot in a pious family, where example, which is, often more powerful than precept, made a good, a permanent impression on their minds. PARENTS! *Bring up your children in the nurture, and admonition of the Lord.* They are the hope of the church; for families are nurseries, in which young ones are raised up, and prepared for usefulness in public life. Be careful that the stream be not poisoned at the fountain-head. It is easiest to bend the twig when it is green. Impressions made in early life are, with difficulty, if ever eradicated. It is dangerous not to raise up a spiritual seed to the Redeemer. Do you not wish your children to serve him after you have gone to your fathers, and sleep in the dust? A pious education is the best estate you can give them. It has often been remarked by practical writers, on this subject, that both defection and reformation in religion commonly begin *in families.* It is an absurdity to suppose that a parent can be righly exercised about the interests of his own soul, if he has not the salvation of his children at heart. The Father of mercies does not

always

always anfwer the prayers of pious parents, on behalf of their children, *when they are prefented to him;* fometimes not before the parents have gone to the eternal world. Many fuch prayers, we have reafon to believe, lodged at the throne of grace, are yet unanfwered; but will be punctually attended to, at the proper time.

UPON THE WHOLE, Had I a thoufand mouths, and a thoufand tongues, I would employ them in recommending the Redeemer's fervice to you all; old and young. *Chufe ye, this day, whom ye will ferve.* Said Elijah to the people, when the competition was betwixt him and Baal, *if the Lord be God, follow him; but, if Baal,* who, when his deluded votaries call upon him, is either deaf or on a journey, *follow him.* How honorable, how eafy, how delightful is the Redeemer's fervice! *Wifdom's ways are ways of pleafantnefs, and all her paths are peace.* Then *give no fleep to your eyes, nor flumber to your eye-lids, until you find a place for the Lord, an habitation for the God of Jacob.*

F I N I S.

Errata to be corrected with the reader's pen.
Page 7, line 23, for *elu-* read *elat-*.—Page 8, line 16, for *part*, read *beft.*—Page 9, line 9, for *Shemei,* read *Shimei.*

DRAUGHT

OF THE

FORM

OF THE

GOVERNMENT AND DISCIPLINE

OF THE

PRESBYTERIAN CHURCH

IN THE

UNITED STATES OF AMERICA.

Propofed, by the Synod of NEW-YORK and PHILADELPHIA, for the confideration of the Prefbyteries and Churches under their care.

NEW-YORK:

Printed by S. and J. LOUDON, No. 5, *Water-Street.*

M,DCC,LXXXVII.

THE Synod of New-York and Philadelphia, *at their meeting, held in Philadelphia,* May, 1787, *appointed the Rev.* Dr. John Rodgers, Dr. Alexander MacWhorter, Mr. Alexander Miller and Mr. James Wilson, *Ministers, a Committee, to print One Thousand Copies of the draught of the Form of Government and Discipline, as now amended by the Synod, to be distributed among the Presbyteries and Churches under their care.*

The Committee was also appointed to print the last paragraph of the 20th *Chapter of the Westminster Confession of Faith ; the 3d paragraph of the* 23d *Chapter ; and the* 1st *paragraph of the* 31st *Chapter, as now proposed to be altered by the Synod:*————*Further, the Committee was appointed, to revise the Directory for the Public worship of God, and to print it, when revised and amended by them, together with the draught of the form of Government and Discipline : And the Synod agreed, that these be called, when revised and adopted,* the Confession of Faith, and Directory for the Public Worship of God, of the Presbyterian Church in the United States of America.

The Committee, considering that a power of making verbal alterations, in the draught of the Form of Government and Discipline, was committed to them by the Synod, and being fully sensible that they are liable to make mistakes in this particular, have thought proper to print, all the words which they have changed, in Italics.————

INTRODUCTION.

THE Synod of NEW-YORK and PHILADELPHIA, *judging it expedient to afcertain and fix the* fyftem of union, and the form of the Government *and* Difcipline *of the Prefbyterian Church in thefe United States,* under their care, *have* thought proper to lay down, *by way of introduction,* a few *of the* general principles, by which they have been *hitherto* governed, and *which are the ground work* of the *following* plan. This, *it is* hoped, will, in fome *meafure,* prevent *thofe* rafh *mifconftructions* and uncandid reflections, *which ufually* proceed from an imperfect view of any fubject; as well as make the feveral parts *of the fyftem plain, and* the whole *plan perfpicuous, and fully* underftood.

The Synod are unanimoufly of opinion;

I. That " God alone is Lord of the con-
" fcience, and hath left it free from the doc-
" trines and commandments of men; which are
" in any thing contrary to his word, or befide
" it in matters of faith or worfhip:" Therefore, they confider the rights of private judgement, in all matters that *refpect* religion, as univerfal and unalienable : They do not even wifh to fee any religious conftitution aided by the civil power, further than may be neceffary for protection and fecurity, and, at the fame time, may be equal and common to all others.

II. That, in perfect confiftency with the above principle of common right, every Chriftian

Church,

Church, or union and affociation of particular Churches, *are* entitled to declare the terms of admiffion into *their communion*, and the qualifications of *their* minifters and members, as well as the whole fyftem of *the* internal government which Chrift hath appointed: That, in the exercife of this right, they may, notwithftanding, err, in making the terms of communion *either* too lax or too narrow: yet, even in this cafe, they do not infringe the liberty, or *encroach upon the* rights of others, but only make an improper ufe of their own.

III. That our bleffed Saviour, for the edification of *the* vifible Church, which is his body, hath appointed officers, not only to preach the Gofpel *and adminifter the Sacraments*; but alfo to exercife difcipline, for the prefervation both of truth and duty: and, that it is incumbent upon *thefe officers*, and upon the whole Church, in whofe name they act, to cenfure, or caft out, the erroneous and fcandalous; *obferving*, in *all* cafes, the rules *contained* in the word of God.

IV. That truth is in order to goodnefs; and that no opinion can be either more pernicious or more abfurd, than that which brings truth and falfehood upon a level, and reprefents it of no confequence what a man's *fentiments* are: On the contrary, They are of opinion, that foundnefs in the faith lays a proper foundation for holy practice; for, if it were otherwife, it would be of no *importance* either to difcover truth or to embrace it.

V. That while, under the conviction of the above principle, They think it neceffary to make effectual provifion, that all, who are admitted

as

as Teachers, be found in the faith; They also believe, that there are truths and forms, with respect to which men of good characters and principles may differ: And, in all these, They think it the duty, both of private Christians and Societies, to *exercise* mutual forbearance towards each other.

VI. That though the character, qualifications, and authority of Church-officers, are laid down in the *holy* Scriptures, as well as the proper method of *their* investiture and institution; yet the election of the persons, to the exercise of this authority, in any particular society, is in that society.

VII. That all Church power, whether exercised by the body in general, or, in the way of representation, by delegated authority, is only ministerial and declarative: *That is to say*, that the Holy Scriptures are the only rule of faith and manners; that no Church judicatory ought to pretend to make laws, to bind the conscience, in virtue of their own authority; *and that all* their *decisions should* be founded upon the revealed will of God: *Now* though it *will* easily be admitted, that all Synods and Councils may err, through the frailty inseparable from humanity; yet there is much greater danger, from the unused claim of making laws, than from the right of judging upon laws already made, and common to all who profess the Gospel; although it is right, as necessity requires in the present state, be lodged with fallible men.

VIII. *Lastly*, That, if the above Scriptural and rational principles be stedfastly adhered to, the vigour and strictness of *their* discipline will contribute to the glory and happiness of any

Church

Church. Since *discipline* must be purely moral and spiritual in its object, and not attended with any civil effects, it can derive no force whatever, but from its' own justice, the approbation of an impartial public, and the countenance and blessing of the great Head of the Church universal.

The FORM, &c.

Of the Church.

JESUS CHRIST, who is now exalted, far above all principality and power, hath erected, in this world, a kingdom, which is his Church.

The universal Church consists of all those persons, in every nation, together with their children, who make profession of *the* holy religion *of Christ*, and submit to his laws.

As this immense multitude cannot meet *together*, in one place, to hold communion, or *to* worship God, it is reasonable, and *warranted by Scripture example*, that they should be divided into many particular Churches.

A particular Church consists of a number of professing Christians, with their offspring, voluntarily associated together, for divine worship and *godly* living, *agreeably* to the holy Scriptures; and *submitting to* a certain form of government.

Of the Officers of the Church.

Extraordinary Officers. Our blessed Lord, at first, collected his Church, out of different nations, and formed it into one body, by the mission of men endued with miraculous gifts, which have, long since, ceased. The

(8)

Perpetual Officers The ordinary and perpetual Officers, in the Church, are, *Bishops* or *Pastors*; the representatives of the People, usually stiled *Ruling Elders*; and *Deacons*.

Of Bishops or Pastors.

Names, &c. The *pastoral* office is the first, in the Church, both *for* dignity and usefulness. *The person who fills this office*, hath, in Scripture, obtained different names expressive of *his* various duties: As *He* has the oversight of the flock of Christ, he is *called* Bishop * : As He feeds them with spiritual food, he is *stiled* Pastor : As He serves Christ in his church, he is termed Minister: As *it* is *his duty* to be grave, and prudent, and an example of the flock, and to govern well in the house and kingdom of Christ, he is *denominated* Presbyter or Elder : As He is the messenger of God, he *is addressed as the* Angel *of the Church* : As He is sent to declare the will of God *to* sinners, and to beseech *them* to be reconciled to God through Christ, he is *represented as* Ambassador : And, as He dispenses the manifold grace of God, and the ordinances *instituted by* Christ, he is *spoken of as* Steward of the mysteries of God.

Of Ruling Elders.

Name, &c. Ruling Elders are properly the representatives of the people, chosen by them, for the purpose of exercising government and discipline,

---

* As the office and character of the Gospel Minister is particularly and fully described, in the holy Scriptures, under the title of Bishop; and as this term is peculiarly expressive of his duty, as an Overseer of the flock, it ought not to be rejected.

in conjunction with Paſtors *or Miniſters*. This office has been underſtood, by a great part of the Proteſtant reformed Churches, to be deſignated, in the Holy Scriptures, by the title of Governments; and of thoſe who rule well, but do not labour in word and doctrine.

Of Deacons.

Name, &c. The Scriptures clearly point out Deacons as diſtinct officers in the Church, whoſe buſineſs it is, not to adminiſter any of the ordinances of the Goſpel, but to take care of the Poor, and to diſtribute among them the collections which may be raiſed for their uſe. To them alſo may be properly committed the management of the temporal affairs of the Church.

Of the Ordinances in a particular Church.

Ordinances of the Church. The Ordinances, eſtabliſhed by Chriſt the Head, in a particular Church, *which is* regularly conſtituted with its proper officers, are, Prayer; ſinging Praiſes; reading, expounding, and preaching the Word of God; adminiſtring Baptiſm and the Lord's Supper; public ſolemn Faſting and Thankſgiving; Catechiſing; making collections for the Poor and other pious purpoſes; exerciſing Diſcipline; and bleſſing the People.

Of Church Government, and the ſeveral kinds of Judicatories.

Different Judicatories. It is abſolutely neceſſary that the government of the Church be exerciſed under ſome certain and definite form: And we hold it expedient, and agreeable to ſcripture and

B the

the practice of the primitive Christians, that the Church be governed by Congregational, Presbyterial, and Synodical Assemblies. *In full consistency with this belief*, we embrace, in the spirit of charity, those Christians who differ from us, in opinion or in practice, on these subjects.

Their Powers.
These Assemblies ought not to possess any civil jurisdiction, nor to inflict any civil penalties. Their power is wholly moral or spiritual, and that only ministerial and declarative. They possess the right of requiring obedience to the laws of Christ; and of excluding the disobedient and disorderly from the privileges of the Church. To give efficiency, however, to this necessary and scriptural authority, they possess the powers requisite for obtaining evidence and inflicting censure: They can call before them any offender against the order and government of the Church: They can require members, of their own society, to appear and give testimony on the cause; but the highest punishment, to which their authority extends, is to exclude, the contumacious and impenitent, from the Congregation of believers.

Of the Congregational Assembly or Judicatory, usually stiled the Church Session.

Constituent Members of the Church Session.
The Church Session consists of the Minister or Ministers, and Elders of a particular Congregation.

Its power.
The Church Session is competent to the spiritual government of the congregation: For which purpose, they have power to inquire into the knowledge and Christian conduct

duct of *all its* members; to call before them offenders and witnesses, *who are of* their own *denomination*; to admonish; to rebuke; to suspend or exclude, from the Sacraments, those who are found to deserve the censures of the Church; to concert the best measures for promoting the spiritual interests of *the* Congregation; and to appoint Delegates to the higher Judicatories of the Church.

How to be convened. The Minister shall have a right to convene the Session when he may judge it requisite: And he ought, in all cases, to convene them, when requested by any two or more of the Elders.

Registers to be kept. We think it proper, that every *Church* Session keep a fair register, of Births; *of* Baptisms; *of* Marriages; of persons admitted to the Lord's table; of Deaths in the society; and *of* other removals.

Of the Presbyterial Assembly.

Necessity of the Presbytery. The Church being divided into many separate Congregations, *these* need mutual counsel and assistance, in order to preserve soundness of doctrine, and regularity of discipline; and to enter into common measures, for the promoting of knowledge and religion, and for *the* preventing *of* the encroachments of infidelity and error. Hence arise the importance and usefulness of Presbyterial and Synodical Assemblies.

Constituent Members thereof. A Presbytery consists of all the *Ministers*, and one ruling Elder from each Congregation, within a certain district. Every Congregation, which has a settled Pastor,

tor, has a right to be represented, in Presbytery, by one Elder; and every Collegiate Church, by two or more Elders, in proportion to its Ministers. Where there are two or more Congregations, united under one Pastor, all such Congregations shall have but one Elder to represent them. Every Congregation, which has no settled *Minister*, and is able and willing, in the judgment of Presbytery, to support *one*, shall be entitled to be represented, by a ruling Elder, in this *Judicatory* : and where there are two or more such Congregations, united for the maintenance of the Gospel, and, in their united state, are of the description aforesaid, then such united Congregations may be represented by one Elder. Every Elder, not known to the Presbytery, shall produce a certificate of his regular appointment, from *the* Church which he represents.

Quorum of the Presbytery. Any three Ministers, and as many Elders as may be present, belonging to the Presbytery, being met, at the time and place appointed, shall be a Judicatory, competent to the dispatch of business ; notwithstanding the absence of the other Members.

Powers of the Presbytery. &c. The Presbytery *have* cognizance of all things, that regard the welfare of the particular Churches within their bounds, which are not cognizable by the Session : *They* have also a power of receiving and issuing appeals from the Sessions ; and references, brought before them in an orderly manner ; of examining, and licensing Candidates for the Gospel ministry ; of ordaining, settling, removing, or judging Ministers ; of examining, and approving or censuring the records of the Sessions ;

Seſſions; of reſolving queſtions of doctrine or diſcipline, ſeriouſly and reaſonably propoſed; or condemning erroneous opinions, that injure the purity or peace of the Church; of viſiting particular churches, to inquire into their ſtate, and redreſs the evils that may have ariſen within them; of uniting, or dividing Congregations, at the requeſt of the people; and of ordering whatever pertains to the ſpiritual concerns of the Churches under their care: and it ſhall be the duty of the Preſbyteries to report, to the Synod, licenſures, ordinations, *the* diſmiſſing or receiving of Members, and the removal of Members by death.

How to be convened. The *Preſbytery* ſhall meet on their own adjournments; and, when any emergency ſhall require a meeting, ſooner than the time to which the Judicatory ſtands adjourned, the Moderator ſhall, with the concurrence, or at the requeſt, of two Miniſters and two Elders, the Elders being of different Congregations, call a meeting of the Preſbytery, by a circular letter ſent to every Miniſter, and to the Seſſion of every vacant Congregation having a right to ſend a Repreſentative to the Judicatory, in due time previous to the meeting, which time ſhall be aſcertained and recorded by each Preſbytery, and ſhall not be leſs than ten days: and nothing ſhall be tranſacted, at ſuch ſpecial meeting, beſides *the* particular buſineſs for which the Judicatory has been thus convened.

Opening of the Preſbytery. At each meeting of Preſbytery, a ſermon ſhall be delivered, if convenient; and every particular ſeſſion ſhall be opened and concluded with prayer: The roll ſhall be called, and the meeting recorded by the Clerk, who

who shall enter the names of the Members present, and also of those Ministers who are absent.

Of the Synodical Assembly.

Constituent Members of a Synod. As a Presbytery is the Convention of the Bishops and Elders, within a certain district; so a Synod is the Convention of several Presbyteries, within a larger district.

Powers thereof. The Synod have power to admit and judge of appeals, regularly brought up from the Presbyteries; to give their judgment on all references, in ecclesiastical cases, made to them; to review the Presbytery books; to redress whatever hath been done by Presbyteries contrary to order; to take effectual care that Presbyteries observe the Constitutions of the Church; to make such regulations, for the benefit of their whole body, and of the Presbyteries and Churches under their care, as shall be agreeable to the word of God, and not contradictory to the decisions of the General Council; and to propose, to the General Council, for their adoption, such measures as may be of common advantage to the whole Church.

Of the General Council.

Stile of the highest Judicatory of the Presbyterian Church. The General Council *is* the highest Judicatory of the Presbyterian Church; and shall represent, in one body, all the particular Churches of *this* denomination; and shall bear the stile and title of THE GENERAL COUNCIL OF THE PRESBYTERIAN CHURCH IN THE UNITED STATES OF AMERICA.

The

Constituent Members of the General Council. The General Council shall consist of an equal delegation of *Bishops* and Elders, from each Presbytery, in the following proportion : *viz.* each Presbytery, consisting of not more than six Ministers, shall send one Minister and one Elder ; each Presbytery, consisting of more than six Ministers and not more than twelve, shall send two Ministers and two Elders ; and in like proportion, for every six Ministers, in any Presbytery : And these Delegates, so appointed, shall bear the title of COMMISSIONERS TO THE GENERAL COUNCIL.

Quorum thereof. Any fourteen, or more, of these Commissioners, one half of whom shall be Ministers, being met, on the day, and at the place appointed, shall be competent to form a General Council, *and to proceed to business.*

Powers of the Council. The Council shall receive and issue all appeals and references, which may be regularly brought before them from the inferior Judicatories ; *they* shall review the minutes and proceedings of every Synod, to approve or censure them ; *they shall* give their advice and instructions, in all other cases submitted to them ; *and they shall* also constitute the bond of union, peace, correspondence, and mutual confidence, among all our Churches.

Other powers of the Council. To the Council also belongs *the* power of consulting, reasoning, and judging, in controversies respecting doctrine and discipline ; of reproving, warning, or bearing testimony against error in doctrine, or immorality *in* practice, in any Church, Presbytery, or Synod ; of corresponding with foreign Churches ; of putting a stop to schismatical contentions *and* disputations :

disputations : and, in general, of recommending and attempting reformation of manners ; and of promoting charity, truth, and holiness, through all the Churches : and of erecting new Synods, when they judge it necessary.

<small>Restriction of the power of the Council.</small> *Before any overtures or regulations, proposed by* the Council *to be established as* standing rules, *shall be obligatory on the Churches*, it shall be necessary to transmit them to all the Presbyteries, and to receive the returns of, at least, a majority of the Presbyteries, in writing, approving thereof.

Of Electing and Ordaining Ruling Elders and Deacons.

Having defined the Officers of the Church, and the Assemblies by which it shall be governed, it is proper here to prescribe the modes in which ecclesiastical Rulers shall be ordained to their respective offices.

<small>Mode of electing Ruling Elders, &c.</small> Every Congregation shall elect persons, to *the* office *of Ruling Elder, and to the office of Deacon*, or either of them, in the mode most approved and in use in that Congregation.

<small>How to be ordained.</small> When any person *shall have been elected to either of* these offices, *and shall have declared his willingness to accept thereof*, he shall be set apart in the following manner.

<small>Engagements required of Elders and Deacons.</small> After sermon, the Minister shall *propose* to him, in the presence of the Congregation, the following questions : *viz.*

I.

I. Do you believe the Scriptures, of the Old and New Testament, to be the word of God, the only infallible rule of Faith and Practice?

II. Do you sincerely receive and adopt, the Confession of Faith of this Church, as containing *the* System of doctrine taught in the holy Scriptures?

III. Do you approve of the Government and Discipline of the Presbyterian Church, as exercised in these United States?

IV. Do you accept the office of Ruling Elder [or Deacon as the case may be] in this Congregation, and promise faithfully to perform all the duties thereof?

To be set apart by prayer. After *having answered these questions in the affirmative,* he shall be set apart, by prayer, *to the office of Elder [or Deacon as the case may be;] and the Minister shall give him, and the Congregation, an exhortation suited to the occasion.*

Of Licensing Candidates, or Probationers, to preach the Gospel.

Presbyteries ought to license Probationers. The holy Scriptures require, that some trial be previously had, of those who are to be ordained to the ministry of the Gospel, that this sacred office may not be degraded, by being committed to weak and unworthy men; and that the Churches may have an opportunity of judging of the competency of the talents of those by whom they are to be instructed and governed. For this purpose *Presbyteries* shall licence Probationers, to preach the Gospel; that, after a competent trial of their talents, and receiving, from the Churches, a good report; They may, in due time, ordain *them* to the pastoral office.

Testimonials to be produced by Candidates applying to be licensed. It is proper and requisite, that Candidates, applying to the Presbytery to be licensed to preach the Gospel, produce satisfactory testimonials of their good moral character, and of their being regular members of some particular Church: And it is the duty of the Presbytery, for their further satisfaction with regard to the real piety of such Candidates, to examine them respecting their experimental acquaintance with religion, and the motives which influence them to desire the sacred office. And it is recommended, that the Candidate be *also* required to produce a diploma, of Bachelor or Master of Arts, from some College or University; or at least authentic testimonials of his having gone through a regular course of learning.

Trials in order to Licensе. Because it is highly reproachful to religion, and dangerous to the Church, to intrust the holy ministry to weak and ignorant men, the Presbytery shall try each Candidate, *as to his* knowledge of the Latin language, and of the Original languages in which the holy Scriptures were written: They shall examine *him*, on the Arts and Sciences; on Theology, natural and revealed; and on Ecclesiastical history. And, in order to make trial of *his* talents to explain and vindicate, and practically to enforce the doctrines of the Gospel, the Presbytery shall require of *him*, an Exegesis on some common head of divinity; a Homily; a Presbyterial exercise; a Lecture or explication of a portion of Scripture; and a popular Sermon:

Sermon: Or other similar exercises, to be held, at several successive sessions, till *They* shall have obtained satisfaction, as to *his* piety, literature, and aptness to teach in the Churches.

<small>The study of Divinity must continue at least two years before licence.</small> That the most effectual measures may be taken, to guard against *the admission of* insufficient men into the sacred office, it is recommended, that no Candidate, except in extraordinary cases, be licensed; unless, after his having completed the the usual course of academical studies, he shall have studied divinity, at least two years, under some approved Divine, or Professor of Theology.

<small>Engagements required of Probationers, before licence.</small> Before the Presbytery proceed to licence the Candidate, the Moderator shall requre of him the following engagements: *viz.*

I. Do you believe the Scriptures, of the Old and New Testament, to be the word of God, the only infallible rule of Faith and Practice?

II. Do you sincerely receive and adopt, the Confession of Faith of this Church, as containing *the* system of doctrine taught in the holy Scriptures?

III. Do you promise to study the peace, unity, and purity of the Church?

IV. Do you promise to submit yourself, in the Lord, to the government of this Presbytery, or of any other Presbytery in the bounds of which you may be?

<small>Manner of licensing.</small> The Candidate having answered these questions in the affirmative, and the Moderator having offered up a prayer suitable to the occasion, He shall address himself to the Candidate,

Candidate, to the following purpose: "In the name of the Lord Jesus Christ, and by that authority, which he hath given to his Church for its edification, we do licence you, to preach the Gospel, wherever God in his providence may call you thereto: and, for this purpose, may the blessing of God rest upon you, and the Spirit of Christ fill your heart. *Amen.*" And record shall be made of the licensure, in the following form: *viz.*

Form of licence. At the day of the Presbytery of having received sufficient testimonials, in favour of of his having gone through a regular course of literature; of his good moral character; and of his being in the communion of the Church; proceeded to take the usual parts of trial for his licensure: And he having given satisfaction, as to his accomplishments in literature; as to his experimental acquaintance with religion; and as to his proficiency in Divinity, and other studies; the Presbytery did, and hereby do express their approbation of all these parts of trial: and he having adopted the Confession of Faith of this Church, and satisfactorily answered the questions, appointed to be put to Candidates to be licensed, the Presbytery did, and hereby do licence him, the said , to preach the Gospel of Christ, as a Probationer for the holy ministry, within the bounds of this Presbytery, or wherever he shall be orderly called.

Testimonials of a Probationer. When any Candidate shall, by the permission of *his* Presbytery, remove without its limits, an extract of this record, accompanied with a Presbyterial recommendation,

commendation, signed by the Clerk, shall be his testimonials, to the Presbytery under whose care he shall come.

Of the Election, and Ordination, of Bishops or Pastors.

A Church disposed to prepare a Call in order to ordination, shall ask the assistance of a Minister.

When any Probationer *shall have* preached, so much to the satisfaction of any Congregation *as* that the people appear disposed to receive him as their *minister*, the Session shall solicit the *presence* and counsel of some neighbouring Minister, *to assist them* in preparing a Call for him; unless highly inconvenient on account of distance: in which case they may proceed without such assistance.

The day for preparing the Call shall be previously appointed on a Lord's day.

On a Lord's day, immediately after public worship, it shall be intimated from the Pulpit, that all *the* members of that Congregation are requested to meet, on   ensuing, at the Church, or usual place for holding public worship; then and there, if it be agreeable to them, to prepare a Call *for*   to be their Pastor.

The Minister shall receive the votes of none but regular members, and who punctually pay towards the support of the Church.

On the day appointed, the Minister, whose assistance has been obtained, shall preach a sermon, at the usual season for public worship; and, after sermon, *He* shall announce to the People, that he will immediately proceed to take the votes of the Electors of that Congregation, in the case of   whether or not he shall be chosen to be their *Minister.* In this election, no person shall be
entitled

entitled to vote, who refuses to submit to the censures of the Church, regularly administred; or who does not contribute his just proportion, according to his own engagements, or, the rules of that Church, to all its necessary expences.

<small>When the People are not unanimous the Minister shall certify the number and circumstances of the Dissentients.</small> When the votes are taken, if it appear that a great proportion of the People are averse from the Candidate, and cannot be induced to concur in the call, the assisting *Minister* shall endeavour to dissuade the Congregation from prosecuting it further. But if the People be nearly, or entirely, unanimous; or if the majority shall insist upon their right to call a Minister; then in that case, the Minister, after using his utmost endeavours to persuade the Congregation to unanimity, shall proceed to draw a call in due form, and to have it subscribed by the Electors; certifying, at the same time, the number and circumstances of those who do not concur in the Call: *all which proceedings shall* be laid before the Presbytery, together with the call.

<small>The form of a Call.</small> The Call shall be in the following, or like form : *viz.*

The Congregation of   being, on sufficient grounds, well satisfied of the ministerial qualifications of you
and having good hopes, from our past experience of your labours, that your ministrations in the Gospel will be profitable to our spiritual interests, do earnestly call, and desire you, to undertake the Pastoral office in said Congregation; promising you, in the *discharge* of your duty, all proper support, encouragement, and obedience,

in the Lord : And, that you may be free from worldly cares and avocations, we hereby promife, and oblige ourfelves, to pay to you, the fum of   in regular *   payments, during the time of your being, and continuing, the regular Paftor of this Church. In teftimony whereof, we have refpectively fubfcribed our names, this   day of   A. D.
Attefted by A. B. *Moderator of the meeting.*

A Call may, in certain cafes, be fubfcribed by Elders or Deacons. But if any Congregation fhall choofe to fubfcribe their Call, by their Elders and Deacons, or either, they fhall be at liberty fo to do : but it fhall, in fuch cafe, be fully certified, to the Prefbytery, by the Minifter who prefided, that they have been appointed, for this purpofe, by a public vote of the Congregation ; and that the Call has been, in all other refpects, prepared as above directed.

A call fufficient both for ordination & inftalment. When a Call fhall be prefented to any Minifter or Candidate, it fhall always be viewed as a fufficient petition from the people for his inftalment. The acceptance of a Call, by a Minifter or Candidate, fhall always be confiderd as a requeft, on his part, to be inftalled at the fame time. And when a Candidate fhall be ordained, in confequence of a Call from any Congregation, the Prefbytery fhall always, at *the fame* time, ordain and inftal him Paftor of that Congregation.

The

---

* This blank to be filled up with the words, quarterly, half yearly, or yearly, as may beft fuit the Congregation.

The Call must be presented to the Presbytery. The Call, thus prepared *, shall be presented to the Presbytery, under whose care the person called shall be; that, if the Presbytery think it expedient to present the Call *to him*, it may be accordingly presented: And no Minister or Candidate shall receive a Call, but through the hands of the Presbytery.

How to proceed when the Call is to the Licentiate of another Presbytery. If the Call be to the Licentiate of another Presbytery, in that case the Commissioners, deputed from the Congregation to prosecute the Call, shall produce, to that Judicatory, a certificate from their own Presbytery, regularly attested by the Moderator and Clerk, that they are in order. If that Presbytery present the Call to their Licentiate, and he be disposed to accept it, they shall then dismiss him from their jurisdiction, and require him to repair to that Presbytery, into the bounds of which he is called, and there to submit himself to the usual trials preparatory to ordination.

Trials for Ordination. Trials for ordination, especially in a different Presbytery from that in which

---

* Inasmuch as the comfort and honor of the ministry greatly depends, on the easy and decent provision which is made for their families after their death; it is highly expedient, that each Congregation should deposit, in the widows fund, such a sum as shall be sufficient to secure, to the family of their Pastor after his death, one of the annuities promised by them to the Contributors: provided that the Corporation shall stipulate with them, that the said annuity shall be paid, to the family of their Pastor, and to the families of his successors in the same charge forever, who shall die during the continuance of their pastoral relation to the said Congregation. And provided they further engage, that no deposition, suspension, or removal, of any of their Pastors, shall ever deprive their families of the expected annuities: provided that such deposed, suspended, or removed Pastor shall continue, during his life, to pay his annual rate to the fund, or shall settle in another Congregation that has made a similar provision for their Pastor and his family.

which the Candidate was licenfed, fhall confift of a careful examination, *as to his acquaintance with experimental religion*; *as to his knowledge* of Philofophy, Theology, Ecclefiaftical hiftory, the Greek and Hebrew languages, and fuch other branches of learning as to the Prefbytery may appear requifite; *and as to his knowledge* of the Conftitution, the rules and principles of the Government and Difcipline of the Church; together with fuch written difcourfes, founded on the word of God, as to the Prefbytery fhall feem proper. The Prefbytery, being fully fatisfied with his qualifications for the facred office, fhall appoint a convenient day for his ordination, which ought to be, if convenient, in that Church of which he is to be the *Minifter*.

Prefbytery being conftituted a fermon fhall be preached, &c. The day appointed for ordination being come, and the Prefbytery convened, a member of the Prefbytery, previoufly appointed to that duty, fhall preach a fermon adapted to the occafion. The fame, or another member appointed to prefide in this bufinefs, fhall afterwards briefly recite from the pulpit, in the audience of the people, the proceedings of the Prefbytery preparatory to this tranfaction: He fhall point out the nature and importance of the ordinance; and endeavour to imprefs the audience with a proper fenfe of the folemnity of the tranfaction.

Engagements required of thafe who are ordained. Then addreffing himfelf to the Candidate, he fhall propofe to him the following queftions: *viz.*

I. Do you believe the Scriptures, of the Old and New Teftament, to be the word of God, the only infallible rule of Faith and Practice?

D   II.

II. Do you sincerely receive and adopt, the Confession of Faith of this Church, as containing *the* system of doctrine taught in the holy Scriptures ?

III. Do you approve of the Government and discipline of the Presbyterian Church, as exercised in these United States ?

IV. Do you promise subjection to your **Brethren** in the Lord ?

V. Have you been induced, as far as you know your own heart, to seek the office of the holy ministry, *from* love to God, and a sincere desire to promote his glory in the Gospel of his Son ?

VI. Do you promise to be zealous and faithful in maintaining the truths of the Gospel, and the purity and peace of the Church ; whatever persecution, or opposition, may arise unto you on that account ?

VII. Do you engage to be faithful and diligent, in the exercise of all private and personal duties, which become you as a Christian and a Minister of the Gospel ; as well as in all relative duties, and the public duties of your office, endeavouring to adorn the profession of the Gospel by your conversation ; and walking, with exemplary piety, before the flock, over which God shall make you Overseer ?

Engagements required of the People. The Candidate having answered these questions in the affirmative, the Moderator shall demand of the People :

I. Do you, the People of this Congregation, continue to profess your readiness to receive ――――, whom you have called, to be your *Minister* ?

II.

II. Do you promise to receive the word of truth from his mouth, with meekness and love; and to submit to him, with humility, in the due exercise of Discipline?

III. Do you promise to encourage him, in his arduous labour, and to assist his endeavours for your instruction and spiritual edification?

IV. And do you engage to continue to him, while he is your Pastor, that competent worldly maintenance which you have promised; and whatever else you may see needful, for the honour of religion, and his comfort among you?

Mode of ordination. The People having answered these questions, in the affirmative, by holding up their right hands, the Candidate shall kneel down, in the most convenient part of the Church: Then the presiding Bishop shall, by prayer, and with the laying on of the hands of the Presbytery, according to the Apostolic example, solemnly ordain him to the holy office of the Gospel ministry. Prayer being ended, he shall rise from his knees; and the Minister who presides shall first, and afterwards all the members of the Presbytery in their order, take him by the right hand, saying, in words to this purpose, "We give you the right hand of Fellowship, to take part of this ministry with us." After which the Minister presiding, or some other appointed for the purpose, shall give a solemn charge, in the name of God, to the newly ordained Bishop, and to the people, to persevere in the discharge of their mutual duties; and shall then, by prayer, recommend them both to the grace of God, and his holy keeping: and finally, after singing of a psalm, *shall* dismiss the Congregation with the usual blessing. And the Presbytery shall duly record the transaction.

Of

Of Translation, or removing a Minister from one Charge to another.

Translation to be made by the Presbytery. No Bishop shall be translated from one Church to another, nor shall he receive any Call for that purpose, but by the permission of the Presbytery.

Mode of procedure in translations. Any Church, desiring to call a settled Minister from his present charge, shall, by Commissioners properly authorized, represent to the Presbytery the ground on which they plead his removal. The Presbytery, having maturely considered their plea, may, according as it appears more or less reasonable, either recommend to them to desist from prosecuting the Call; or may order it to be delivered, to the Minister to whom it is directed, together with a written citation, to him and his Congregation, to appear before the Presbytery at *their* next meeting. This citation shall be read from the pulpit in that Church, by a member of the Presbytery appointed for that purpose, immediately after public worship; so that, at least, two sabbaths shall intervene, betwixt the citation, and the meeting of the Presbytery at which the cause of translation is to be considered. The Presbytery, being met, and having heard the parties, shall, upon the whole view of the case, either continue him in his former charge, or translate him, as they shall deem to be most for the peace and edification of the Church; or refer the whole affair to the Synod, at their next meeting, for their advice and direction.

When

Mode of procedure when the Minister is of another Presbytery. When the Congregation, calling any settled Minister, is within the limits of another Presbytery, that Congregation shall obtain leave, from the Presbytery to which they belong, to apply to the Presbytery of which he is a member: And that Presbytery, having cited him and his Congregation as before directed, shall proceed to hear and issue the cause. If they agree to the translation, they shall release him from his present charge; and having given him proper testimonials, shall require him to repair to that Presbytery, within the bounds of which the Congregation calling him lies, that the proper steps may be taken for his regular settlement in that Congregation: And the Presbytery, to which the Congregation belongs, having received an authenticated certificate of his release, under the hand of the Clerk of that Presbytery, shall proceed to instal him, in the Congregation, as soon as convenient. *Provided always,* that no Bishop or Pastor shall be translated, without his own consent previously obtained.

Instalment constitutes the pastoral relation &c. When any Minister is to be settled in a Congregation, the instalment which consists in constituting a pastoral relation between him and the people of that particular Church, may be performed, either by the Presbytery, or by a Committee appointed for that purpose; as may appear most expedient: and the following order shall be observed therein.

Notice of the day must be given. A day shall be appointed for the instalment, at such time as may appear most convenient, and due notice thereof given to the Congregation.

When

A Sermon shall be delivered, &c.

When the Presbytery, or Committee, shall be convened and constituted, on the day appointed, a sermon shall be delivered, by some one of the members previously appointed thereto; immediately after which, the Bishop, who is to preside, shall state to the Congregation the design of their meeting and briefly recite the proceedings of the Presbytery relative thereto. And then, addressing himself to the *Minister* to be installed, shall propose to him the following or similar questions:

Installment consists in mutual engagements of Minister and People.

I. Are you now willing to take the charge of this Congregation, as their Pastor, agreeably to your declaration at accepting their Call?

II. Do you conscientiously believe and declare, as far as you know your own heart, that, in taking upon you this charge, you are influenced by a sincere desire to promote the glory of God, and the good of his Church?

III. Do you solemnly promise, that, by *the assistance of* the grace of God, you will endeavour faithfully to discharge all the duties of a Pastor to this Congregation; and will be careful, to maintain a deportment in all respects becoming a Minister of the Gospel of Christ, agreeably to your Ordination engagements? To all *these* having received satisfactory answers, He shall propose to the People the same, or *like* questions, as those directed under the head of ordination; which having been also satisfactorily answered, by holding up their right hand, in testimony of assent, He shall solemnly pronounce and declare the said Minister to be regularly constituted the Pastor of that Congregation.

tion. A charge shall then be given to both parties, as directed in the affair of ordination; and, after prayer, and singing a psalm adapted to the transaction, the Congregation shall be dismissed with the usual benediction.

Elders and Heads of families shall give their right hand to their Minister. It is highly becoming, that, after the solemnity of the instalment, the heads of Families of that Congregation who are then present, or at least the Elders, and those appointed to take care of the temporal concerns of that Church, should come forward to their Pastor, and give him their right hand, in token of cordial reception and affectionate regard.

Of resigning a Pastoral Charge.

The Congregation must be cited and heard. When any *Minister* shall labour under such grievances, in his Congregation, as that he shall desire leave to resign his pastoral charge, the Presbytery shall cite *the* Congregation to appear, by their Commissioners, at their next meeting, to shew cause, if any they have, why the Presbytery should not accept the resignation. If the Congregation fail to appear, or if their reasons for retaining their Pastor be deemed by the Presbytery insufficient, he shall have leave granted to resign his pastoral charge; of which due record shall be made, and that Church shall be held to be vacant, till supplied again, in an orderly manner, with another *Minister:* And if any Congregation shall desire to be released from their Pastor, a similar process, *mutatis mutandis,* shall be observed.

Of

Of Missions.

When vacancies become so numerous, in any Presbytery, that they cannot be supplied with the frequent administration of the Word and ordinances, it shall be proper for such Presbytery, or any vacant Congregation within their bounds, with the leave of the Presbytery, to apply to any other Presbytery, or to any Synod, or to the General Council, for such assistance as they can afford. And, when any Presbytery shall send any of their Ministers or Probationers to distant vacancies, the Missionary shall be ready to produce his credentials to the Presbytery or Presbyteries, through the bounds of which he may pass, or at least *to* a Committee thereof, and obtain their approbation. And the General Council may, of their own knowledge, send missions, to any part, to plant Churches, or to supply vacancies: And, for this purpose, may direct any Presbytery to ordain *Evangelists*, or *Ministers* without relation to particular Churches: *Provided always*, that such missions be made with the consent of the parties appointed; and that the Judicatory sending them make the necessary provision for their support and reward in the performance of this service.

Of Moderators.

A Moderator necessary.   It is equally necessary in the Judicatories of the Church, as in other assemblies, that there should be a Moderator or President; that the business may be conducted with order and dispatch.

The

The authority and duty of the Moderator. The Moderator is to be considered as possessing, by delegation from the whole body, all authority necessary for the preservation of order; for convening and adjourning the Judicatory; and directing its operations according to the rules of the Church. He is to propose to the Judicatory every subject of deliberation that comes before them. He may propose what appears to him the most regular and speedy way of bringing any business to issue. He shall prevent the members from interrupting each other; and require them, in speaking, always to address the Chair. He shall prevent a speaker from deviating from the subject; and from using personal reflections. He shall silence those who refuse to obey order. He shall prevent members who attempt to leave the Judicatory without leave obtained from him. He shall, at a proper season, when the deliberations are ended, put the question and call the votes. If the Judicatory be equally divided he shall possess the casting vote. If he be not willing to decide, he shall put the question a second time: and if the Judicatory be again equally divided, and he decline to give his vote, the question shall be lost. In all questions he shall give a concise and clear state of the object of the vote; and the vote being taken, shall then declare how the question is *decided*. *And he* shall likewise, *when properly advised*, convene the Judicatory, by his circular letter, before the ordinary time of meeting.

The Minister perpetual Moderator of the Church Session. The Pastor of the Congregation shall always be the Moderator of the Church Session; except when, for prudential reasons, it may appear adviseable

viseable that some other Minister should be invited to preside: in which case the Pastor may, with the concurrence of the Session, invite such other Minister as they may see meet, belonging to the same Presbytery, to preside in that affair. In this Judicatory, therefore, the Moderator is continual: but, in the vacancy of any Church, the Moderator shall be the Minister sent to them by the Presbytery; or invited by the Session to preside on a particular occasion. In Congregations, where there are Colleagues, they shall, when present, alternately preside in the Session.

The Moderators of the other Judicatories how to be chosen. The Moderator of the Presbytery shall be chosen from year to year, or at every meeting of the Presbytery, as the Presbytery may think best. The Moderator, of the Synod, and of the General Council, shall be chosen at each meeting of those Judicatories: and the last Moderator present shall open the meeting with a sermon, and shall hold the chair till a new Moderator be chosen.

Of Privilege.

It shall be the privilege of any member of a Judicatory to speak, in his proper order, to any question, *with* leave from the Moderator. The Moderator shall give leave to the person who first rises: but if two, or more members, are judged to have risen at the same time, the Moderator shall determine which shall speak first. Any member shall have a right to propose any question, relative to the business of the Church, *or to* the interests of religion, and to have it put to vote; provided only, that his motion be seconded

conded by another member. If any member conceive his privileges to be unjuſtly controuled by the Moderator, he may appeal to the Judicatory, who ſhall determine the point of privilege by a vote ; and the Moderator and member muſt ſubmit to the ſuffrage of the Judicatory.

Of Clerks.

Every Judicatory ſhall chooſe a Clerk, to record their tranſactions, whoſe continuance ſhall be during pleaſure. It ſhall be the duty of the Clerk, beſides recording the tranſactions, to preſerve them carefully ; and to grant extracts from them, whenever properly required : and ſuch extracts, under the hand of the Clerk, *ſhall* be conſidered *as* authentic vouchers, of the fact which they declare, in any eccleſiaſtical Judicatory, and to every part of the Church.

Of vacant Congregations aſſembling for Public Worſhip.

Conſidering that the number of our Congregations is ſo greatly ſuperior to the number of *Miniſters* who are to ſupply them, and that this diſproportion is daily increaſing, in the extended and growing ſettlements on the frontiers ; and conſidering the great importance of weekly aſſembling the people, for the public worſhip of God ; in order thereby to improve their knowledge ; to confirm their habits of worſhip, and their deſire of the public ordinances ; to augment their reverence *for the moſt high God* ; and to promote the charitable affections *which* unite men moſt firmly in ſociety : It is recommended, *that* every vacant Congregation meet together,

on

on the Lord's day, at one or more places, for the purpose of prayer, *singing* praises, and reading the holy Scriptures, together with the works of such approved Divines, as the Presbytery, within whose bounds they are, may recommend, and they may be able to procure; and that the Elders or Deacons be the persons who shall preside, and select the portions of Scripture, and of the other books, to be read; and to see that the whole be conducted in a becoming and orderly manner.

Of Commissioners to the General Council.

Commissioners shall be appointed at last stated meeting of the Presbytery. The Commissioners to the General Council shall always be appointed, by the Presbytery from which they come, at its last stated meeting immediately preceding the meeting of the General Council; provided, that there be a sufficient interval, between that time and the meeting of the Council, for the Commissioners to attend their duty in due season: otherwise, the Presbytery may make the appointment at any stated meeting, not more than seven months preceding the meeting of the Council. And as much as possible to prevent all failure in the representation of the Presbyteries, arising from unforeseen accidents to those first appointed, it may be expedient for each Presbytery, in the room of each Commissioner, to appoint also an alternate Commissioner, to supply his place, in case of necessary absence.

Form of a Commission. Each Commissioner, before his name shall be enrolled as a member of the Council, shall produce, from his Presbytery,

a

commiſſion under the hand of the Moderator *and* Clerk, in the following or like form : *viz.*

" The Preſbytery of   being met at
           on the   day of   doth
hereby appoint   Biſhop of the
Congregation of   [or   ruling
Elder in the Congregation of   as
the caſe may be ;]" (to which the Preſbytery may, if they think proper, make a ſubſtitution in the following form, " or in caſe of his abſence, then   Biſhop of the Congregation of   [or   ruling Elder in the Congregation of   as the caſe may be ;]") to be a Commiſſioner, on behalf of this Preſbytery, to the next General Council of the Preſbyterian Church in the United States of America, to meet at   on the
day of   A. D.   or wherever, and whenever the ſaid Council may happen to ſit ; to conſult, vote, and determine, on all things that may come before that body, according to the principles and conſtitutions of this Church, and the Word of God. And of his diligence herein, he is to render an account at his return.
    Signed, by order of the Preſbytery,
                        Moderator,
                        Clerk."

And the Preſhytery ſhall make record of the appointment.

<small>Commiſſions ſhall be delivered to the Clerk at the firſt Seſſion.</small> Theſe commiſſions ſhall, if poſſible, be delivered to the Clerk of the Council, in proper ſeaſon, *that he may* have the rolls of the Council completed before the firſt ſeſſion. Commiſſions, not *produced at the opening of the Council,* ſhall afterwards

wards be delivered only in the intervals between the seſſions. Every *Commiſſioner* ſhall have a right to deliberate in the Council; but none ſhall be entitled to vote, until their names have been enrolled by the Clerk, and their commiſsions publicly read, and filed among the papers of the Council.

The Council ſhall meet once a year.
The General Council ſhall meet, at leaſt, once in every year, on the Tueſday of   and afterwards on their own adjournments. If there be not a ſufficient number, for the tranſaction of buſineſs, convened before 12 o'clock, on that day, thoſe who are preſent ſhall have power to adjourn, from day to day, till a ſufficient number ſhall have met to conſtitute a Council.

And ſhall be opened with a Sermon.
On the day, to which the General Council ſtands adjourned, and between the hours of eleven and twelve, the Moderator of the laſt General Council, if preſent; or, in caſe of his abſence, the ſenior *Miniſter* preſent, ſhall open the meeting with a ſermon. After ſermon, the Members being in the houſe where the Council is to hold its ſeſſions, the ſame *Miniſter* who preached ſhall, by prayer, publicly implore the bleſſing and direction of Almighty God; and ſhall continue to preſide till a new moderator be choſen. For this purpoſe he ſhall call for the commiſſions of thoſe preſent; which being read, and the names of the Members enrolled in order, *if there be a Quorum, they* ſhall *chuſe* a Moderator.

Mode of diſſolving the Council.
Each ſeſſion of the Council, as of all the other Judicatories of the Church, ſhall be introduced and concluded with prayer. And the whole buſineſs of the

the Council being *finifhed*, and the vote being taken for diffolving the prefent Council, the Moderator fhall fay from the Chair : " By virtue of the authority delegated to me by the Church, let this General Council be diffolved ; and I do hereby diffolve it, and require another Council, chofen in the fame manner, to meet at on the   day of A. D.   ." After which he fhall pray, and return thanks to God for his great mercy and goodnefs, and pronounce, on thofe prefent, the *Apoftolic* benediction.

Expences of Delegates to be defrayed. In order, as far as poffible, to procure a refpectable and full delegation to all our Judicatories, it is proper, that the expences of Minifters and Elders, in their attendance on thefe Judicatories, be defrayed, by the bodies which they refpectively reprefent.

Forms of Procefs in the Judicatories of this Church.

With regard to Scandals, or offences that may arife in our Churches, we agree to obferve the following rules of proceeding.

I. Inafmuch as all baptized perfons are Members of the Church, they are under its care, and fubject to its government and difcipline ; and, when they have arrived at the years of difcretion, they are bound to perform all the duties of Church-members.

II. No accufation fhall be admitted, as the foundation of a procefs before an ecclefiaftical Judicatory, but where fuch offences are alledged, as appear, from the Word of God, to merit the public notice and cenfure of the Church :

and,

and, in the accufation, the times, places, and circumftances, fhould be afcertained, if poffible; that the accufed may have an opportunity to prove an *alibi*; or to extenuate, or alleviate his crime.

III. No complaint or information, on the fubject of perfonal and private injuries, fhall be admitted; unlefs thofe means of reconciliation, and of privately reclaiming the offender, have been ufed, which are required by Chrift, Mat. XVIII. 15, 16. And, in all cafes, the ecclefiaftical Judicatories, in receiving accufations, in conducting proceffes, or inflicting cenfures, ought to avoid, as far as poffible, the divulging of offences, to the fcandal of the Church: becaufe the unneceffary fpreading of fcandal hardens and enrages the guilty, grieves the godly, and difhonours religion. And if any private Chriftian fhall induftrioufly fpread the knowledge of an offence, unlefs in profecuting it before the proper Judicatories of the Church, he fhall be liable to cenfure, as an uncandid flanderer of his brother.

IV. When complaint is made of a crime, cognizable before any Judicatory, no more fhall be done at the firft meeting, unlefs by confent of parties, than to give the accufed a copy of each charge with the names of the witneffes to fupport it; and a citation of all concerned, to appear at the next meeting of the Judicatory, to have the matter fully heard and decided: Notice fhall be given to the parties concerned, at leaft ten days, previoufly to the meeting of the Judicatory.

V.

V. The Judicatory, in many cafes, may find it more for edification, to fend fome Members to converfe, in a private manner, with the accufed perfon; and, if he confefs guilt, to endeavour to bring him to repentance; than to proceed immediately to citation.

VI. When an accufed perfon, or a witnefs, refufes to obey the citation, he fhall be cited a fecond and a third time; and if he ftill continue to refufe, he fhall be excluded from the communion of the Church, for his contumacy; until he repent.

VII. No crime fhall be confidered as eftablifhed by a fingle witnefs.

VIII. The oath, or affirmation, to be taken by a witnefs, fhall be in the following, or like terms: "*I* folemnly promife, in the prefence of the omnifcient and heart-fearching God, that *I* will declare the truth, the whole truth, and nothing but the truth, according to the beft of *my* knowledge, in the matter in which *I am* called to witnefs, as *I* fhall anfwer it to the great Judge of quick and dead."

IX. The trial fhall be open, fair, and impartial: the witneffes fhall be examined in the prefence of the accufed, or at leaft after he fhall have received due citation to attend; *and he* fhall be permitted to afk any queftions tending to his own exculpation.

X. No witnefs, afterwards to be examined, fhall be prefent, during the examination of another witnefs, on the fame caufe.

XI. The teftimony, given by witneffes, muft be faithfully recorded, and read to them, for their approbation or fubfcription.

XII. The judgment shall be regularly entered on the records of the Judicatory; and the parties shall be allowed copies of the whole proceedings, if they demand them: And, in case of references or appeals, the Judicatory *appealed from* shall send authentic copies of the whole *process* to the higher Judicatories.

XIII. The person found guilty shall be admonished, or rebuked, or excluded from Church privileges, as the case shall appear to deserve; and this only till he give satisfactory evidence of repentance.

XIV. The sentence shall be published, only in the Church or Churches which have been offended: or, if it be a matter of small importance, and it shall appear most for edification not to publish it, it may pass only in the Judicatory.

XV. Such gross offenders, as will not be reclaimed by the private or public admonitions of the Church, are to be cut off from its communion, agreeably to our Lord's direction, *Mat. XVIII.* 17. and the Apostolic injunction respecting the incestuous person, *I Cor. V.* 1——5. But as this is the highest *censure* of the Church, and of the most solemn nature, it is not to be *inflicted*, without the advice and consent of, at least, the Presbytery under whose care the particular Church is, to which the offender belongs; or the advice of a higher Judicatory, as the case may appear to require.

XVI. All processes, in cases of scandal shall commence, within the space of one year, after the crime shall have been committed; unless it shall have become recently flagrant.

XVII.

XVII. When any Member shall remove from one *Congregation* to another, he shall produce proper testimonials of his Church-membership, before he be admitted to Church-privileges; unless the Church, to which he removes, has other satisfactory means of information.

Of Process against a Bishop or Minister.

As the success of the Gospel, in a great measure, depends upon the credit and good report of its Ministers, each Presbytery ought, with the greatest attention, to watch over all their Members; and *to* be careful to censure them, when necessary, with impartiality; either for personal crimes, which they may commit in common with other men: or those that are vocational, arising from the manner in which they may discharge their important office.

I. Process, against a Gospel Minister, shall always be entered before the Presbytery of which he is a member: *But*, in case of crimes committed without the limits of that Presbytery, evidence shall be taken, at the instance of *the* Presbytery within which the offence has been committed; and the whole proof, authenticated under the hand of the Moderator and Clerk, shall be transmitted to the Judicatory before which he is to be tried.

II. Process, against a Gospel Minister, shall not be entered upon; unless some person or persons undertake to make out the charge; or when common fame so loudly proclaims the scandal, that the Presbytery find it necessary to prosecute, and search into the matter, for the honour of religion.

III.

III. The succefs of the Gospel greatly depends on *the unblemished* character of *its Ministers, their* soundness in the Faith, and holy, and exemplary conversation. It is the duty of all Christians to be very cautious in taking up an ill report of any man, but especially of a Minister *of the* Gospel. If, therefore, any man know a Minister guilty of a private censurable fault, he should warn him in private; but if he persist in it, or it become public, he should apply, to some other Bishop of *the* Presbytery, for his advice in the matter.

IV. When complaint is laid before the Presbytery, it must be reduced to writing, and nothing farther be done at the first meeting, unless by consent of parties, than giving the Minister a full copy of the charges, with the names of the witnesses annexed thereto; and citing all parties, and their witnesses, to appear and be heard at the next meeting; which meeting shall not be sooner than ten days after such citation.

V. At the next meeting of the Presbytery, the charges must be read to him, and his answers heard and recorded. If it appear necessary to proceed farther, the Presbytery ought to labour to bring him to confession; and if he confess, and the matter *be* base and flagitious; such as drunkenness, uncleanness, or crimes of a higher nature; however penitent he may appear, to the satisfaction of all, the Presbytery must, without delay, suspend him from the exercise of his office, or depose him from the ministry; and appoint him a due time to confess publicly before the Congregation offended, and *to* profess his repentance.

VI. The prosecutor *shall* be previously warned, that, if he fail to prove the charges, he must himself be censured, as a slanderer of the Gospel ministry.

VII. If a Minister, accused of atrocious crimes, being three times duly cited, shall refuse to attend the Presbytery, he must be immediately suspended: and if, *after another citation*, he still refuse to attend, he shall be deposed as contumacious.

VIII. If the Minister, when he appears, will not confess, but denies the facts alledged against him; if, on hearing the witnesses, the charges appear important and well supported, the Presbytery must, nevertheless, censure him; and suspend or depose him, according to the nature of the offence.

IX. Heresy and schism may be of such a nature as to infer deposition: but errors ought to be carefully considered; whether they strike at the vitals of religion, and are industriously spread; or whether they arise from the weakness of the human understanding, and are not likely to do much hurt.

X. *A Minister, under process for heresy or schism*, should be treated with christian and brotherly tenderness; frequent conferences *ought to be held with him*, and *proper* admonitions *administred*: *yet*, in some more dangerous cases, suspension becomes necessary; but a Synod should be consulted in such cases.

XI. If the Presbytery find, on trial, that the matter complained of amounts to no more than such acts of infirmity, as may be amended and the People satisfied, so as little or nothing remains to hinder his usefulness; they shall take all prudent measures to remove the offence.

XII.

XII. A Minister, deposed for scandalous conduct, may not be restored, on his deepest sorrow for sin, without some time of eminent and exemplary, humble and edifying conversation, to heal the wound made by his scandal.

XIII. As soon as a Minister is deposed, his Congregation shall be declared vacant.

CONFESSION OF FAITH.

Chap. XX.

IV. And becauſe the powers which God hath ordained, and the liberty which Chriſt hath purchaſed, are not intended by God to deſtroy, but mutually to uphold and preſerve one another; they who, upon pretence of Chriſtian liberty, ſhall oppoſe any lawful power, or the lawful exerciſe of it, whether it be civil or eccleſiaſtical, reſiſt the ordinance of God. And for their publiſhing of ſuch opinions, or maintaining of ſuch practices, as are contrary to the light of nature, or to the known principles of Chriſtianity, whether concerning faith, worſhip, or converſation; or to the power of godlineſs; or ſuch erroneous opinions or practices, as either, in their own nature, or in the manner of publiſhing or maintaining them, are deſtructive to the external peace and order which Chriſt hath eſtabliſhed in the Church; they may lawfully be called to account, and proceeded againſt by the cenſures of the Church.

Chap. XXIII.

III. Civil Magiſtrates may not aſſume to themſelves the adminiſtration of the Word and Sacraments; or the power of the keys of the kingdom of Heaven; or, in the leaſt, interfere in matters of Faith. Yet, as nurſing Fathers, it is the duty of Civil Magiſtrates to protect the Church of our common Lord, without giving the preference to any denomination of Chriſtians above the reſt, in ſuch a manner, that all eccleſiaſtical perſons whatever ſhall enjoy the
full,

full, free, and unqueſtioned liberty of diſcharging, every part of their ſacred funƈtion, without violence or danger. And, as Jeſus Chriſt hath appointed a regular Government and Diſcipline in his Church, no Law, of any Commonwealth, ſhould interfere with, let, or hinder, the due exercife thereof, among the voluntary members of any denomination of Chriſtians, according to their own profeſſion and belief. It is the duty of Civil Magiſtrates to proteƈt the perſon and good name of all their people, in ſuch an effeƈtual manner as that no perſon be ſuffered, either upon pretence of religion or of infidelity, to offer any indignity, violence, abuſe, or injury to any other perſon whatſoever: and to take order, that all religious and eccleſiaſtical Aſſemblies be held, without moleſtation or diſturbance.

Chap. XXXI.

1. * For the better government and further edification of the Church, there ought to be ſuch Aſſemblies as are commonly called Synods or Councils: and it belongeth to the Overſeers and other Rulers of the particular Churches, by virtue of their office, and the power which Chriſt hath given them for edification and not for deſtruƈtion, to appoint ſuch Aſſemblies; and to convene together in them, as often as they ſhall judge it expedient for the good of the Church.

---

* *This is propoſed to be ſubſtituted in room of the firſt and ſecond ſeƈtions of this Chapter.*

THE
DIRECTORY,

FOR THE

PUBLIC WORSHIP OF GOD,

OF THE

PRESBYTERIAN CHURCH,

IN THE

UNITED STATES OF AMERICA;

As revised by the COMMITTEE OF SYNOD appointed for that Purpose.

Let all things be done decently, and in order.
1 Cor. XIV. 40.

CONTENTS.

Preface.
Of the Sanctification of the Lord's Day.
Of the Assembling of the Congregation, &c.
Of the public reading of the holy Scriptures.
Of the singing of Psalms.
Of public Prayer before Sermon.
Of the Preaching of the Word.
Of Prayer after Sermon.
Of the Administration of Baptism.
Of the Administration of the Lord's Supper.
Of the Admission of Persons to Sealing-Ordinances.
Of the Mode of inflicting Church-Censures.
Of the Solemnization of Marriage.
Of the Visitation of the Sick.
Of the Burial of the Dead.
Of Fasting; and of the Observation of Days of Thanksgiving.
Of the Ordination of Ministers of the Gospel.
The Directory for Secret and Family Worship.

PREFACE.

THE Presbyterian Church in America, from small beginnings, through the great goodness of God, hath risen to be a numerous and respectable body. It is of the last importance, that great care be taken to preserve, in this extensive community, not only soundness of doctrine, but also purity of manners, and regularity of worship.

This Church firmly believes, that her doctrines, and modes of worship, are most agreeable to the Word of God; to the Practice of the Primitive Church in the three first Centuries; and to the best reformed Churches. She thinks it the indispensible duty of all her people to use their utmost endeavours, to have regular settled Ministers of their own persuasion; and stated worship, in their own way, every Lord's day.

At the same time, the Presbyterian Church maintains a high respect for the other Protestant Churches of this Country; though several of them differ from her in some forms of government and Modes of worship: particularly for the regular Congregational Churches to the eastward; for the Associate, Low Dutch, and German, reformed Churches; and for the Lutheran and Episcopal Churches.

In places where there are only a few Presbyterians, and they are not able to have worship usually in their own way; it is recommended to them, to attend with the Christian brethren, of any of the above denominations, which may be most convenient, rather than spend their Sabbaths without public worship. But this Church warns all her People against illiterate, vagrant, and

and defigning perfons, who, under pretence of greater zeal and ftrictnefs than others, only go about to make a party. It is much better for them, to ftay at home on the Lord's day with their families, than to encourage thofe men, who, by condemning regular, known and pious Churches, give too much reafon to fufpect that their own views are dangerous and wrong.

Although the Prefbyterian Church believes her Government and worfhip, as well as her Faith, to be the pureft and beft; yet thefe are far from being perfect. This imperfection, however, is not fo much in her conftitution, as in carrying her government, and modes of worfhip into effect. The Form of government and difcipline is intended to obviate the imperfection, in the one cafe; and the following directory for worfhip, in the other.

One great and apparent imperfection, attending the public worfhip of this Church, as well as that of other denominations (for which we have great reafon to be deeply humbled before God) is the manifeft deficiency of folemn gravity, holy reverence, and a devotional fpirit, in the time of performing divine fervice. It is abfolutely neceffary that fomething be done to revive the fpirit and appearance of devotion. Where there is real devotion; there the appearance of it will be. This, we doubt not, is the cafe with a number, through divine grace, in all our Congregations. It is readily granted, that there may be the appearance, without the fpirit of devotion; but there cannot be the fpirit, without the appearance: and, did we attend more to the appearance, it might have a happy tendency to awaken and revive a devotional fpirit.

Many

Many things seem to contribute to banish the appearance of devotion from our worshipping Assemblies.

I. Persons going out and in, during divine service, is an odious practice. It is highly offensive to God, disturbs the Congregation, and mars their worship; and is never to be allowed, but in cases of absolute necessity. The Rulers of every Church ought to be careful to correct this disorder.

II. Another evil, increasing in our public worship, and tending to destroy the spirit and appearance of devotion, is, that many, in some of our Congregations, do not join in singing the praises of God. Every person ought to keep his eyes fixed upon his book, his heart engaged, and his voice employed in this delightful service; and to sing, with solemn reverence and composure, as in the presence of the most High. None can justly pretend, as an excuse, their want of voice, or their want of an ear for music; for there is no person who cannot, at least in a low voice, follow the tune: And, if the Officers of the Church be careful, that all have books and do sing, there is reason to hope, that, with the divine blessing, the spirit and appearance of devotion will be restored to this branch of our worship.

III. There is a want of devotion, awfully apparent in our Congregations, during the time of public prayer. Some are gazing about, some turning their back to the Minister, and others putting themselves into different attitudes of ease; and but few, either are in the posture, or have the appearance of devotion. It is the indispensible duty of the whole Congregation, seriously and

and devoutly, to join with the Minister in offering up the desires of their hearts unto God. There ought not to be a wandering heart, a gazing eye, a careless or indevout posture, in any part of divine service. The scriptural postures, in prayer, are, in general, standing or kneeling; the former of which is in use, with us, in the Church; and the latter, in the Family. In this duty, all ought to put themselves into the most devout attitude, as in the presence of the holy God, having their eyes fixed, covered or closed; and so continue throughout the whole of the service: and we doubt not but a due attention to the posture in prayer would have a happy tendency to bring on a praying frame of mind, and to revive a devotional spirit.

IV. As the reading of the holy Scriptures is a very important part of divine worship, it is much to be lamented, that this should be neglected in any of our Congregations. It is provided for, in the Directory, that, where it has not been used, it should be introduced and faithfully practised. In order to give solemnity to this part of worship, and to testify our reverence for the Word of God, it would be decent, and not improper, for the whole Congregation to stand up, during the reading of the Scriptures; as was the usage under the Old Testament dispensation, and among the primitive Christians. It is also recommended, that all have their Bibles; and that they, silently and devoutly, follow the Minister while he is reading. Thus the spirit of devotion will be promoted and cherished.

V. There are also some things amiss, while the Minister is preaching, which should be corrected. None ought to stand up; much less to

turn

turn their back upon the Minister; to place themselves in sluggish or carelefs postures; or to indulge to sleep, whispering or laughing. All ought, seriously and gravely, to attend to the whole of the instruction or exhortation; and to receive it with faith and love. Were these things duly observed, during the preaching of the Word, there would probably be fewer complaints among us of its want of success.

Now may God, of his infinite mercy, grant, that solemn reverence, and a devotional spirit, may be revived and flourish, in all our Churches, through Jesus Christ our Lord. *Amen.*

THE
DIRECTORY, &c.

Of the Sanctification of the LORD'S DAY.

IT is the duty of every person to remember the Lord's Day, and to prepare for it, before its approach. All worldly business, should be so ordered, and seasonably laid aside, as that we may not be hindered thereby from sanctifying the Sabbath, as the holy Scriptures require.

The whole day is to be kept holy to the Lord, and to be employed in the public and private exercises of religion. Therefore, it is requisite, that there be an holy resting, all the day, from unnecessary labours; and an abstaining from those recreations, which may be lawful on other days; and also, as much as possible, from worldly thoughts and conversation.

Let the provisions, for the support of the family on that day, be so ordered, that servants or others be not improperly detained from the public worship of God; nor hindered from sanctifying the Sabbath.

Let every person and family, in the morning, by secret and private prayer, for themselves and others, especially for the assistance of God to their Minister, and for a blessing upon his ministry; by reading the scriptures; and by holy meditation; prepare for communion with God in his public ordinances.

Let

Let the people be careful to assemble at the appointed time, that, being all present at the beginning, they may unite, with one heart, in all the parts of public worship : and let none unnecessarily depart, till after the blessing be pronounced.

Let the time, after the solemn services of the congregation in public are over, be spent in reading ; meditation ; repeating of sermons ; catechising ; religious conversation ; prayer for a blessing upon the public ordinances ; the singing of psalms, hymns, or spiritual songs ; visiting the sick ; relieving the poor ; and in performing such like duties of piety, charity and mercy.

Of the assembling of the Congregation, and their behaviour during Divine Service.

When the time appointed for public worship is come, let the people enter the Church, and take their seats, in a decent, grave, and reverent manner. And, after the Congregation is assembled, the Minister shall begin the service with prayer, to the following purpose :

‘ Holy, holy, holy, Lord God Almighty, who
‘ art, and wast, and art to come ; We, who are
‘ unworthy of the least of all thy mercies, humbly
‘ present ourselves in thy courts, to offer homage,
‘ adoration, and praise, to Thee, our Creator, our
‘ Redeemer, and our God. Enable us, O Lord,
‘ by thy good Spirit, to attend to the holy duties
‘ to which thou art calling us at this time, without
‘ distraction of mind, and with reverence and godly
‘ fear. Admit us, we beseech thee, with humble
‘ boldness, to enter into the holiest, by the blood
‘ of Jesus, by the new and living way, which he
‘ hath consecrated for us, through the vail.——

H Instruct-

'Inftruct us from thy holy word. May we read
it with wife and underftanding hearts. Prepare
us for finging thy praifes, that we may make melody in our hearts unto the Lord, and offer
up an acceptable fervice to our God. Teach
us to pray, infpire us with a fpirit of devotion,
enable us to exercife faith in all the parts of
divine worfhip. And let all be done to the
glory of the Father, of the Son, and of the
Holy Ghoft; and gracioufly accept us, through
Jefus Chrift our Lord. Amen.'

This, and all the other prayers in the Directory, may and ought to be varied, according to the variety of circumftances which may occur; agreeably to the views and judgment of every minifter. Thus the fpirit of prayer will be encouraged; and the undue reftraint of this fpirit, which is the too frequent effect of Forms of prayer, will be guarded againft.

In the time of public worfhip, let all the people attend with gravity and reverence; forbearing to read any thing, except what the minifter is then reading or citing; abftaining from all whifperings, from falutations of perfons prefent or coming in; and from gazing about, fleeping, fmiling, and all other indecent behaviour.

If any one be prevented from being prefent at the beginning of fervice, he ought not, when he enters the Church, to betake himfelf to his private devotion; but to compofe his mind, and reverently join in the public worfhip, with the Congregation.

Of the public reading of the Holy Scriptures.

The reading of the holy Scriptures, in the Congregation, is a part of the public worfhip of God; and

and ought to be performed by the Ministers and Teachers.

All the canonical books, of the old and new Testament, shall be publicly read, from the most approved translation, in the vulgar tongue, that all may hear and understand.

How large a portion shall be read at once is left to the discretion of every Minister: however, in each service, he ought to read, at least, one chapter; and more, when the chapters are short, or the connection requires it. He may, when he thinks it expedient, expound any part of what is read; always having regard to the time, that neither reading, singing, praying, preaching, or any other ordinance, be disproportionate the one to the other; nor the whole rendered too short or too tedious.

Of the singing of Psalms.

It is the duty of Christians to praise God, by singing psalms and hymns, publicly in the Church, as also privately in the family.

In singing the praises of God, we are to sing with the spirit, and with the understanding also; making melody, in our hearts, unto the Lord. It is also proper, that we cultivate some knowledge of the rules of music; that we may praise God with our voices, as well as with our hearts.

The whole congregation should be furnished with books, and ought to join in this part of worship. It is proper to sing without parceling out the psalm, line by line. The practice of reading the psalm, line by line, was introduced in times of ignorance, when many in the Congregation could not read: therefore, it is recommended, that it be laid aside, as far as convenient.

The proportion, of the time of public worſhip to be ſpent in ſinging, is left to the prudence of every Miniſter: but it is recommended, that more time be allowed, for this excellent part of divine ſervice, than has been uſual in moſt of our Churches.

Of public Prayer before Sermon.

After the introductory prayer, reading the word, and ſinging praiſe; the Miniſter is to proceed to a more extenſive adoration of God, confeſſion of ſin, thankſgiving for mercies, ſupplication for bleſſings, and interceſſion for others; in a longer prayer, to this effect:

'O God, thou art our God, early will we
'ſeek thee; our God, and we will praiſe thee;
'our father's God, and we will exalt thee:
'Thou art very great, cloathed with honor and
'majeſty. Thou covereſt thyſelf with light as
'with a garment; and in thee is no dark-
'neſs at all.

'Thou art God thyſelf alone; and, beſides thee,
'there is none elſe. The heavens declare thy
'glory, and the firmament ſheweth forth thy
'handy work. The inviſible things of God,
'from the creation of the world, are clearly
'ſeen, being underſtood by the things that are
'made, even thine eternal power and Godhead.

'Thou art tranſcendently great in all thy
'perfections. Thou art glorious in holineſs,
'fearful in praiſes, doing wonders. Who, in
'the heavens, can be compared unto the Lord?
'Who, among the ſons of the mighty, can be
'likened unto thee, O Lord God of hoſts? As

'the

' the heavens are high above the earth, so are
' thy thoughts above our thoughts, and thy ways
' above our ways. All nations, before thee, are
' as the drop of a bucket, or the small dust of the
' balance; and thou takeſt up the iſles as a very
' little thing: They are as nothing, and counted
' to thee leſs than nothing and vanity.

' Thou art the eternal, immortal and un-
' changeable God. Before the mountains were
' brought forth, or ever thou hadſt formed the
' earth and the world, from everlaſting to ever-
' laſting thou art God; the ſame, yeſterday, to day,
' and forever.

' Thou art the omnipreſent God. None can
' hide himſelf in ſecret places, that thou canſt not
' ſee him, for thou filleſt heaven and earth with
' thy preſence.

' Thou art the omniſcient Jehovah. All
' things are naked and opened unto the eyes of him
' with whom we have to do. Thou underſtandeſt
' our thoughts afar off: There is not a word in
' our tongue, but, lo! O Lord, thou knoweſt it
' altogether.

' Thy wiſdom is unſearchable. Thine under-
' ſtanding, O Lord, is infinite. Thou telleſt the
' number of the ſtars, and calleſt them all by their
' names. Thou art wonderful in counſel, excel-
' lent in working, wiſe in heart, and mighty in
' ſtrength. O the depth of the wiſdom and know-
' ledge of God! how unſearchable are his judg-
' ments, and his ways paſt finding out?

' Thy ſovereignty is inconteſtable. Thou
' doſt, according to thy will, in the armies of hea-
' ven, and among the inhabitants of the earth,
' and none can ſtay thy hand, or ſay unto thee,
' what doeſt thou.

' Thy

'Thy power is irresistible We know, O
God that thou canst do every thing. All power is thine, both in heaven and in earth: Thou killest, and thou makest alive: Thou woundest, and thou healest: And there is none that can deliver out of thy hand.

'Thou art a God of unspotted purity, and perfect rectitude. Thou art holy, O thou that inhabitest the praises of Israel. Holy and and reverent is thy name; and we give thanks at the remembrance of thy holiness. Thou art of purer eyes than to behold iniquity; neither shall evil dwell with thee.

'Thy justice is inflexible, thy truth inviolable, and the treasures of thy goodness inexhaustible. Thou art righteous, O Lord, in all thy ways, and holy in all thy works. Thy righteousness is as the great mountains: All thy ways are truth and judgment. Thou art God, and thy mercy endureth forever. Thy loving kindness is great towards us, and thy truth endureth to all generations. Thou hast proclaimed thy name, the Lord, the Lord God, merciful and gracious, slow to anger, abundant in goodness and truth, keeping mercy for thousands, forgiving iniquity, transgression and sin.

'These, O Lord, are but part of thy ways; for who by searching can find out God? who can find out the Almighty to perfection?

'We praise thee as a God of ineffable glory. Thou hast prepared thy throne in the heavens; and the Seraphim vail their faces before thee. Thou makest thine Angels spirits, and thy ministers a flame of fire: Thousand thousands minister unto thee, and ten thousand times ten
'thousand

'thousand stand before thee. Thou art worthy,
' O Lord, to receive blessing and honor and glo-
' ry and power; for thou hast created all things,
' and for thy pleasure, they are and were crea-
' ted. The earth is full of thy riches : thy
' kingdom ruleth over all : a sparrow falls not
' to the ground without our father ; and the
' hairs of our head are all numbered.

' Thou madest man at first of the dust of the
' ground, and didst breathe into him the breath
' of life, and he became a living soul. Thou
' hast made, of one blood, all the nations of men,
' for to dwell on all the face of the earth, and
' hast determined the times before appointed,
' and the bounds of their habitation.

' We adore thee, as the one, living, and true
' God, the Father, the Word, and the holy
' Ghost. We give honor to the Son as to the
' Father ; and to the comforter the holy Spirit,
' who is sent to teach us all things, and to bring
' all things to our remembrance. We praise
' thee, O Father, Son, and Holy Ghost, the Cre-
' ator, the Redeemer, and the Sanctifier. Thou hast
' made us, and not we ourselves ; and therefore
' we are not our own but thine, thy people,
' and the sheep of thy pasture. In thee we live,
' and move, and have our being. Thou hast re-
' deemed us from evil. We are bought with a
' price. It is of thy mercy that we are not con-
' sumed, even because thy compassions fail not.
' Thou hast appointed us a high priest, in whose
' name we may come boldly to the throne of
' grace. We make mention of the righteouf-
': ness of Christ, and of his only.

' Most merciful God, we come unto thee,
' in humble dependence upon his atonement
' and intercession, and confess our sins, which

' are

' are many and great. Againſt thee, thee only
' have we ſinned, O God; and to us belongeth ſhame
' and confuſion of face. Behold we are vile,
' what ſhall we anſwer thee? We will lay our hand
' upon our mouth. Thou putteſt no truſt in
' thy ſaints; yea the heavens are not clean in thy
' ſight. How much more abominable and fil-
' thy is man, who drinketh iniquity like water?
' We have ruined ourſelves; but in thee is our
' help. If thou Lord ſhouldſt mark iniquities,
' O Lord, who ſhall ſtand? But there is for-
' giveneſs with thee that thou mayeſt be feared:
' with thee there is mercy; yea, with our God,
' there is plenteous redemption.

' O Lord, thou madeſt man upright, but he
' hath ſought out many inventions. Our firſt
' parents rebelled againſt thee; and we are tranſ-
' greſſors from the womb. We are a ſeed of
' evil doers. We have dealt very treacherouſly.
' By one man's diſobedience, many were made
' ſinners. By one man ſin entered into the
' world, and death by ſin; and ſo death paſſed
' upon all men, for that all have ſinned. Behold,
' we are ſhapen in iniquity. We are by nature
' children of wrath, even as others. All fleſh
' have corrupted their way; we are all gone a-
' ſide; we are altogether become filthy: there is
' none righteous; there is none that doth good;
' no not one.

' Our underſtandings are darkened by reaſon
' of ſin; our wills are ſtubborn and perverſe;
' and our affections are alienated from thee. We
' are wiſe to do evil, but to do good we have
' no knowledge. Our neck hath been an iron
' ſinew; and we have made our heart as the
' adamant. We have followed after vanities,

' and

' and forsaken our mercies. We have set
' our affections on things beneath; and our
' hearts have departed from the living God.
' We are prone to evil as the sparks fly upward.
' Our hearts are deceitful above all things, and
' desperately wicked. O Lord, we lament our
' irregular appetites, and inordinate passions.
' We bewail our pride, our carnality, and world-
' ly mindedness. Our sins are attended with ex-
' ceedingly great aggravations. We have sin-
' ned against the clearest light, the tenderest
' love, and the most faithful warnings of God,
' of parents, of ministers, and of our own con-
' sciences. And now, O Lord, what shall we
' say, for we have forsaken thy commandments:
' we have sinned, what shall we do unto thee,
' O thou preserver of men?

' Glory, glory to thy name in the highest,
' that there is any hope for the lost and sinful
' children of men; that thou hast entertained
' purposes of mercy towards any of the guilty
' race; that the joyful sound of peace and re-
' conciliation with God hath reached our ears.
' We thank thee, that thou hast so loved the
' world as to give thine only begotten Son, that
' whosoever believeth in him should not perish,
' but have everlasting life.

' In the all prevailing name of Jesus of Naza-
' reth, a name with which thou art ever well
' pleased, we present our prayers and supplica-
' tions to thee. And now, Lord, what wait we
' for? Our eyes are unto thee, and our hope is
' in thee, through Christ Jesus our Redeemer.
' Deliver us from all our transgressions; and, O
' God, be merciful to us sinners. Wash us
' thoroughly from our iniquity, and cleanse us

' from

'from our sins: For we acknowledge our tranf-
'greffions; and our fin is ever before us. Juf-
'tify us freely by thy grace, through the re-
'demption that is in Chrift Jefus our Lord.

'Create in us a clean heart, O God, and re-
'new a right fpirit within us. Work in us the
'work of faith with power. Difpofe us to a
'godly forrow for our fins, and give us repentance
'unto life. Shed abroad thy love in our hearts
'by the holy Ghoft given unto us. Teach us
'thy ftatutes, and give us underftanding that we
'may know thy teftimonies. May we know
'God and Jefus Chrift, whom to know is eter-
'nal life. Put thy fear, O Lord, into our
'hearts, that we may never depart from thy law.
'Hide pride from our eyes; and cloath us with
'humility. Enable us to put on the ornament
'of a meek and quiet fpirit. O God of peace,
'let not anger reft in our bofoms. Fill us with
'charity and brotherly love, that we may keep
'the unity of the fpirit in the bond of peace.
'May our confciences be always tender. May we
'abftain from all appearance of evil. Difpofe us
'to contentment with the allotments of thy pro-
'vidence; and form us to fubmiffion and refig-
'nation to thy will. May we ever poffefs our
'fouls in patience, and feel an holy indifference
'to all the objects of time and fenfe. O Lord, fur-
'nifh us with hope, which maketh not afhamed;
'that living hope which is, as an anchor to the
'foul, both fure and ftedfaft.

'Enable us, O Lord, to be circumfpect in all
'our converfation, watching over our thoughts,
'our lips, and our lives. May the grace of
'God teach us, that denying ungodlinefs and
'worldly lufts, we may live foberly, righteouf-

'ly

'ly and godly in this present world; looking for
'that blessed hope, and the glorious appearing
'of the great God, and our Saviour Jesus
'Christ, who gave himself for us, that he might
'redeem us from all iniquity, and purify unto
'himself a peculiar people, zealous of good
'works. Lord, quicken us in the ways of right-
'eousness. Let us ever practise the things which
'are honest in the sight of all men. May we
'be diligent in every duty, performing it with
'a ready mind, and with joy and gladness of
'heart. May we have grace always to live in
'the exercise of devotion and piety towards God;
'of truth, charity and righteousness towards
'men; and to maintain chastity, temperance
'and sobriety towards ourselves. Grant that
'we may increase in all godliness; that we
'may grow in grace, and in the knowledge of
'our Lord and Saviour Jesus Christ.

'O Lord, who art the confidence of all the
'ends of the earth, preserve us from temptation;
'support us under afflictions; comfort us in sor-
'rows; make us useful in life, and prepare us
'for death: And when we have done serving
'thee here below, admit us, we beseech thee, to
'that state of rest and perfection, which thou
'hast reserved for thy people in the heavenly
'world.

'And now, O Lord our God, we desire to
'lift up our hearts to thee, in a grateful ac-
'knowledgment of all thy mercies and benefits
'to us. We praise thee, as the King of Kings,
'and Lord of Lords, full of compassion and
'goodness to the children of men. We thank
'thee, that thou hast formed us reasonable crea-
'tures, capable of knowing, serving, and enjoy-
'ing

'ing thee. We bless thee for thy preserving
' care; for our lives, our health, our food and
' raiment; for our friends, our comforts, and all
' our temporal enjoyments. Above all we praise
' thee, O most merciful Father, for spiritual bles-
' sings in heavenly places in Christ Jesus.

' We thank thee, O Lord, for the early intima-
' tions of good will to fallen man; that the seed of
' the woman should bruise the serpent's head.
' We adore thee for the wonderful and mysterious
' incarnation of thine only begotten Son. We
' praise thee, that when the fulness of time was
' come, thou didst send forth thy Son made of a
' woman, made under the law, to redeem them
' that were under the law, that we might receive
' the adoption of sons. We thank thee for his
' gracious undertaking; for his exemplary life;
' his soul saving doctrines; for the stupen-
' dous miracles whereby he confirmed his divine
' mission; and, in a special manner, for his me-
' ritorious death and sufferings. We bless thee
' that he was delivered for our offences, and rose
' again for our justification; that he hath as-
' cended to his father and our father, to his God
' and our God; and that he ever liveth to make
' intercession for us.

' We thank thee, O Lord God of grace, for
' the holy Spirit, and for his sanctifying and com-
' forting influences upon the souls of men; for
' the covenant of grace and all the precious pro-
' mises thereof; for thy Word; for the gospel
' ministry, and the institution of all thine ordinan-
' ces; for Sabbaths; and for sanctuary blessings.
' We praise thee for the strivings of thy Spirit,
' and for the remonstrances and admonitions of
' our consciences; for enlightening, renewing,
' justifying,

'justifying, adopting and sanctifying grace ; for
'sweet communion with thee in thine ordinan-
' ces ; for gracious answers to our prayers ;
' for succour in temptations ; for support un-
' der troubles ; and for the joyful hopes of a
' glorious immortality.

'Now, O thou most High, when we pray unto
' thee, we would remember and make supplica-
' tion for all the children of men. Extend, we
' beseech thee, thy mercy to a guilty world ;
' and let all the ends of the earth see the salva-
' tion of our God. Let thy gospel be preached
' unto every creature ; and add, unto thy church
' daily, such as shall be saved. Give unto thy
' Son the Heathen for his inheritance, and the ut-
' termost parts of the earth for his possession. O
' Lord, gather, into the gospel Church, thine
' ancient people the Jews ; hasten the latter day
' glory; accomplish all the purposes of thy grace;
' remove every thing which is a let or hin-
' drance to the advancement of the Redeemer's
' kingdom ; take away all error and idolatry,
' Antichristian superstition, and Mahometan
' delusion.

'We pray for thy blessing upon thy Church
' universal, and upon every branch of it in par-
' ticular. O Lord, pity any part of thy Church
' which may be suffering affliction or persecu-
' tion. Let not the rod of the wicked rest upon
' the lot of the righteous ; strengthen the faith
' and patience of thy suffering saints, that they
' may hope and quietly wait for the salvation of
' the Lord. Pour out thy Spirit upon all thy
' Churches ; revive thy work in the midst of the
' years ; cause pure and undefiled religon uni-
' versally to prevail ; arise, have mercy upon
' Zion,

'Zion, and let the time to favour her, yea, the
'set time, come.

'Heavenly Father, do thou bless all the Mi-
'nisters of thy Gospel; purify the sons of Levi,
'and make those holy who bear the vessels of the
'Lord; make them burning and shining lights
'in thy golden candlesticks; and may they turn
'many to righteousness, and shine as stars in the
'firmament of glory forever and ever.

'O Lord, we pray for thy special favour to
'thy Churches in this land. Be very gracious
'to all the Congregations and Ministers of this
'Church. Bless our Presbyteries, our Synods,
'and our General Council. May their deliberations
'at all times have a happy tendency to promote true
'religion, and to advance, more and more, the
'interest of the Redeemer's kingdom. Make
'all our people holy in their lives, and godly in
'their conversation. May they be an ornament
'to their profession; and may our Church be
'a praise in the land.

'O thou, who art King among the nations,
'visit all the nations and kingdoms of the earth
'with thy goodness, thy mercy, and thy sal-
'vation.

'Deal favorably, O Lord, with the land in
'which we live. O the hope of Israel, the Sa-
'viour thereof in time of trouble, be not as a
'stranger in our land, and as a way-faring man,
'that turneth aside to tarry for a night. Make
'this Emmanuel's land. May it be a valley of
'vision, a land wherein truth, peace and right-
'eousness shall always dwell.

'Give, O Lord, we intreat thee, prosperity
'to the Inhabitants of this country, in their hus-
'bandry, their trades and their merchandize.
'Make not our heaven brass, nor our earth iron;

'but

' but grant us, we pray thee, rain in due ſeaſon;
' and reſerve unto us the appointed weeks of
' harveſt. Let our land yield her increaſe, and
' our trees their fruit. Abundantly bleſs our
' proviſion, and ſatisfy our poor with bread.

' O Lord, bleſs all in authority over us, ſu-
' preme and ſubordinate. Counſel our Counſel-
' lors, and teach our Senators wiſdom. Make
' our Officers peace, and our Exactors righteouſ-
' neſs. [It is proper, that ſpecial petitions be
' here offered up; for the Congreſs of the Uni-
' ted States; for the particular States, their Go-
' vernors and other Rulers; for the State, in
' which the Congregation may be, its Govern-
' or, Legiſlature, and other Rulers, Judges and
' Magiſtrates; as well as for the whole body of
' the people.] May all our Magiſtrates and Ru-
' lers rule in the fear of God; be able men,
' men of truth, fearing God, and hating covet-
' ouſneſs. May judgment run down as waters,
' and righteouſneſs as a mighty ſtream.

' O Lord, we pray for all Schools, Colleges,
' and other Seminaries of learning. From theſe
' fountains may ſtreams iſſue, which ſhall make
' glad the city of our God. Bleſs all Teachers in
' them; and may the youth be trained up in
' the fear of the Lord.

' Moſt gracious God, we beſeech thee to ex-
' tend compaſſion to the ſons and daughters of
' affliction. Heal the ſick; eaſe the pained;
' ſupport the diſtreſſed; ſuccour the tempted;
' comfort mourners; reſtore, to their right mind,
' thoſe who are deprived of the uſe of their rea-
' ſon: be the God of the widow, the father of
' the fatherleſs, and the orphan's ſtay. [It is
' proper here, if any have deſired the prayers
' of the Church, that ſpecial petitions be offered
' up for them.]   ' And

'And now, O Lord our God, we commit
'ourselves unto thee; we hope in thy mercies;
'and we wait for thy salvation. Pardon the ini-
'quity of our holy things. We ask and offer
'all, in the name of our once crucified but now
'exalted Redeemer, the Lord Jesus Christ; to
'whom, with the Father, and the Spirit of all
'grace, be ascribed glory, honor, dominion and
'praise, for ever and ever. *Amen.*'

We judge this to be a convenient order in the the public prayers of the Church; yet the Minister, as in prudence he shall think meet, is to alter and change this order; to leave out any petitions or parts of it; to add to or vary it, according to the numerous patterns of prayer in the Scriptures.

We recommend it to all Ministers ordinarily to use scriptural language in their public prayers, and that they be careful not to be tedious in this part of the service. We think that the prayer before sermon ought not usually to be shorter than twelve, nor longer than eighteen or twenty minutes.

As the prayer, which Christ taught his disciples, is both a pattern for prayer, and itself a most comprehensive prayer, we recommend it to be used in the prayers of the Church: and we think the most proper place for this purpose is, either at the conclusion of the introductory prayer, or at the end of this prayer.

Let a Psalm be also sung here, before the minister proceed to his Sermon.

Of the preaching of the Word.

The Preaching of the Word, being an institution of God for the salvation of men, should be so performed, that the workman need not be a-
shamed,

shamed, but may save himself and those that hear him.

Every man, who undertakes this sacred Work, should be careful that he be called of God, and regularly called and introduced by the Church, according to the order of the Scriptures.

The subject of his Sermon is to be some verse or verses of scripture, holding forth some principle of religion, inculcating some duty, or reproving some sin. Let him not use a text merely as a motto, but be careful that the doctrine proposed be fairly contained in it. It is proper also, that large portions of Scripture be sometimes expounded, and particularly improved, for the instruction of the People in the meaning and use of the sacred Oracles.

Let the introduction of his discourse be brief and perspicuous, and ordinarily drawn from the text or context; that, by a natural and easy transition, it may lead him to the subject, which he intends to consider. Let not the divisions be too numerous. Let the doctrines be plain, the explications easy, the illustrations clear, the arguments convincing, the inferences natural; and the application solemn, affectionate, powerful and persuasive.

This method of preaching requires much study, meditation and prayer. Ministers ought, in general, to write their sermons, and not to indulge themselves in loose extempore harangues, but to carry beaten oil into the sanctuary of the Lord. They ought so to digest their sermons, and commit them to memory, as not, ordinarily, to use their notes in public. But if any choose to have their notes before them, let them use them with the glance of the eye, but not read their sermons from the pulpit.

The servant of Christ is to prepare for the sanctuary, and to conduct the services thereof, in such a manner, that his hearers may be edified; and may feel the word of God to be quick and powerful, and a discerner of the thoughts and intents of the heart. Whatever the peculiarities of a Minister's method may be, he is to perform his whole ministry;

I. Faithfully, having a single eye to the honor of Christ, and sincerely seeking the salvation of the people.

II. Painfully; not doing the work of the Lord negligently.

III. Plainly; that the feeblest mind may understand; delivering the truth, not in the enticing words of man's wisdom, but in demonstration of the Spirit and of power.

IV. Wisely; adapting all his doctrines, exhortations and reproofs, in such a manner as may be most likely to be successful; neither neglecting the meanest, nor sparing the greatest in their sins.

V. Gravely and decently, as becometh the Oracles of God; avoiding all such improper gestures and phrases as may cause sensible men to despise him and his ministry.

VI. With meekness and tender affection; that the people may see the whole of his ministrations proceed from love, holy zeal, and a hearty desire to do them good.

VII. As taught of God, and fully persuaded in his own mind, that what he delivers is the truth

truth of Chrift; expreffing himfelf in language agreeable to Scripture, avoiding terms of art, and the phrafes of Philofophers. He is alfo to live the doctrine which he teaches, being an example to the flock, in humility, circumfpection and godly converfation; that he may have comfort in this life, many feals to his miniftry, and, when he has finifhed his labours of love, a crown of glory in the world to come.

VIII. As one, primary defign, of the public ordinances of the Sabbath, is, to pay acts of focial homage to the moft high God, the Minifter is to be careful not to make his fermons too long, fo as to interfere therewith. He is particularly to guard againft fhortening the devotional, and more important parts of the fervice, to make way for long difcourfes. But, when there is only one public fervice in the day, as is the cafe, in the winter, in many of our country Churches, the fermon, with all the other parts, may be fomewhat longer, than where there are two or more fervices. And, when there are two or more public fervices, ftatedly every Lord's day, we think the fermons, in general, ought not to be fhorter than thirty, nor longer than forty or forty-five minutes.

Of Prayer after Sermon.

The fermon being ended, the Minifter is to pray, turning fome of the principal parts of his fermon into confeffion, humiliation, petition, thankfgiving and praife, as the nature of the fubject may direct. In a fpecial manner he is,

' To give thanks, for the great love of God
' in fending his only begotten Son to be the Sa-
' viour of the world; for the communications of

' the

' the Holy Ghost ; for the light, liberty, privi-
' leges and rich blessings of the gospel ; for e-
' lecting love, redeeming mercy, sanctifying
' grace, and the joyful hopes of glory.

' To pray for the continuance of the gospel,
' with all its ordinances, in their purity, spiritu-
' ality and power ; for a blessing to accompany
' the word of his grace, with which they have
' been now favoured ; for preparation for death
' and judgment ; for the forgiveness of the ini-
' quities of our most holy services ; and for the
' acceptance of our persons and offerings, through
' the merits and mediation of our great High
' Priest and Saviour, the Lord Jesus Christ '

After this prayer, let a psalm be sung. Then let there be a collection for the poor, or other uses of the Church ; and let every one lay by, upon the first day of the week, as God hath prospered him, agreeably to the Apostolic direction. Then let the Minister dismiss the Congregation with a solemn blessing, to the following or like purport :

' The grace of the Lord Jesus Christ, and the
' love of God, and the communion of the holy
' Ghost, be with you all. *Amen.*'

Of the Administration of Baptism.

Baptism is not to be unnecessarily delayed, nor to be administred, in any case, by any private person ; but by a Minister of Christ, called to be the Steward of the mysteries of God.

It is usually to be administred in the Church, in the presence of the Congregation ; and it is convenient that it be performed immediately after sermon.

After

After previous notice is given to the Minister, the child to be baptized is to be presented, by one or both the parents, signifying their desire that the child may be baptized.

Before baptism, the Minister may, occasionally, use some words of instruction, respecting the institution, nature, use and ends of this ordinance: Shewing ;

'That it is instituted by Christ ; that it is a
'seal of the righteousness of faith ; that the
'seed of the faithful have no less a right to this
'ordinance, under the gospel, than the seed of
'Abraham to circumcision, under the Old Tes-
'tament ; that Christ commanded all nations
'to be baptized ; that he blessed little children,
'declaring that of such is the kingdom of hea-
'ven ; that children are federally holy, and
'therefore ought to be baptized ; that we are,
'by nature, sinful, guilty and polluted, and have
'need of cleansing by the blood of Christ, and
'by the sanctifying influences of the Spirit of
'God.'

The Minister is also to exhort the parents to the careful performance of their duty : requiring ;

'That they teach the child to read the word
'of God ; that they instruct it in the principles
'of our holy religion, as contained in the Scrip-
'tures of the old and new Testament, and ex-
'cellently summed up in the Confession and Ca-
'techism of this Church; that they pray with and
'for it ; that they set an example of piety and
'godliness before it ; and endeavour, by all the
'means of God's appointment, to bring up their
'child in the nurture and admonition of the
'Lord.'

Then

Then the Minister is to pray for a blessing to attend this ordinance, in the following or like manner :

 ‘ Most merciful, holy, and eternal God, we
‘ pray for thy blessing upon these parents and
‘ their child. The souls of parents and the
‘ souls of children are thine. Enable these pa-
‘ rents, in faith and love, to offer up their child
‘ to thee, at this time, in this holy ordinance of
‘ baptism. Sanctify this child by thy grace.
‘ May its original guilt be done away, through
‘ the blood of the Lamb, that was slain. Wash
‘ this child in the laver of regeneration. In-
‘ graft it into Christ ; and make it an heir of
‘ glory. Join the inward baptism of the Spirit
‘ with the outward baptism of water. Gracious-
‘ ly bless and sanctify this holy ordinance to the
‘ spiritual benefit of this child. Ratify in hea-
‘ ven what we now do upon earth. Hear us,
‘ O our God, accept and answer us, only for
‘ the sake of our divine Redeemer. *Amen.*’

Then the Minister, either taking the Child in his arms, or leaving it in the arms of the parent, shall call the child by its name, and say ;

 ‘ I baptize thee, in the name of the Father,
‘ and of the Son, and of the Holy Ghost.’

As he pronounces these words, he is to baptize the Child with water, by pouring or sprinkling it on the face of the Child, without adding any other ceremony.

This being performed he shall pray to this or the like purpose :

 ‘ O thou most glorious, condescending, and
‘ gracious God, Father, Son, and Holy Ghost ;
‘ we give thee hearty thanks, for the covenant of
‘ grace, and for all the institutions of thy mercy.
‘ Follow

'Follow with thy blessing this holy ordinance of baptism, which has now been administred in thy name. O Lord, enable these parents to live in the faithful discharge of every christian duty, towards this Child. Receive it into thy fatherly care and protection. May it live and grow up before thee, and do worthily in its day and generation. Sanctify it by thy Spirit; uphold it by thy power. May it be a useful member of thy Church here; and be kept, by faith, unto salvation, through Jesus Christ our Lord. Amen.'

This will form a part of the concluding prayer of public worship.

It is proper, that baptism be administred in the presence of the Congregation: yet there may be cases, when it will be expedient to administer this ordinance in private houses; of which the Minister is to be the Judge.

Of the Administration of the Lord's Supper.

The Communion, or Supper of the Lord, is to be celebrated frequently; but how often may be determined by the Minister and Eldership of each Congregation, as they may judge most for edification: but, we think it ought to be administered, at least, once in every quarter of the year. The time for the celebration of this ordinance, we judge convenient after the morning sermon: But if any choose to celebrate it in the afternoon, they are at their liberty.

The ignorant and scandalous are not to be admitted to the Lord's supper.

It is proper that public notice should be given to the Congregation, at least, the sabbath before the administration of this ordinance, and that, on

some

some day of the week, something be taught concerning its nature, and a due preparation for it, that all may come in a suitable manner to this holy feast.

When the sermon is ended, the Minister shall shew ;

' That this is an ordinance of Christ, by reading
' the words of institution, either from one of the
' Evangelists, or from 1 Cor. XI *chapter*, which,
' as to him may appear expedient, he may ex-
' plain and apply; that it is to be observed in
' remembrance of Christ, to shew forth his death
' till he come ; that it is of inestimable benefit,
' to strengthen his people against sin ; to sup-
' port them under troubles ; to encourage and
' quicken them in duty ; to inspire them with
' love and zeal ; to increase their faith, and ho-
' ly resolution, and to beget peace of conscience,
' and comfortable hopes of glory.'

He is to warn the profane, the ignorant, and scandalous, and those that secretly indulge themselves in any known sin, not to approach the holy Table.

On the other hand, he shall invite to this holy Table, such as, sensible of their lost and helpless state by sin, depend upon the atonement of Christ for pardon and acceptance with God ; such as, being instructed in the Gospel doctrine, have a competent knowledge to discern the Lord's body ; and such as desire to forsake the ways of sin, and are determined to lead a life of practical godliness.

The table, on which the elements are placed, being decently covered, the bread in convenient dishes, and the wine in large cups ; and the Communicants orderly and gravely sitting around it,

(or

(or in their seats before the table) in the presence of the Minister: Let him take a portion of the bread in one hand, and one of the cups in the other; and then pray for a blessing, to this or the like effect:

'O thou eternal God, Father, Son, and holy
'Spirit; We adore thee as the fountain of be-
'ing and blessedness. We praise thee, that
'thou hast erected a Church in this fallen world;
'that we are called to be members of it; and
'that thou hast appointed various ordinances to
'be observed therein.

'Now, O Lord, we are invited to come and
'eat of Wisdom's bread, and to drink of the
'wine that she hath mingled. Cause us so to
'hunger and thirst after righteousness, that we
'may be filled. Draw us, and we will run after
'thee. Bring us into thy chambers, that we
'may be glad and rejoice in thee, and remem-
'ber thy love more than wine.

'Most gracious God, we give thee glory for
'all the purposes of thy love; for the mission,
'sufferings and death of Jesus Christ, in whose
'name alone we have access to the throne of
'thy grace, and hope for everlasting life. We
'thank thee for this holy ordinance. We de-
'voutly pray for thy divine blessing upon us,
'in our attendance upon this feast of love.

'Bless, O Lord, these elements of bread and
'wine. May we receive them as the Symbols
'of the broken body, and shed blood, of our
'Lord and Saviour Jesus Christ. May we, by
'faith, eat the flesh, and drink the blood, of the
'Son of God. O let this cup of blessing, which
'we bless, be to us the communion of the blood of
'Christ; let this bread, which we break, be to us
'the communion of the body of Christ.

L 'Most

'Most merciful Father, keep our hearts and
'minds in the whole of this duty; and pre-
'serve us from the suggestions of the evil one.
'May our souls feel the lively exercises of every
'grace. Suit thy mercy to our various circum-
'stances. May we be joined to the Lord in a
'new and everlasting covenant, and made one
'spirit with him. May thy continual grace
'and aid further, and assist us, in the perform-
'ance of every duty of the Christian life. Seal
'unto us, we beseech thee, the remission of all our
'sins, the gift of the Holy Ghost, and the pro-
'mise of eternal life.

'Now unto him who is able to keep us
'from falling, and to present us faultless before
'the presence of his glory with exceeding joy,
'to the only wife God our Saviour be glory
'and majesty, dominion and power, both now
'and ever. *Amen.*'

The elements being now set apart by prayer, the Minister is to take the bread, and break
it, into small portions, in the view of the people. While he is performing this sacramental
action, let him make such observations, upon
the body of Christ Jesus, which was broken
for us, as to him may appear proper.

Then he is to say in expressions of this sort:

'Our Lord Jesus Christ, on the same night
'in which he was betrayed, having taken bread,
'and blessed and broken it, gave it to his Disci-
'ples; as I, ministring in his name, give this
'bread unto you; saying, [here the Bread is
'to be distributed] Take, eat; this is my Body,
'which is broken for you: this do in remem-
'brance of me.'

After having given the Bread, he shall take
the Cup, and say: 'After

'After the same manner, our Saviour also
'took the Cup, and, having given thanks, as
'hath been done in his name, he gave it to the
'Disciples; saying, [while the Minister is re-
'peating these words let him give the Cup] This
'Cup is the New Testament in my blood, which
'is shed for many, for the remission of sins: Drink
'ye all of it.'

The Minister himself is to communicate, at such time as may appear to him most convenient.

The Minister may, in a few words, put the Communicants in mind;

'Of the grace of God, in Jesus Christ, held
'forth in this sacrament, and of their obligation
'to be the Lord's; and may exhort them, to
'walk worthy of the vocation wherewith they are
'called; and, as they have professedly received
'Christ Jesus the Lord, that they be care-
'ful so to walk in him; and to maintain good
'works.'

It may not be improper for the Minister to give a word of exhortation also to those who have been only spectators, reminding them;

'Of their duty; stating their sin and danger,
'by living in disobedience to Christ, in neglect-
'ing this holy ordinance; and calling upon them
'to be earnest in making preparation for at-
'tending upon it, at the next time of its cele-
'bration.'

Then the Minister is to pray and give thanks to God;

'For his rich mercy, and invaluable good-
'ness, vouchsafed to them in that sacred com-
'munion; to implore pardon for the defects
'of the whole service; and to pray for the ac-
'ceptance of their persons and performances;
                                          'for

'for the gracious assistance of the Holy Spirit,
'to enable them, as they have received Christ
'Jesus the Lord, so to walk in him ; that they
'may hold fast that they have received, that no
'man take their crown ; that their conversa-
'tion may be as becometh the gospel ; that they
'may bear about with them, continually, the
'dying of the Lord Jesus ; that the life also of
'Jesus may be manifested in their mortal body ;
'that their light may so shine before men, that
'others, seeing their good works, may glorify
'their Father who is in heaven.'

The collection, for the poor, and to defray the expence of the elements, may be made after this, or at such other time as may seem meet to the Eldership.

Now let a psalm or hymn be sung, and the Congregation dismissed, with the following or some other gospel benediction ;

'Now the God of peace, that brought again
'from the dead our Lord Jesus, that great shep-
'herd of the sheep, through the blood of the
'everlasting covenant, make you perfect in every
'good work to do his will, working in you that
'which is well pleasing in his sight, through Je-
'sus Christ; to whom be glory forever and ever.
'*Amen.*'

It has been customary, in some parts of our Church, to observe a Fast before the Lord's Supper ; to have Sermon on Saturday and Monday ; and to assemble two or three Ministers, with their Congregations, on such occasions. Whereas these seasons have been blessed to many souls, and may tend to keep up a stricter union of Ministers and Congregations ; we think it not improper, that they, who chuse to continue

nue in this practice, should dispense the Sacrament, in this way, once a year : but we judge it highly expedient and necessary, that each Congregation celebrate the Communion, as before directed, at least once in each quarter of the year.

Of the Admission of Persons to Sealing-Ordinances.

Children, born within the pale of the visible Church, and dedicated to God in baptism, are Christians. They are under the inspection and government of the Church-Session ; and are to be taught to read, and repeat the Catechism, the Apostles Creed, and the Lord's prayer. They are to be taught to pray, to abhor sin, to fear God, and to obey the Lord Jesus Christ : And, when they come to years of discretion, if they be free from scandal, appear sober and steady, and to have sufficient knowledge to discern the Lord's body, they ought to be informed, it is their duty, and their privilege, to come to the Lord's Supper.

The years of discretion, in young Christians, cannot be precisely fixed. This must be left to the prudence of the Eldership. The Officers of the Church are the sole Judges of the qualifications of those to be admitted to Sealing-Ordinances ; and of the time when it is proper to admit young Christians to them.

Those, who are to be admitted to Sealing-Ordinances, shall be examined, as to their knowledge and belief of the following things : viz.

' That the Scriptures, of the Old and New
' Testament, are the Word of God, the only in-
' fallible rule of faith and practice ; that these
' contain, plainly and sufficiently, every doc-
' trine

' trine needful for salvation ; that there is one,
' only, living, and true, God, possessed of every
' perfection and excellency, the Creator, the
' Preserver, and the Governor of the universe ;
' that there are three Persons in the Godhead,
' the Father, the Son, and the Holy Spirit, and
' that these three are one ; that all men are in a
' lost estate, and, as sinners, stand justly condemn-
' ed by the law of God, and are liable to his
' wrath and curse ; that Jesus Christ, the on-
' ly begotten Son of God, who is God and
' man in one person, came into this world, to
' seek and to save them that are lost ; that he
' suffered, and made atonement, in their room
' and stead ; that he died for their offences, and
' rose again for their justification ; that he sit-
' teth at the right hand of God in heaven, ma-
' king continual intercession for them ; that the
' enlightening and sanctifying influences of the
' Holy Ghost are absolutely necessary, to lead
' us into the saving understanding of the sacred
' Scriptures, to renew the heart, and to enable
' a Christian to live Godlily in the world ; and
' that watchfulness over the life, holy meditation,
' a conscientious attendance upon public, pri-
' vate, and secret worship ; together with the
' steady practice of righteousness, truth, sinceri-
' ty, and charity, towards men ; and of sobriety,
' chastity, and temperance, towards ourselves ;
' are the indispensible duties of every Christian.'

— When the knowledge, of those who are to be admitted to sealing-ordinances, is judged to be satisfactory ; and nothing appears in their life and conversation to hinder their admission ; the Minister shall, either in private, or in the

presence

presence of the Session, or in the presence of the Congregation, as shall be most expedient, ask the profession of their faith, in the following or like manner :

' Do you believe Jesus Christ to be the Son of
' God ? Do you assent to the Covenant of grace,
' and acknowledge the obligation of your bap-
' tismal engagements ? Do you take God, the
' Father, Son, and Holy Ghost, to be your God?
' Do you renounce your former sins? And do you
' promise, through grace, to live in the diligent
' practice of all the duties required in the
' Gospel ?'

It is not improper that this be accompanied with suitable exhortation and prayer. And the persons, so professing their Faith, are, immediately thereupon, entitled to sealing-ordinances.

Unbaptized persons are not members of the visible Church ; they are not Christians : Therefore, when they offer themselves, they are to be considered as candidates for admission into the Church, and to be taught the doctrines of the Gospel as above directed.

When their knowledge shall be deemed satisfactory, and nothing appears in their life against their admission, it is most expedient, in ordinary cases, that they should publicly profess their Faith, in the presence of the Congregation ; [in the same, or like manner, as directed above in the admission of young Christians to Sealing-Ordinances:] After which they ought to be immediately baptized, and admitted to all the privileges of the Church.

Of the mode of inflicting Church-Censures.

The power, which Christ hath given the Rulers of his Church, is for edification, and not for destruction. As, in the preaching of the Word, the wicked are, ministerially and doctrinally, separated from the good; so, by discipline, the Church authoritatively makes a distinction between the holy and the profane. In this she acts the part of a tender Mother, correcting her Children only for their good: And that every one of them may be presented faultless, in the day of the Lord Jesus.

When any person, belonging to the Congregation, is reported of, as being guilty of a scandalous and censurable offence; the Church-Session shall consider it as their duty, to enquire into the matter; to call the person before them, and to deal with him, according to the rules of the Church.

When any member shall have been guilty of a fault, deserving censure, the Judicatory shall proceed with all tenderness, and restore their offending brother in the spirit of meekness; considering themselves, lest they also be tempted. Censure ought to be inflicted with the greatest possible solemnity; that it may be the means of impressing the mind of the delinquent with a proper sense of his danger, while he stands excluded from the privileges of the Church of the living God: and that, with the divine blessing, it may lead him to repentance; and earnestly to desire to be reconciled to the Lord whom he hath offended, and to his Church, which he hath, by his sin, scandalized and grieved.

When any person shall voluntarily confess himself guilty of an offence; and the offence be of a smaller nature; and He shall appear penitent, the Judicatory may give him an admonition, to be more watchful for the future, without proceeding to suspend or exclude him from privileges.

When the Judicatory has resolved to pass sentence, suspending a member from Church-privileges, the Moderator shall address him, to the following or like purpose:

'Whereas you are guilty [by your own con-
'fession, or convicted by sufficient proof as the
'case may be], of the sin of [here mention the
'particular offence] we declare you suspended
'from the privileges of the Church; till you give
'satisfactory evidence of the sincerity of your
'repentance.'

We now solemnly rebuke you for your sin. Consider, that this is one of those works of the flesh, which exclude from the kingdom of Heaven. You must have been far left of God, thus to crucify afresh the Son of God, and put him to open shame. Seriously reflect, that the wrath of God is revealed, from Heaven, against all unrighteousness; and that you shall have his wrath poured out upon you to the uttermost; unless you repent. Out of Christ, there is no safety: for our God is a consuming fire. But, while faithfulness to your soul obliges us to warn you of your danger, we call upon you to repent; to turn unto the Lord, who will have mercy upon you; and to our God, who will abundantly pardon. O be persuaded to flee to the blood of sprinkling. Apply anew to Christ Jesus the Lord: for he is able to save them to the uttermost, that come unto God by him, seeing he ever liveth to make intercession for them.

M   Then

Then let the Minister pray, in the following or like manner:

'O Lord, do thou, who hast given authori-
'ty to thy servants to bind and to loose upon
'earth, bless thine own ordinance. May this
'person be recovered from the snare of the De-
'stroyer. None are able to pluck the people
'of Christ out of his hand. Do thou, O com-
'passionate Redeemer, who didst pray for Pe-
'ter, in the hour of temptation, that his Faith
'might not fail, and, who didst restore him after
'he had fallen, grant repentance unto this Of-
'fender. May his heart be filled with godly
'sorrow, which worketh repentance not to be
'repented of. O Lord, deal not with him, ac-
'cording to the demerit of his sin; but do thou
'magnify thy grace, by the forgiveness of all his
'iniquities. Bless thy Church, O thou King of
'Saints, and preserve thy servants from such
'heinous offences. Let the time to favour Zi-
'on come, when the people shall be subdued
'under the anointed of the Lord. Enable us,
'O Lord, to watch and pray, that we enter not
'into temptation. Let not the Adversary tri-
'umph over thy chosen. Hear us, most gra-
'cious God, for the sake of Jesus Christ, the on-
'ly Mediator between God and man. *Amen.*'

It is most expedient, that all this should pass only before the Judicatory. But, if any Church think it most expedient to rebuke the Offender publicly, this solemn exclusion, from the privileges of the Church, may be in the presence of the Congregation.

After a person has been excluded from Church privileges, it is not fit, that he be given over as lost. The Minister, and Elders, and other Christians,

tians, should take occasion to converse with him; as well as pray frequently in private, that it would please God to give him repentance. And it may not be improper, at times, particularly on days preparatory to the dispensing of the Lord's Supper, that the prayers of the Church be offered up, for those unhappy persons, who by their wickedness, have shut themselves out from this holy communion.

When the Judicatory shall be satisfied, as to the reality of the repentance of any Offender, he shall, on his earnest importunity, be admitted to profess his repentance; and be restored to the privileges of the Church.

It is most proper, that Penitents, appointed by the Session to be restored to Church-privileges, should be reconciled in the presence of the Congregation : [yet this is not so indispensible, but that a Judicatory may, on good grounds, do it by themselves] and it shall be done in the following or like manner :

The Minister, having called the Penitent, in the presence of the Congregation, shall say :

'Do you now profess your repentance for
'your sin; your sincere desire to be restored to
'the privileges of the Church; and your pur-
'pose, through the assistance of the grace of
'God, to live as it becometh the Gospel ?'

Upon his answering in the affirmative, the Minister shall address him thus :

Dear Brother, it gives us sincere pleasure to be allowed to entertain a hope, that you have seen your folly, your sin, and your danger, and have been led to flee for refuge to the only hope set before us in the Gospel. Permit me to remind you, that you have now to do with the

heart-

heart-searching God. It is easy to impose upon the Church; you may deceive man, but God cannot be deceived, and may not be mocked. Oh! that your heart may be right with him. If you, in this solemn manner, profess repentance, while you feel no true repentance, but are still drawn with the Cords of sin, be afraid: for the bands of mockers shall be made strong. But, Brothen, we hope better things of you; and things which accompany salvation, though we thus speak. Suffer me to remind you, that much circumspection is necessary; and that a humble, holy walking with God is your special duty. You have grieved the people of God, and given occasion to the Adversary to blaspheme. I beseech you, endeavour, by your modest unaffected piety, to edify the one, and to stop the mouth of the other. Your late fall has, no doubt, convinced you of the great need you have of the grace and Spirit of God. Live in constant dependance thereon: and may you be enabled, for the future, to adorn the doctrine of God our Saviour in all things.

Then let the Minister pray to the following purpose:

' Most gracious God, thou art the Father of
' mercies; thou art the God of all grace, and
' of all consolation. Judgment is thy strange
' work. There is forgiveness with thee, that
' thou mayest be feared. With the Lord there
' is mercy, and with him is plenteous redemp-
' tion. We desire, O God, to join with this
' person in confessing his iniquity. O may his
' sin be ever before him. May he be washed in
' the fountain opened for sin. Lord thou hast
' said, there is joy in heaven over one sinner that
' repenteth, more than over ninety and nine just
' persons,

'persons, who need no repentance. O Lord,
'we beseech thee to magnify thy grace by sa-
'ving this precious soul. Do thou loose in Hea-
'ven, as we now, in thy name, loose him on
'earth. O Lord, hide thy face from his sins;
'and blot out all his iniquities. Create in him
'a clean heart, O God; and renew a right
'spirit within him. Restore unto him the joy of
'thy salvation; and uphold him with thy free
'Spirit. Bless all thy Church. Keep us from
'falling. Sanctify us wholly in body and spirit:
'And may we all, at last, be presented faultless,
'before the presence of thy glory, with exceed-
'ing joy: for the sake of Jesus Christ, for whom
'we thank thee; and may, Blessing, and honour,
'and glory, and power, be unto him that sitteth
'upon the throne, and unto the Lamb, forever
'and ever. *Amen*.'

Then the Minister shall say to the Penitent:
'By virtue of the authority which Christ hath
'left in the Church, for its edification, I pro-
'nounce you loosed from the sentence of exclu-
'sion, and received again to all the privileges
'of the Gospel. Go and sin no more, lest a
'worse thing befal you.'

When any person has been, with the advice of the Presbytery, (as directed in the Form of government &c.) adjudged to be cut off from the communion of the Church, it is proper that the sentence be pronounced against him; even although, as is to be expected in such cases of contumacy and wickedness, he should pretend to despise the censures of the Church, and either cast off all profession of religion, or go to another denomination. The design of excommunication is, both to operate upon the Offender as

the

the means of reclaiming him, and alſo to purge out the old leaven from the Church, that others may not be reproached for his vileneſs, or contaminated with his example.

The Miniſter ſhall, after the advice of the Preſbytery has been obtained, at leaſt two Lord's days before the excommunication, give the Congregation a ſhort narrative of the ſeveral ſteps which have been taken with their ſcandalous and obſtinate brother, and inform them, that it has been found neceſſary to reſolve to cut him off from their communion.

On the forenoon of the Lord's day appointed for the purpoſe, after all the other parts of worſhip are over, before pronouncing the bleſſing, the Miniſter ſhall denounce this awful ſentence, in the following or like manner :

He ſhall begin by ſhewing the authority of the Church to caſt out unworthy members, from Mat. XVIII. 15, 16, 17, 18; 1 Cor. V. 1, 2, 3, 4, 5; and ſhall briefly explain the nature, uſe, and conſequences of this tremendous cenſure; warning the people, to avoid all unneceſſary intercourſe with him who is caſt out, and to let him be unto them as an Heathen man and a Publican.

Then he ſhall ſay : (for it is not to be expected the perſon will be preſent)

' Whereas A. B. hath been, by ſufficient
' proof, convicted of [here inſert the ſin,] and,
' after much admonition and prayer, obſtinately
' refuſeth to hear the Church, and hath manifeſt-
' ed no evidence of repentance : Therefore, in
' the name and by the authority of the Lord Je-
' ſus Chriſt, I pronounce him ſhut out from the
' Church of God, and delivered unto Satan, that
' his ſpirit may be ſaved in the day of the Lord
' Jeſus.' Then

Then the Minister shall pray, to the following purpose:

'Holy, holy, holy, Lord God Almighty; thou
'art of purer eyes than to behold iniquity, or
'to look upon sin. Evil shall not dwell with
'thee, nor fools stand in thy sight. O Lord,
'do thou bless this ordinance which thou hast
'instituted. As we have, by thy appointment,
'shut out this obstinate sinner from the Church
'of the living God; do thou bind in hea-
'ven, whom we now, in thy name, bind upon
'earth. Let not thy Church or people be con-
'taminated with this unworthy member, whom,
'as old leaven, we have now purged out. Let
'not his sins prove a reproach to our most holy
'profession. But, O most merciful God, thou
'seekest not the destruction of the sinner. Take
'not, we beseech thee, thy holy Spirit wholly
'from this unhappy Person. O cause him to
'feel the tremendous danger of being without
'God, and without hope in the world. Con-
'vince him, by thy Spirit, of sin, of righteouf-
'nefs, and of judgment. O Lord, from a deep
'sense of guilt, may he, in due time, be laid
'under the happy necessity, of seeking the
'peace of God and of his Church; that so he,
'who hath been bound with much grief and re-
'luctance, may be loosed with the joy of all
'Saints. And, O Lord, may thy people, warn-
'ed by this dreadful example, fear and do no
'more presumptuously. O Lord, hear, answer,
'and do, for the sake of Jesus Christ: and to
'thy name be ascribed glory, dominion, and
'praise, world without end. *Amen.*'

It may perhaps happen, that some, whom God hath given up to a seared conscience and to hardness of heart, will affect to despise this sentence, and to be highly offended with the Church. But in general excommunicated persons, when they coolly reflect on their sin, and remember that this is the ordinance of Christ, will it is hoped be wounded in their hearts and pricked in their reins. Like Cain, when God pronounced sentence upon him for the murder of his brother, they will find their punishment greater than they are able to bear. Knowing themselves to be an execration and a curse in the earth, they will, for the most part, be desirous of being delivered from this unhappy condition. As the Father ran to meet the prodigal son, when he was yet a great way off; so the Church should cherish every symptom of humility and repentance.

When the Church-Session shall have obtained satisfaction, as to the sincerity of his penitence, and have consulted the Presbytery, the Minister shall, at least two Lord's days before, inform the Congregation of the steps which have been taken with the excommunicated person; and that it is resolved to restore him to Church-privileges.

On the day appointed for his absolution, when all the other parts of divine service are over, before pronouncing the blessing in the forenoon, the Minister shall call upon the excommunicated person, and propose to him, in the presence of the Congregation, the following questions:

‘ Do you, from a deep sense of your great
‘ wickedness, freely confess your sin, obstina-
‘ cy and presumption, in thus rebelling against
‘ God, and in refusing to hear his Church;

‘ and

'and do you acknowledge that you have been,
' in juſtice and mercy, cut off from the commu-
' nion of the Saints ? Anſwer, I do. Do you
' now voluntarily profeſs your ſincere repent-
' ance, and deep contrition, for your ſin and ob-
' ſtinacy ; and do you humbly aſk the forgive-
' neſs of God and of his Church ? Anſwer, I
' do. Do you ſincerely promiſe, through di-
' vine grace, to live in all humbleneſs of mind
' and circumſpection ; and to endeavour to a-
' dorn the doctrine of God our Saviour, by
' having your converſation as becometh the Goſ-
' pel ? Anſwer I do.'

Here the Miniſter ſhall give the Penitent a ſuit-
able exhortation ; addreſſing him in the bowels of
brotherly love, encouraging and comforting him.
Then he ſhall pronounce the ſentence of abſolu-
tion, in the following words :

' Whereas you, A. B. for your ſin and obſti-
' nacy, have been ſhut out from the communion
' of the Faithful, but have now manifeſted ſuch
' repentance as ſatisfies the Church: In the name
' of the Lord Jeſus Chriſt and by his authority,
' I declare you abſolved, from the ſentence of ex-
' communication formerly denounced againſt
' you ; and I do, with pleaſure, receive you in-
' to the communion of the Church, that you
' may be a partaker of all the benefits of the
' Lord Jeſus to your eternal ſalvation.'

Here the Miniſter ſhall pray to the following
effect :

' Almighty God, and moſt merciful Father,
' thou wilt not execute the fierceneſs of thine
' anger, thou wilt not return to deſtroy ; for thou
' art God, and not man, the holy One in the
' midſt of us. Thy thoughts are not as our
' thoughts ;

'thoughts; therefore the sons of men are not
'confumed. Thou art a faithful God, keeping
'mercy for thousands, forgiving iniquity, tranf-
'greffion, and fins, and that will by no means
'clear the guilty. We humbly adore and yield
'thee hearty thanks, for the exceeding great
'riches of thy grace in Chrift Jefus. In him
'thou art reconciling the world unto thyfelf;
'not imputing unto them their trefpaffes or their
'fins. Encouraged by the numberlefs intima-
'tions of thy mercy and grace, O Lord, we pre-
'fent this Penitent unto thee. Againft thee,
'thee only, has he finned, and in thy fight done
'this evil. O Lord, he hath hardened himfelf
'againft reproof. Like profane Efau, he hath de-
'fpifed his birth-right. He hath counted it a
'fmall thing to be cut off from the Church of
'the living God. We muft confefs before thee,
'O thou moft High, that he hath trodden un-
'der foot the fon of God, and hath counted the
'blood of the covenant wherewith he was fanc-
'tified, an unholy thing. O Lord, let him not
'be like Efau, who found no place for repent-
'ance, though he fought it carefully with tears.
'We befeech thee, O our God, to fill his heart,
'more and more, with godly forrow. May he
'receive, from the Prince and Saviour exalted,
'true repentance, and remiffion of fins. May
'his heart be fprinkled from an evil confcience,
'and his body wafhed with pure water. Re-
'ceive him, O Lord, into thy fold, as we now,
'in thy name, receive him again into the Church.
'May his foul be bound in the bundle of life.
'Preferve him from temptation; and may he
'henceforth live in thy fear. O God, blefs all
'thy people. May their love be confirmed to
'this

' this penitent. Let him that thinketh he stand-
' eth take heed left he fall. Let no evil furmi-
' fing, againft their brother, find place in their
' hearts : but may love, which covereth a mul-
' titude of fins, poffefs every foul. Forgive, we
' befeech thee, all our fins, and preferve us un-
' to thy heavenly kingdom and glory : for the
' fake of Jefus Chrift, who is our Advocate in
' heaven ; and who, with the Father, and the
' Holy Spirit, ever liveth and reigneth, in one
' undivided Godhead. *Amen.*'

Of the Solemnization of Marriage.

Marriage is not a facrament, nor peculiar to the Church of Chrift. It is proper that every Commonwealth, for the good of fociety, make laws to regulate Marriage, which all Citizens are bound to obey.

Chriftians ought to marry in the Lord ; therefore it is fit, that their marriage be folemnized by a lawful Minifter, that fpecial inftruction may be given them, and fuitable prayers made, when they enter into this relation.

Marriage is to be between one man and one woman only ; and they are not to be within the degrees of confanguinity or affinity prohibited by the word of God.

The parties ought to be of fuch years of difcretion as to be capable of making their own choice ; and if they be under age, or live with their parents, the confent of the parents, or others under whofe care they are, ought to be previoufly obtained, and well certified to the Minifter, before he proceeds to folemnize the marriage.

Parents ought neither to compel their children to marry contrary to their own inclinations, nor deny their consent without just and important reasons.

Marriage is of a public nature. The welfare of civil society, the happiness of families, and the credit of religion are deeply interested in it. Therefore the purpose of marriage ought to be sufficiently published a proper time, previously to the solemnization of it. It is enjoined on all Ministers to be careful that, in this matter, they neither transgress the laws of God, nor the laws of the community: And that they may not destroy the peace and comfort of families, they must be properly certified, with respect to the parties applying to them, that no just objections lie against their marriage.

Marriage must always be performed before a competent number of witnesses; and the Minister is to give a certificate of the marriage, when required.

When the parties present themselves for marriage, the Minister is to desire, if there is any person present who knows any lawful reason why these persons may not be joined together in the marriage relation, that they will now make it known, or ever after hold their peace.

No objections being made, he is then severally to address himself to the parties to be married, in the following or like words:

' You, sir, declare, in the presence of God,
' that you do not know any reason, by precon-
' tract or otherwise, why you may not lawfully
' marry this woman.'

Upon his declaring he does not, the Minister shall address himself to the Bride, in the same or similar terms:

' You

'You, Madam, declare, in the prefence of God, that you do not know any reafon, by precontract or otherwife, why you may not lawfully marry this man.'

Upon her declaring fhe does not, he is to pray to the following import :

'Moft holy, and moft gracious God, we adore thee as the Maker of our bodies, and the father of our fpirits. Be pleafed to accept our grateful acknowledgments, that thou haft made us rational creatures ; and that thou haft made us capable of the various bleffings of the focial life. We adore thee for the inftitution of marriage ; and that thou haft made it honourable in all. Be pleafed to blefs thefe perfons who are about to be joined to each other in this intimate and tender relation. While they join hands may they join hearts ; and being united to each other in the marriage covenant, may they be united to the Lord Jefus in that covenant, which is ordered in all things and fure. May they enter upon this important relation in the fear of the Lord ; and have abundant caufe to adore and rejoice in that providence that hath formed it between them. We devoutly pray for thy gracious prefence with us ; for the pardon of our fins ; and for the acceptance both of our perfons and fervices ; for the fake of Jefus Chrift, thy Son, our only Lord and Saviour. *Amen*'

The Minifter fhall then proceed to give them fome inftruction, from the Scriptures, refpecting the inftitution and duties of this ftate, fhewing ;

'That God has inftituted marriage for the comfort and happinefs of mankind, in declaring a man fhall forfake his father and mother and cleave unto his wife, and that marriage is ho-
'nourable

'nourable in all; that he hath appointed vari-
'ous duties, which are incumbent upon those
'who enter into this relation; such as, a high e-
'steem and mutual love for another; bear-
'ing with each other's infirmities and weak-
'nesses, to which human nature is subject in its
'present lapsed state; to encourage each other un-
'der the various ills of life; to comfort one a-
'nother in sickness; in honesty and industry to
'provide for each others temporal support; to
'pray for and encourage one another, in the
'things which pertain to God, and to their im-
'mortal souls; and to live together as the heirs
'of the grace of life.'

Then the Minister shall cause the bridegroom and bride to join their right hands, and shall pronounce the marriage covenant, first to the man, in these words:

'You, sir, take this woman, whom you hold
'by the hand, to be your lawful and married
'wife; and you promise, and covenant, in the
'presence of God and these witnesses, that you
'will be unto her a loving and faithful husband,
'until you shall be separated by death.'

The Bridegroom shall express his consent, by saying, 'Yes I do.'

Then the Minister shall address himself to the woman in these words:

'You, Madam, take this man, whom you
'hold by the hand, to be your lawful and mar-
'ried husband; and you promise, and cove-
'nant, in the presence of God and these wit-
'nesses, that you will be unto him a loving,
'faithful, and obedient wife, until you shall be
'separated by death.'

The Bride shall express her consent, by saying, 'Yes, I do.' Then

Then the minifter is to fay;

'I pronounce you, Hufband and Wife, ac-
'cording to the ordinance of God; what there-
'fore God hath joined together, let not man put
'afunder.'

After this the Minifter may exhort them, in a
few words, to the mutual difcharge of their duty.

Then let him conclude with a prayer to this
effect.

'Moft merciful and gracious God, in whom
'all the families of the earth are bleffed, we pray
'for thy blefling to defcend upon thefe perfons,
'whom now, in thy holy providence, thou haft
'brought into the marriage relation. May they
'enter upon a family ftate in thy fear, and live
'in thy favour. Blefs them with all fpiritual
'and temporal bleffings; Blefs them in their
'bafket, and in their ftore. May they dwell to-
'gether in love, as joint heirs of the grace of
'life, that their prayers may not be hindered.
'We commit them, O Lord, to thy indulgent
'providence, praying, that goodnefs and mercy
'may attend them all the days of their appoint-
'ed time. We thank thee, for the prefent
'joyful occafion; and that the voice of the
'bridegroom and of the bride is ftill heard
'among us. May we rejoice in thy fear.
'Keep us back from fin. Pardon all our tranf-
'greffions. Help us all to live in the faithful
'difcharge of the duties which are incumbent
'upon us, in our various relations. Guide us
'by thy counfel through this world, and after-
'wards admit us to that ftate of perfection,
'where there will be neither marrying nor giv-
'ing in marriage, but where we fhall be as the
'angels of thy prefence: And now to the Fa-
'ther, the Son, and the Holy Ghoft, be afcribed
'everlafting praifes. '*Amen.*' Let

Let the Minister keep a proper register, of the names of all persons whom he marries, and of the time of their marriage, for the perusal of all whom it may concern.

Of the Visitation of the Sick.

When persons are sick, it is their duty, before their strength and understanding fail them, to send for their Minister, and to make known to him, with prudence, their spiritual state; or to consult him on the concerns of their precious souls: And it is his duty to visit them, at their request, and to apply himself, with all tenderness and love, to administer spiritual good to their immortal souls.

He shall instruct the sick, out of the Scriptures, that diseases arise not out of the ground, nor do they come by chance; but that they are directed and sent by a wise and holy God, either for correction of sin, for the trial of grace, for improvement in religion, or for other important ends; and that they shall work together for good to all those who make a wise improvement of God's visitation, neither despising his chastening hand, nor waxing weary of his rebukes.

If the Minister apprehend him to be grosly ignorant, he shall examine him upon the most plain and important principles of religion; and instruct him, in the nature of repentance and faith, and the way of acceptance with God, through the mediation and atonement of Jesus Christ.

He shall exhort the sick to examine himself; to search his heart, and try his former ways, by the word of God; and assist him, by mentioning some of the obvious marks and evidences of sincere piety.

If

If the sick shall signify any scruple, doubt or temptation, under which he labours, the Minister, must endeavour to resolve his doubts, and administer instruction and direction, as the case may seem to require.

If the sick appear to be a stupid, thoughtless and hardened sinner, he shall endeavour to awaken his mind; to arouse his conscience; to convince him of the evil and danger of sin; of the curse of the law, and the wrath of God due to sinners; to bring him to a humble and penitential sense of his iniquities; and to state before him the fulness of the grace and mercy of God, in and through the glorious Redeemer; the absolute necessity of faith and repentance, in order to his being interested in the favour of God, or his obtaining everlasting happiness.

If the sick person shall appear to have knowledge, to be of a tender conscience, and to have been endeavouring to serve God in uprightness, though not without many failings and sinful infirmities; or if his spirit be broken with a sense of sin, or through apprehensions of the want of the divine favour; then it will be proper to administer consolation and encouragement to him, by setting before him the freeness and riches of the grace of God, the all-sufficiency of the righteousness of Christ, and the supporting promises of the gospel.

The Minister must endeavour to guard the sick person against ill-grounded persuasions of the mercy of God, without a vital union to Christ; and against unreasonable fears of death and desponding discouragements; against presumption upon his own goodness and merit, upon the one hand; and against despair of the mercy and grace of God in Christ Jesus, on the other.

In one word, it is the Minister's duty to administer to the sick person instruction, conviction, support, consolation or encouragement, as his case may seem to require.

At a proper time, when he is most composed, the Minister, if desired, shall pray with and for him, in the following or like manner.

'O thou, sovereign, great and glorious Jeho-
' vah, we bow down before thee, and acknowledge
' our absolute dependance upon thee. Thou
' hast made it our duty to pray with and for the
' sick and the afflicted. Enable us, at this time,
' to pray in faith, to confess our sins with peni-
' tential sentiments of heart, and to draw near
' to thee, in humble dependance upon the a-
' tonement of our Lord and Saviour Jesus Christ.
' We acknowledge, that we are guilty sinners,
' sinners by nature and sinners by practice. Sin is
' the procuring cause of all the calamities which
' come upon us. Sin has introduced sickness,
' pain, misery and death into our apostate world.
' Affliction cometh not forth of the dust, neither
' doth trouble spring out of the ground. O
' Lord, thou killest and thou makest alive, thou
' woundest and thou healest, thou layest on beds
' of sickness, and thou raisest up again. Thou
' hast brought us into this world, thou continu-
' est us in it, and takest us out of it according to
' thy holy pleasure. We know and are assured,
' that the God of all the earth always does that
' which is right.

' O most merciful Father, extend compassion
' to this person on a bed of sickness, languish-
' ment and distress. Shew unto him why thou
' contendest with him, and why thou afflictest
' him very sore. Rebuke him not in thine an-
' ger,

'ger, nor chasten him in thy hot displeasure.
'When thou with rebukes dost chasten man for
'sin, thou makest his beauty to consume away
'like a moth. Let him neither despise the chast-
'ning of the Lord, nor faint when he is rebu-
'ked of him. Remove thy stroke, we pray thee.
'O spare a little, that he may recover strength,
'before he go hence, and be here no more.
'Sanctify to him this visitation of thy provi-
'dence. Enable him to make a suitable improve-
'ment of it, for his soul's good. Prepare him
'for all the events of thy will. If thou art pleas-
'ed to recover him from this affliction, and to
'add unto his days, we pray that he may rise to
'health and strength, with a faithful remem-
'brance of thy correcting hand, and with full
'purposes of holiness and new obedience.
'When thou hast tried him, O Lord, let him
'come forth as gold which has been tried.
'Speak the word and he shall be healed. Deal
'bountifully with him and he shall live and
'praise thee. But if this sickness be unto death,
'and thou hast determined to finish his days by
'the present visitation, O Lord, have mercy
'upon his precious soul. Pardon all his sins.
'Give him clear evidences of an interest in thy
'favour. May he find, by sweet experience,
'his soul united to Jesus by a new and living
'faith. Save him from the temptations of Sa-
'tan. Take away the sting of death, and cause
'him to triumph over the grave ; and, when
'his flesh and his heart faileth, be thou the
'strength of his heart, and his portion forever.
'O Lord, we wait for thy salvation. We com-
'mit him unto thee, praying, that if he live, he
'may live to thee, and if he die, that he may
'die

' die to thee, that whether he liveth or dieth he
' may be thine. Hear us, O our God, and an-
' swer us, only for the sake of our divine Re-
' deemer; to whom, with the Father, and Spi-
' rit of all grace, be given glory, and honour,
' and dominion, and power, forever and ever.
' Amen.'

The Minister shall admonish him to settle his worldly affairs; to make restitution or satisfaction where he hath done any wrong; to be reconciled to those with whom he may have been at variance; to forgive all men their trespasses against him, as he expects forgiveness from God; and, if he be rich, to dispose of some part of his worldly substance for charitable purposes, or for the Church of Christ.

Lastly, the Minister may improve the present occasion to exhort those about the sick, to consider their mortality; to turn to the Lord and make their peace with him; in health to prepare for sickness, death and judgment.

Of the Burial of the Dead.

When any Christian departs this life, let the corpse be taken care of in a decent manner, and be kept a proper and sufficient time before interment.

When the season for the funeral comes, let all who are present, conduct themselves with gravity. We highly disapprove of the use of spirituous liquors at the funeral of any persons of our communion; and we recommend the utter abolition of a custom so offensive and improper. It is decent and proper, that persons be interred, in a manner suitable to their rank and condition while living.

Let the Christian friends, who attend at the house of the funeral, apply themselves to serious meditation and discourse; and the Minister, if present, may exhort them to consider the frailty of life, and the importance of being prepared for death and eternity.

Then let the dead body be decently attended to the grave, and there immediately interred without any ceremony.

Of Fasting ; and of the observation of days of Thanksgiving.

There is no day under the Gospel commanded to be kept holy, except the Lord's day, which is the christian sabbath.

Those seasons, vulgarly called holidays, not being appointed in the word of God, but having been introduced in times of superstition, and abused to much sin, are not to be observed by the people of our communion.

Nevertheless to observe days of fasting and thankfgiving, as the extraordinary dispensations of divine providence may direct, we judge both scriptural and rational.

Fasts and thankfgivings may be observed by individual Christians, or families, in private, by particular Congregations, by a number of Congregations contiguous to each other, by the Congregations under the care of a Presbytery, or of a Synod, or by all the Congregations of our Church.

It must be left to the judgment and discretion of every Christian and family to determine, when it is proper to observe a private fast or thanksgiving ; and to the Church-session to determine for particular Congregations; and to the Presbyteries or Synods to determine for larger districts. When it is deemed expedient that a fast or thankfgiving fhould be general, the call for them muft be judged of by the Synod or General Council. And if at any time the civil power fhould think it proper to appoint a faft or thankfgiving, it is the duty of the Minifters and people of our communion, as we live under a chriftian government, to pay all due refpect to the fame.

Public notice is to be given a convenient time before the day of fafting or thankfgiving comes, that perfons may fo order their temporal affairs, that they may properly attend to the duties thereof.

There fhall be public worfhip upon all fuch days; and let the prayers, pfalms, portions of fcripture to be read, and fermons, be all, in a fpecial manner adapted to the occafion.

On faft days, let the Minifter point out the authority and providences calling to the obfervation thereof; and let him fpend a more than ufual portion of time in folemn prayer, particular confeffion of fin, efpecially of the fins of the day and place, with their aggravations, which have brought down the judgments of heaven. And let the whole day be fpent in deep humiliation and mourning before God.

On days of thankfgiving, he is to give the like information, refpecting the authority and providences which call to the obfervance of them; and to fpend a more than ufual part of the time in the giving of thanks, agreeably to the occafion, and in finging pfalms or hymns of praife.

It is the duty of people, on thefe days, to rejoice with holy gladnefs of heart; and to manifeft felt the liberality, which is their great duty upon such occasions, by sending portions and giving gifts. But let trembling be so joined with our mirth, as that no excess or unbecoming levity be indulged.

Of the Ordination of Ministers of the Gospel.

The Ordination of a Person, to the Work of the Gospel Ministry, is the setting Him apart to this holy Office, agreeably to the Institution of Christ, the great Head of the Church. This is the Business of the Presbytery.

When the Person to be ordained has passed through the Trials prescribed in the Form of Government and Discipline, or such others as shall be deemed satisfactory; the Presbytery being met for his ordination, the Sermon being ended, and the Engagements, directed in the Form of Government, &c. being taken, the Person, who is to be ordained, shall kneel down in the most convenient part of the Church, and the Minister, who has been appointed to preside, shall lay his Right Hand upon his Head, and then all the other Ministers of the Presbytery present, shall also lay their Right Hands upon his Head; and the presiding Minister shall pray in the following or like manner:

' Holy, holy, holy, Lord God Almighty, We
' adore Thee, as the one, living, and true God,
' the Creator and the Preserver of all things.
' We adore Thee as the God and Father of our
' Lord Jesus Christ, and in him reconciling the
' world unto Thyself, not imputing their trespas-
' ses unto them. We most devoutly praise Thee
' for the unspeakable Gift of a Saviour, and for

' the

' the Plan of faving loft Men through him; for his
' Incarnation, his Atonement, his Refurrection
' and Afcenfion to Glory. We praife Thee,
' that, when He afcended up on high, He led
' Captivity captive, and gave Gifts unto Men:
' that he gave fome, Apoftles; and fome, Pro-
' phets; and fome, Evangelifts; and fome, Paf-
' tors and Teachers; for the perfecting of the
' Saints, for the Work of the Miniftry, for the
' edifying of the Body of Chrift.

' We thank Thee, O Lord, that Thou art
' raifing up and qualifying Men for this great
' Work, from age to age, and throughout the
' feveral Parts of thy Church. We thank
' Thee, that thou haft inclined the heart of this
' thy Servant to devote Himfelf to the Lord, in
' the Work of the Miniftry. We pray that
' Thou wouldft gracioufly accept of the Dedi-
' cation which He now makes of Himfelf to
' Thee, in the Gofpel of thy Son.

' We do, in the name of the Father, and of
' the Son and of the Holy Ghoft, ordain him
' Bifhop of this Church; and fet him apart to the
' Office of the holy Miniftry. We moft humbly
' pray, that thou wouldeft gracioufly approve
' and ratify in heaven, what we now do in thy
' name, upon earth.

' O moft merciful God, grant this thy fervant a
' double portion of thy Spirit. Enable him to
' be diligent and faithful in the difcharge of the
' great duties of his miniftry. May he be wife
' in winning fouls to Chrift. Make him an e-
' minent bleffing to thy Church in general, and
' to thefe thy People, over whom thou art fet-
' ting him, in particular. Enable him, O Lord,
' to take heed unto himfelf, and to his doctrine,
' and to continue in them, that he may both fave
' himfelf, and them that hear him. ' Gra-

'Gracious God, pardon all our sins, and hear
'us, for the sake of Jesus Christ our Lord:
'And let the Glory be to the Father, and to
'the Son, and to the Holy Spirit, now and for
'ever. *Amen.*'

Prayer being ended, and the Person ordained having risen from his knees, the Minister, who presides, shall give him the Bible, addressing him in words to the following import:

'You have now received authority to preach
'the Gospel, and to administer all the Ordinances
'instituted by Christ. In token whereof, take this
'holy book, which contains your commission; stu-
'dy it carefully; and conduct yourself, in every
'part of your office, in conformity to it.'

Then he shall take him by the Right Hand; saying, in words to this purpose; 'We give
'You the Right Hand of Fellowship, to take
'part of this Ministry with us.'' Or thus:
'In token of our acceptance of you, to take
'part with us in this sacred Ministry, to which
'we have now set you apart, we do, agreeably
'to the Apostolic example, give you the Right
'Hand of Fellowship.' Then the Ministers who laid hands upon him, shall, in their order, take him by the right hand.

The Minister who presided, or some other appointed to the business, shall then address him on the Nature and Importance of the Office to which he has been set apart: charging him,

'To take heed unto himself, and to all the
'flock, over which the Holy Ghost hath made
'him Overseer; to feed the Church of God,
'which he hath purchased with his own blood;
'to love Christ, and to feed his sheep: shewing
'him, that a Bishop must take the oversight of
'them,

'them, not by constraint, but willingly; not for
' filthy Lucre, but of a ready Mind; neither as
' being Lord over God's Heritage, but as an
' Example to the Flock, in Word, in Conversa-
' tion, in Charity, in Spirit, in Faith, in Purity:
' Exhorting him, that he neglect not the Gift
' that is in him, but that he meditate upon these
' things, and give himself wholly to them, that
' his profiting may appear unto all; that he take
' heed, not only to Himself, but also to his Doc-
' trine; and that he continue stedfast therein;
' that he bear patiently all the Trials to which
' the faithful discharge of the duties of his office
' may at any time subject him, in humble depen-
' dance upon the grace and faithfulness of his
' Lord, who has promised to be with his Mini-
' sters even to the end of the world; that he
' preach the word, be instant, in season and out
' of season, reprove, rebuke, exhort, with all
' long-suffering and doctrine; and that he rule
' well his own house; encouraging him to hope
' and expect, that, when the chief Shepherd
' shall appear, he shall receive a Crown of Glory
' that fadeth not away.'

After this, the same Minister, or another as may be most convenient, shall address the Congregation (if the person has been ordained to a particular charge) on the inestimable blessing of a judicious and faithful administration of the Word and the ordinances of the Gospel in a stated way. He shall lay before them the duties, which a People owe their Minister, with the obligations to a conscientious discharge thereof: shewing them;

' That they are bound to esteem and honour
' him for his works sake; to attend upon his
                                    ' ministry

' miniſtry with diligence and ſteadineſs, and to
' ſtudy to profit thereby; to receive, with meek-
' neſs, his admonitions and reproofs, and to ſubmit
' to the diſcipline of Chriſt's houſe, adminiſtred
' by him, in conjunction with the other officers
' of the Church; to be much in prayer to God
' for him, as one who watches for their ſouls,
' and muſt give an account of his ſtewardſhip;
' to afford, with punctuality and cheerfulneſs,
' the worldly ſupport, which, in this ſolemn
' manner, they have promiſed him, before God,
' and the holy Angels, and his Church; aſſur-
' ing them, that the great Judge of quick and
' dead will, at the laſt day, acknowledge what is
' done unto his ſervants, as done unto himſelf:
' And finally, exhorting them to ſtudy the things
' that make for peace, both with their Miniſter,
' and among themſelves, that he and they may
' appear with joy in the great day of Chriſt.'

The Miniſter having finiſhed this addreſs, ſhall pray, and give thanks, in the following or like manner:

' Moſt merciful Father, we thank Thee for
' the miniſtry of reconciliation; that Thou haſt
' committed this treaſure to earthen veſſels, that
' the excellency of the power may be of God and
' not of man. We thank Thee, that Thou haſt
' provided thy Church in this place with one
' to take the overſight of them in the Lord.
' We beſeech Thee to qualify thy Servant,
' more and more, for the faithful, the honoura-
' ble, and the ſucceſsful diſcharge of his high
' truſt. Encourage his heart, and ſtrengthen
' his hands therein, from day to day. Grant
' him, O Lord, a deep and an abiding ſenſe of
' his dependance upon the influences of the
                                            ' Spirit

'Spirit of Chrift for the fuccefs of his labours. May he have many feals of his miniftry in this place; many as his crown of rejoicing in the prefence of our Lord Jefus Chrift at his coming. Render him, we pray Thee, happily inftrumental in promoting true and undefiled Religion, before the Father, and the Lord Jefus Chrift, throughout the Church in general, as well as in this place. May this Congregation be properly fenfible of the rich blefling Thou haft this day conferred upon them; and may they be enabled to receive and improve it in a fuitable manner. May they grow and increafe, under the miniftry of thy Servant, with the increafe of God. May many be added to them daily, of fuch as fhall be faved in the day of Chrift. We pray that thy Servant and this People may be mutual comforts and bleflings to each other, for a long time to come; and may their appearance, in the day of the Lord, be to their eternal joy, through Jefus Chrift, our Lord. *Amen*.'

A Pfalm fhall then be fung, and the Congregation difmiffed with the ufual Blefling.

The fubjects of the Charges, to the Minifter and People, in the cafe of Ordination, will furnifh proper matter for the addreffes of the like nature, in the cafe of the inftalment of a Minifter formerly ordained.

Every Prefbytery will be beft able to judge of the age at which it is proper to ordain any perfon to the work of the Gofpel Miniftry; but we think that, in ordinary cafes, the Candidate fhould be, at leaft, twenty-four years of age.

The

The Directory for Secret and Family Worship.

Besides the public worship in Congregations, it is the indispensable duty of each person alone, in secret, and of every family by itself in private, to pray to and worship God.

Secret worship is most plainly enjoined by our Lord. In this duty every one, apart by himself, is to spend some time in prayer, reading the scriptures, holy meditation, and serious self examination. The many advantages, arising from a conscientious attendance upon these duties, are best known to those who are found in the faithful discharge of them.

Family worship, which ought to be performed by every family, ordinarily morning and evening, consists in prayer, reading the scriptures, and singing praises.

The Head of the family, who is to lead in this service, ought to be careful that all the members of his houshold duly attend, and that none withdraw themselves unnecessarily from any part of family worship; and that all refrain from their common business, while the scriptures are read, and gravely attend to the same, no less than when prayer or praise is offered up.

Let no idler, or vagrant person, perform worship in families; seeing persons tainted with errors, or aiming at divisions, may be ready to creep into houses and lead captive unstable souls. But this is not to be understood, as prohibiting the Head of a family from inviting a christian friend to pray in his family who may be occasionally present, and whose character, for stedfastness and piety, is established.

At

At family worship, let each family keep by themselves, without inviting persons of other families to join with them.

Let not any society or conference meetings, under pretence of more spiritual advantage, ever interfere with or set aside the due order and regular worship of families; for the latter is a divine institution, and of much greater utility and importance.

Let every Head of a family be careful to catechise and instruct his family, at least once every week; and we think the most proper time for these exercises is on Sabbath evenings. And we judge it would be much more for the edification of Christian families, and for the advancement of true religion, for families, apart by themselves, to spend their Sabbath evenings in catechising, holy conference, repetition of the sermons they heard through the day, in prayer, praise, and other religious duties, than in running about to attend society or other meetings, as the practice of too many is, even to the neglect, we fear, of common family duties.

As many as can conceive prayer ought carefully to improve this gift of God; yet for the sake of the young and more bashful Heads of families, we have subjoined a few forms of Family Prayer, earnestly recommending it to all such, not to be negligent in cultivating a spirit of prayer, and to use these forms no longer than till they shall have learned to express the desires of their hearts to God for their families, with some degree of propriety.

A

A PRAYER for a FAMILY, on the morning of the
   LORD'S DAY.

'O Thou blessed, glorious, and highly exalted
' Lord, our God, we desire, with all humility
' and reverence, to bow down and offer homage
' and worship to Thee, this morning of thy
' holy day. We adore Thee as the King eter-
' nal, immortal, invisible, the only wise God.
' Thou art worthy of all honour, love, worship
' and praise, from all thy intelligent creatures.
' Angels and Arch-angels prostrate themselves
' before thy throne, and they cease not, day or
' night, to ascribe glory, honour, dominion and
' power, to him that sitteth on the throne, and to
' the Lamb forever and ever. We, who are
' worms of the dust, and have our habitation in
' houses of clay, desire to unite with this celestial
' company, in praising, magnifying, and adoring
' thy name. We worship Thee, as our Creator,
' Preserver, Benefactor, and Redeemer. In
' Thee we live, and move, and have our being.

' We acknowledge, before Thee, that we are
' fallen creatures, miserable sinners. We have
' forsaken Thee, the fountain of living waters ;
' and have hewn out for ourselves cisterns, bro-
' ken cisterns, which can hold no water. Behold
' we are vile, we are altogether as an unclean
' thing in thy sight. But glory to thy name in
' the highest, that thou hast opened a door of
' hope for sinners ; that thou hast revealed a
' glorious salvation in the gospel ; that thou hast
' set forth Christ Jesus, to be the propitiation
' for sin ; and caused us to hear the glad tidings
' of peace and reconciliation through faith in his
' name. In his name, we come unto thee, con-
                            ' fessing

'fessing our sins, and making supplication for
' all the mercies which we need.
  ' O Lord, most holy, pardon our sins; blot
' out all our transgressions. Justify us freely by
' thy grace, through the redemption that is in
' Jesus Christ. Receive us into thy favour,
' which is life, and make us the subjects of thy
' loving kindness, which is better than life. A-
' dopt us into thy family, and sanctify us by the
' powerful influences of thy Holy Spirit. Ena-
' ble us to sanctify this thy Sabbath, and to keep
' it holy. Prepare our hearts for all the holy
' duties and services of this day. Let the day-
' spring from on high visit us, and the Sun of
' Righteousness shine upon us, with healing in
' his wings.
  ' We praise thee, O God, that thou hast a-
' dorned thy weeks with sabbaths; that thou
' hast sanctified one day in seven, to be kept ho-
' ly to thyself; and that thou hast brought us
' to see another of the days of the Son of man.
' O that we may be in the spirit on this thy day.
' Let God, who, on the first day of the world,
' commanded the light to shine out of darkness,
' on this first day of the week, shine in our hearts,
' to give us the light of the knowledge of the
' glory of God, in the face of Jesus Christ. This
' is the day, which the Lord hath made, we will
' be glad and rejoice in it. O that we may this
' day experience the power of Christ's resurrec-
' tion. As he was raised from the dead by the
' glory of the Father, so let us be raised from
' a state of death in sin, to walk with him in new-
' ness of life, and be prepared to sit with him in
' heavenly places.

' Prepare

'Prepare us, O our God, for the public
' ordinances of thy house this day. May we,
' with our whole hearts, join in the prayers and
' praises of thy church. Enable us to hear thy
' word with attention, to receive it in faith and
' love, to lay it up in our hearts, and to practise
' it in our lives. Give thy presence, O Lord
' our God, to thy ministering servant, who may
' lead our worship, and speak to us in thy name
' to-day. Give him the tongue of the learned,
' that he may speak a word in season to weary
' souls. May thy saints be refreshed and com-
' forted; may sinners be awakened and con-
' verted: May this be a glorious day in thy
' Zion.

' Accomplish, O Lord, we beseech thee, all
' thy designs of mercy. Let thy gospel be pro-
' pagated from the rising to the setting sun. Let
' it run, have free course and be glorified. Be
' in all the worshipping assemblies of thy peo-
' ple this day. Fill thy Churches with thy glo-
' ry. Clothe thy Ministers with salvation, that
' thy people may shout aloud for joy. Keep our
' hearts, and keep our minds this day. Pre-
' serve us from evil and worldly thoughts. Let
' no vain conversation proceed out of our lips.
' Save us from the temptations of Satan. Hand
' us in peace and safety through all the chang-
' ing scenes of time. Be the stay and staff of our
' souls in the solemn hour of death; and finally
' bring us to glory; only for the sake of our Lord
' and Saviour Jesus Christ, who taught us, when
' we pray, to say;

' Our Father, who art in Heaven, hallowed
' be thy name. Thy kingdom come. Thy will
' be done in earth as it is in heaven. Give us

'this day our daily bread; and forgive us our
'trespasses as we forgive them that trespass
'against us. And lead us not into temptation,
'but deliver us from evil: for thine is the king-
'dom, and the power, and the glory, forever.
'Amen.'

A PRAYER for a FAMILY, on the evening of the LORD'S DAY.

' O Thou holy, ever blessed, and ever glori-
'ous Lord our God: Thou art God over
'all, and rich in mercy to all that call upon thy
'name. Thou art most wise and powerful, the
'King of Kings, and Lord of Lords. Thy
'kingdom is an everlasting kingdom; and thy
'dominion from generation to generation. This
'evening of thy holy day, O Lord, we present
'ourselves before thee, to offer up our evening
'sacrifice of prayer and of praise. Thou hast
'given us to enjoy another Sabbath. Thy days
'are sweet to our souls; thy Sabbaths are our
'delight. We bless and praise Thee, with our
'whole hearts, for another of thy holy days. A
'day spent in thy courts, is better than a thou-
'sand elsewhere. How amiable are thy taber-
'nacles, O Lord of hosts! Thou hast carried
'us to thy house of prayer; thou hast caused
'us to hear thy word, and we have had the
'privilege of joining in the prayers and praises
'of thy people, in thy church.

' Glory to God in the highest, for all his
'mercies and benefits to us. How great are
'the privileges we enjoy, above thousands of
'our fellow creatures, who are as good by na-
'ture as we are. What multitudes are bowing

'down

'down to flocks and stones, are groping in
'more than midnight darkness, and know not
'Thee, the true God, nor Jesus Christ, whom
'thou hast sent; while we are favoured with thy
'Sabbaths and thine ordinances, and enjoy this
'glorious light of thy gospel.

'O Lord, we confess we are unworthy of
'the least of all thy mercies; and that thou art
'distinguishing us above others, is owing to thy
'mere, free, holy, and sovereign pleasure. With
'propriety may we ascribe all to the glory of thy
'name, and say, even so, Father, for so it seemeth
'good in thy sight. We call upon our souls,
'and all within us, to bless and magnify thy
'name, for thy distinguishing favours to us, thine
'undeserving creatures. We praise thee for
'the gift of thine only begotten Son; for the
'redemption of Christ Jesus our Lord; for the
'covenant of mercy; for the means of grace,
'and the hopes of eternal life.

'O thou Father of mercies, forgive what thy
'pure eyes have seen amiss in us this day. For-
'give us, that we have not served thee with more
'love, zeal, and godly sincerity. In all things
'we have sinned, and come short of thy glory.
'Pardon, O Lord, our innumerable failings and
'imperfections. Forgive the iniquities of our
'most holy things. After we have done all, we
'have just reason to acknowledge ourselves un-
'profitable servants. But thou hast declared, O
'God, that they who confess and forsake their
'sins, shall find mercy. Thou art faithful to
'forgive us our sins. We pray, most merciful
'Father, that thou wouldst forgive us, and ac-
'cept of us in the beloved. Accept of us, and
'of our poor and imperfect services. Give
'us

' us grace, O God, that we may never for-
' sake thy ways, nor turn from following af-
' ter thee ; but that, with purpose of heart, we
' may always cleave unto the Lord. Let us not
' count our lives dear unto ourselves so that we
' may finish our course, with comfort and joy,
' to the glory of thy name.

' O Lord our God, we pray that thou wouldst
' follow thy word and ordinances with a blef-
' sing wherever they have been dispensed on this
' thy holy sabbath. Bless all the Ministers of
' thy gospel. Make them faithful to Christ, and
' to the souls of men. Pity the poor, the af-
' flicted, sorrowful and distressed. Enlarge the
' borders of the Redeemer's kingdom. Let all
' the nations flow unto it. Hasten the downfal
' of the man of sin ; and let pure and undefiled
' religion before God, and the Father, be revi-
' ved, and made to flourish in all places.

' Take us, O Lord, under thy protection
' this night. Enable us to close the day with
' thee. May we lie down in peace, and our
' sleep be sweet and refreshing to us. Bring us
' to the light of to-morrow ; and may our souls
' rejoice and praise thee, in the out-goings of
' the morning. Enable us to carry much of the
' Sabbath with us through the week. May we
' set the Lord always before us. Prepare us for
' all that is before us in time. Be our guide
' through life, our support in death, and our
' everlasting portion. Now to the king eternal,
' immortal, invisible, the only wise God ; to the
' Father, the Son, and the Holy Ghost, be ho-
' nour and glory, dominion and praise, through
' Jesus Christ our Lord. *Amen.*'

A MORNING PRAYER for a FAMILY.

'O thou God of all confolation! O thou preferver of men! We adore thee as the fountain of all being, perfection, and bleffednefs. We have lain down flept and awaked in mercy; for the Lord hath fuftained us. Thou haft heard our evening prayer, watched over us in our unguarded moments, and brought us, in circumftances of comfort, to the light of this morning. Day unto day uttereth fpeech, and night unto night fheweth knowledge. Thou drawe.t over us the fhadows of the evening; and thou caufeft the outgoings of the morning. Thou art good to all, and thy tender mercies are over all thy works. We give thee moft fincere thanks for the prefervation of the night paft, and the favours of the morning. No plague has come nigh our dwelling; we live, are in health, and are brought in fafety to the light and comforts of another day. We thank thee, O Lord, that our fleep has not been death, nor our beds our graves; but that thou haft refrefhed and ftrengthened us, and we rejoice before thee.

'Thou O Lord, art the God of the families of Ifrael; thou art the God of our family. O caufe thy blefling to reft upon our houfe, and fill our fouls with joy and gladnefs. We acknowledge before thee, O God, that we are guilty finners. We have finned againft thee, as individuals; we have finned againft thee, as a family. Parents, and children, and all of us, are finners in thy fight. We were fhapen in fin, and brought forth in iniquity: We are altogether as an unclean thing before
'thee,

' thee. Yet, glory to thy name in the highest,
' notwithstanding our unworthiness, thou art
' good, and doing us good continually.
  ' We praise thee for the gospel, for Jesus
' Christ, and the method of salvation through
' faith in him. It is an unspeakable privilege,
' that we have access to the throne of thy grace,
' through the Lord Jesus, thine only begotten
' and eternal Son. O look in compassion upon
' us, and, for Christ's sake, pardon all our of-
' fences. Cast out iniquities into the depths of
' the sea, and remember our transgressions no
' more; but be merciful unto us, as thou art
' unto those that love thy name. Sanctify us
' thoroughly by the power of thy grace; subdue
' all our lusts and corruptions, and make us holy
' as thou, the Lord our God, art holy. Let thy
' peace rule in our hearts, and thy law govern in
' our minds; and let the consolations of our God
' be our strength and our song, in the house of
' our pilgrimage. O thou Father of Mercies,
' be thou the portion of our souls; lift upon us
' the light of thy countenance; put gladness into
' our hearts, more than they have, whose corn
' and wine and oil are increased.
  ' We commit ourselves, O Lord, to thy care
' and keeping this day; watch over us for good;
' compass us about with thy favour, as with a
' shield. Preserve us from evil; yea, the Lord
' preserve and keep our souls; preserve our go-
' ing out and coming in; keep us in health and
' safety; bless our employments; prosper us in
' all our lawful undertakings; give us comfort
' and success in our business; let us eat of the
' labour of our hands; and may it be well with
' us. Prepare us for all the events of this day;
                                            ' for

'for we know not what a day may bring forth.
'Give us grace to do the work of this day, ac-
'cording as the duties of it may require. Give
'us the rule over our spirits, and the govern-
'ment of our passions. Keep us from sin; and
'may we not speak unadvisedly with our lips.
'Make us conscientious in all our dealings.
'Arm us against temptation; uphold us in our
'integrity; and may we be in thy fear all the
'day long.

'Lord, plead thy cause in the world; and
'build up thy Church, in its beauty, glory, and
'purity. Bless ministers and people, rulers and
'ruled. Be gracious to our relatives and friends.
'Dwell in the families that call upon thy name.
'Forgive our enemies; and grant unto us a right
'and charitable frame of spirit, towards all men,
'and all that is their's. Visit those that are in
'affliction. Heal the sick; ease the pained;
'succour the tempted; relieve the oppressed;
'and give joy to those that mourn in Zion.
'Deal with us and our family, according to the
'tenor of the everlasting covenant, which is well
'ordered in all things and sure. This is all our
'salvation, and all our desire. We ask and of-
'fer all in the name of our once crucified, but
'now glorified and exalted Redeemer, in whom
'we desire ever to be found, and to whom,
'with thee, O Father, and the co-equal Spirit
'of grace, be ascribed all blessing, glory, and
'praise, both now and forever. *Amen.*'

An EVENING PRAYER for a FAMILY.

'O thou blessed, ever glorious, and eternal
'Jehovah; we adore thee, as our maker, as
'our

' our preferver, and as our God. Thou art the
' benefactor of the univerfe ; thou giveft life,
' and breath, and being, unto all. Thou haft
' carried us through the toils and bufinefs of
' another day ; thou haft ftrengthened us, fed
' and clothed us all our life long. Having ob-
' tained help of God, we continue to this time.
' We are the monuments of thy fparing mercy ;
' and witneffes for thee, that thou art gracious.
' Thou art God, and not man ; therefore we are
' not confumed. Day unto day, and night unto
' night, do teftify, that thou art good, and doing
' good continually. None who feek, and put
' their truft in thee, fhall ever be put to fhame.
' Thou makeft the outgoings of the morning,
' and of the evening to rejoice over us. By thy
' indulgent goodnefs, and merciful loving kind-
' nefs, we are brought to the clofe of another
' day. Bleffed be the Lord, who daily loadeth
' us with his benefits. We have received the
' mercies of the day, though we have come far
' fhort in the duties thereof.

 ' We thank thee, with our whole hearts, for
' the favours and bleffings of another day, for
' the comfortable ufe of thy good creatures,
' our bodily health our friends and all our
' enjoyments. We blefs thee, that thou haft
' fucceeded us, in the labours of our hands,
' this day ; that no evil accident hath befallen
' us ; that thou haft not made the wildernefs
' our habitation, and a barren land our dwelling.
' We praife thee for our public tranquillity ; and
' that thou haft given us a good land in which
' we dwell fafely. Above all we blefs thee for
' Jefus Chrift, and the glorious plan of reconci-
' liation through faith in his name. Glory to
           ' thy

'thy name, O thou eternal God, that thou haſt
'cauſed us to hear the joyful ſound of ſalva-
'tion through a Redeemer.

'We confeſs, O Lord, that we are ſinners, and
'that we are leſs than the leaſt of all thy mercies.
'This day hath added to the ſins of our lives. Alas!
'we miſpend our time, fail in our duty, follow after
'vanities, and forſake our own mercies. We offend
'with our tongues. Who can underſtand his
'errors? cleanſe us from our ſecret faults. We
'pray thee to grant us repentance for all our
'ſins; forgive us all our treſpaſſes; pardon the
'tranſgreſſions of the day paſt: O that the
'blood of Chriſt may cleanſe us from all iniquity.
'May we lie down this night in peace with
'God; may our ſouls return unto thee, and
'comfortably repoſe in thee as our reſt. May
'we live penitential, believing, humble, and
'thankful lives. Accept us graciouſly, and love
'us freely. Make us holy for thy name's ſake;
'and may we live in thy love, in thy favour and
'friendſhip, all the days of our appointed time.
'We commit ourſelves to thee, O Lord our
'God, and deſire to dwell in the ſecret place
'of the Moſt High, and to abide under the
'ſhadow of the Almighty. Let the Lord be
'our habitation and our heritage forever. Make
'a hedge of protection around us this night,
'around our houſe, and all that we have, that
'no evil may befal us, that no plague may come
'nigh our dwelling. May the God of Iſrael,
'who neither ſlumbers nor ſleeps, be our keeper.
'Refreſh our bodies with quiet and comforta-
'ble reſt, and bring us to the light of another
'day, and fit us for all thy will therein. And
'as we are brought one day nearer to our latter

R 'end

'end, Lord, help us so to number our days, as
' to apply our hearts to true wisdom. When
' we put off our clothes for rest, may we be
' mindful, that we must soon put off these mortal
' bodies, and make our bed in the land of dark-
' ness. O prepare us for the sleep of death,
' that, when we come to resign this mortal breath,
' we may feel, in our souls, the joyful hope of
' an eternal rest with God. Do thou, in whom
' all the families of the earth are blessed, bless
' our family, with all spiritual blessings in Christ
' Jesus ; and grant us all those temporal blessings
' thou seest convenient for us.

'In compassion, O Lord, look upon a lost
' world ; send thy gospel where it is not, and
' make it successful where it is. Let the church
' of Christ every where flourish and prevail ; and
' let not any weapon formed against Zion pros-
' per. Bless our land, that, in the peace there-
' of, we may have peace. Own thy ministers in
' their work ; and rule in the hearts of our
' rulers. Let the rising-generation be blessed
' of thee ; and fill the whole earth with thy
' glory. Do for us, we pray thee, abundantly
' above what we can ask or think, for the sake
' of our divine Redeemer Jesus Christ; to whom,
' with the Father, and the eternal Spirit, be all
' glory, dominion, and power, for ever and ever.
' Amen.'

A MORNING PRAYER for a FAMILY.

'O Lord our God, the God of the spirits
' of all flesh, all are thine ; the souls of parents
' and the souls of children are thine ; and thou
' hast mercy, grace, and goodness, sufficient for
' all. We bow before thee this morning, in a
                                            ' family

'family capacity, to acknowledge our family sins,
'and to praise thee for family mercies, and to
'make supplication unto thee, for family blessings.
'O Lord, thou hast built up our family by thy
'good providence. Thou hast given us chil-
'dren; O that they may be made blessings to
'us; that we may never have reason to wish
'that we had been written childless.

'O Lord, we, and our children, are sinners
'before thee. We lament the original pollution
'of our nature. We are all guilty, parents
'and children, before thee. And wherewith, O
'thou Most High, shall we come into thy sight?
'Should we bring thousands of rams, or ten
'thousands of rivers of oil; should we offer the
'fruit of our body for the sin of our souls; all
'would be to no purpose; all would be in vain.
'But glory, glory to thy name, O thou most
'merciful God, that thou hast provided a Lamb
'for a sacrifice, even thine only begotten Son,
'who hath made atonement for sin. We thank
'thee, that we have heard of the name of Je-
'sus; that there is a way of salvation opened
'through him; that we are favoured with the
'light of the gospel, with thy word and ordi-
'nances, with the means of salvation, and the
'hope of eternal life. We bless thee, that we,
'and our children, have been baptized into thy
'name; that we have had liberty to dedicate
'our little Ones to God; that they have been
'admitted to the seals, and are under the bles-
'sings of the covenant: they are born in thy
'house, and made members of thy family, on
'earth. O thou, who art the God of Abra-
'ham, of Isaac, and of Jacob, the God and Fa-
'ther of the faithful, we humbly beseech thee,

'to

' to form us, and our children, for thy holy
' pleasure. Sanctify our souls; sanctify our
' children. May this be a family in which thou
' wilt delight to dwell: and may we all be made
' the servants of the living God.

' O Lord, grant unto our children a good
' capacity; open their minds to receive instruc-
' tion; may they be fitted for usefulness in the
' world, made pious towards God, and meet for
' everlasting happiness. Enable us to teach
' them, and to set holy examples before them;
' to train them up in the way wherein they
' should go; to bring them up in thy fear, in the
' nurture and admonition of the Lord. Most
' gracious God, pardon all our offences; may
' our sins be forgiven, and our iniquities remem-
' bered no more. May each of us be united to
' Christ Jesus in faith, clothed with the robes
' of his righteousness, and justified freely by his
' grace.

' We thank thee, O Lord, for the mercies
' of the last night; that we have slept, have
' been refreshed with rest, are in health this
' morning, and have this opportunity of paying
' our grateful acknowledgments to thee. Now,
' O bountiful preserver of men, take care of us
' this day; keep us in thy fear; preserve us from
' every hurtful danger; may we walk with thee,
' and be enabled to set the Lord always before us.
' Whether we eat or drink, or whatsoever we do,
' may we do all to the glory of thy name. May
' we glorify thee in our souls, and in our bodies,
' which are thine.

' Most merciful father, extend thy mercy to
' a guilty world; pour out thy Spirit upon all
' flesh; revive thine own work in the midst of
' these

'these years. Bless our friends and relatives,
' Forgive our enemies, and reward our benefac-
' tors. Look, in mercy, upon us worshipping
' before thee this morning. 'May we follow our
' daily business, under a sense of thine all-seeing
' eye. Help us to live in an habitual readiness
' for our last day. O that we may live, as we
' shall wish we had lived, when we come to die.
' Be our friend in life; our hope in death; and
' our everlasting portion. All we ask is in the
' name, and for the sake of our Saviour Jesus
' Christ, who is the Lord our Righteousness; to
' him, with the eternal Father, and the ever
' blessed Spirit of grace, be given all wisdom,
' thanksgiving, and dominion, and might, world
' without end. *Amen.*'

An EVENING PRAYER for a FAMILY.

' O thou eternal God, in the morning we
' seek thee, and in the evening we would cele-
' brate thy praises. We, and our children, by
' thy good hand upon us, have lived another day.
' We are in health, and have enjoyed many
' comforts. We praise and magnify thy name.
' Thou art calling us from our labour, and giving
' us an opportunity to rest a while, and refresh
' these weary bodies. Thou hast dealt bounti-
' fully with us this day. Blessed be the Lord,
' who loadeth us with his benefits. We have
' received from thee our daily bread, and now
' we lie down, and sleep; for thou, O Lord,
' makest us to dwell in safety.
  ' Visit us, O God of our salvation, in the
' night, and enable us to commune with our
' hearts upon our beds. Let the Angels of God
                                    ' encamp

'encamp around us for our protection. Let our
'Heavenly Father give us counsel; and let our
'reins instruct us in the night season. May we
'remember thee, O God, and meditate upon
'thee, in the night watches. We praise thee,
'O Lord, for thy mercies and thy blessings to
'us. We humbly beseech thee to look upon
'thine anointed Son, and, in him, be our recon-
'ciled Father and friend. Forgive us all our
'sins; put us among thy children; speak peace
'to our souls, and may we ever glorify thee.
'Sanctify us more and more. Enable us to die
'daily to sin, and to live unto righteousness.

'Pardon, O Lord, the sins of which we may
'have been guilty the day past. May our hearts
'be less attached to the world; and may we
'serve thee better than we have heretofore done.
'Thou art our life. Hitherto our bread hath
'been given us, and our water hath been sure.
'Thou givest us all things richly to enjoy.
'Merciful Father, accept of our humble thanks,
'for all these thine undeserved mercies. Take
'care of us this night: may we lie down in thy
'fear, and sleep in thy favour; and in the morn-
'ing, when we awake, may our hearts be still
'with God.

'Have mercy upon all we should remember,
'when we bow before thee. Supply the wants
'of the poor and needy; restore a sound judg-
'ment to those whose understanding is taken
'away. Be a husband to the widow, and a
'Father to the fatherless. Heal the sick; spare
'useful lives; comfort those who mourn; and
'prepare the dying for death. Let true and
'undefiled religion prevail, more and more, in
'the world. Water thy church with the dew
'of

'of thy heavenly grace. Bless all the ministers
'of thy gospel; dwell in our land; order the
'seasons in mercy. May our rulers be a ter-
'ror to evil doers, and a praise to them that
'do well.
    'And now, O Lord, we commit ourselves unto
'thee; we hope in thy mercy, and we trust in
'thy name. Prepare us for all the dispensations
'of thy providence towards us. Preserve us
'from all the dangers and snares to which we
'may be exposed. Let neither the fear of man,
'which worketh a snare, nor cruel mockings,
'nor even the fears of suffering death, tempt us
'to make shipwreck of faith and a good consci-
'ence, or to be ashamed of the gospel of Christ.
'Enable us to fight the good fight of faith, and
'to finish our course; that we may receive the
'crown of righteousness, which the Lord, the
'righteous Judge, shall give unto all them that
'love his appearing. And now, to the Father,
'the Son, and the Holy Ghost, three Persons,
'but one God, be ascribed all glory, honour,
'and praise, forever and ever. *Amen.*'

A MORNING PRAYER for a FAMILY.

    'O Lord, thou art the God of the spirits of
'all flesh, the Creator and Preserver of all
'things. We, thine unworthy creatures, bow
'in thy presence, to offer up unto thee, in whom
'we live, move and have our being, our morn-
'ing sacrifice of prayer and praise. We count
'it our highest honour, that we are permitted to
'worship thee. It is our inestimable privilege
'to know the only true God; and to have
'boldness to enter into the holiest by the blood
'of Jesus.   'We

'We acknowledge, before thee, we have for-
feited all title to thy favour; we have rendered ourselves unworthy of thy regard. Thou
madeſt man at firſt upright, but he fought out
many inventions. In one man all have ſinned;
and in the ſame Adam all die. To us belongeth ſhame and confuſion of face. O Lord
moſt holy, we are not only by nature unclean,
but we have broken thy commandments, and
have dared to reſiſt the ordinances of him who
is higher than the higheſt. When the awful
denunciations of thy wrath were ſounding in
our ears, we have hardened our hearts againſt
fear. We have remained unmoved, amidſt
the fulleſt declarations of thy mercy, and the
warmeſt invitations of thy love. Juſtly might-
eſt thou have given us up, to purſue our own
devices, without reſtraint or poſſibility of being
recovered. But, glory to thy great name, the
thoughts of Jehovah are not as our thoughts;
the ways of the Lord are not like the ways of
man. When we were caſt out, as to the loath-
ing of our own ſoul, without eye to pity, and
without hand to help, thine own eye pitied,
thine own arm brought us ſalvation.

'We thank thee, moſt gracious God, that we
are not left to ſay, Will the Lord be pleaſed
with thouſands of rams, or with ten thouſands
of rivers of oil? ſhall we give our firſt-born for
our tranſgreſſion, the fruit of our body for the
ſin of our ſoul? Thou, O Lord, haſt ſhewed
us what is Good. Thou haſt ſet forth thine
own Son, to be the Propitiation, through faith
in his blood. Glory to God in the higheſt,
that peace is now proclaimed on earth, and
good-will is publiſhed to the ſons of men. Now

'there

'there is no condemnation to them who are in
'Christ Jesus, who walk not after the flesh but
'after the Spirit. He is able to save them to
'the uttermost that come unto God by him,
'seeing he ever liveth to make intercession for
'them.

'O Lord, let none of us reject the counsel of
'God against our own souls. Leave us not in
'unbelief. Give us not up to hardness of heart.
'We pray for the gift of thy Holy Spirit. O
'may we be adorned with his fruits. Grant us
'so to feel his quickening grace, and his strength-
'ening influence, that we may be enabled to
'perfect holiness in the fear of the Lord; to
'work out our own salvation, with fear and trem-
'bling: for it is God who worketh in us both
'to will and to do of his good pleasure.

'Almighty God, keep us from every tempta-
'tion. O let not the allurements of the world,
'the deceitfulness of riches, the cares of this
'life, or the ensnaring pleasures of sin, draw off
'our hearts from thee. May we feel the pow-
'ers of the world to come. May we set thee,
'the Lord, always before us; and walk by
'faith, not by sight.

'We beseech thee, O Lord, to bless all our
'friends and relatives, wherever they may be.
'Make them partakers of thy grace, and heirs
'of thy glory. Bless our enemies. Enable us
'to forgive them, and to overcome evil with
'good.

'Accept, O Lord, of our hearty thanks for
'thy preserving care of us through the silent
'watches of the night. We have slept, and are
'refreshed. Thou hast raised us up in health,
'and hast girded us with strength for labour.

'Enable

' Enable us, O our God, to perform the duties of
' the day aright. Let us not be slothful or negligent
' in business.   Whatever our hands find to do,
• may we do it with our might, as unto the Lord.
' May we ever remember, that we are only pil-
' grims and strangers ; and that every return, of
' night and of day, is bringing us nearer our
' eternal home.

 ' Forgive, we beseech thee, all our sins. En-
' able us to cleanse ourselves from all filthiness,
' both of the flesh and spirit, perfecting holiness
' in the fear of God. Hear us, O Lord, in Hea-
' ven, the habitation of thy holiness, and graci-
' ously answer our prayers ; for the sake of Jesus
' Christ, our glorious Redeemer and Advocate.
' *Amen*.'

An EVENING PRAYER for a FAMILY.

 ' Our Father who art in Heaven, thou art the
' hearer of prayer. The gods of the nations
' were idols, silver and gold, the work of men's
' hands ; they saw not ; they heard not ; nor
' could they relieve their deluded worshippers.
• But thou, O our God, art he who stretched
' out the heavens, and who laid the foundations
' of the earth, and formed the spirit of man with-
' in him. Thou upholdest all things by the
' word of thy power. Thine eyes run to and
' fro, throughout the whole earth, beholding the
' evil and the good ; and thine ears are ever
' open to the cries of thy people. We humbly
' present unto thee our evening devotion.

 ' Thou, O Lord, hast preserved us this day ;
' thou hast fed us ; thou hast clothed us ; thou
' hast enabled us to labour ; and thou hast bles-
             ' sed

'fed the work of our hands. It is becaufe of
' our rebellion againſt God, that we muſt eat
' our bread in the ſweat of our brow. But we
' give thee moſt hearty thanks, that, amidſt all
' the toils and burdens of the day, we can refreſh
' our fouls, by meditating on that reſt which
' thou haſt prepared for all thy people.

' Enable us all, O Lord, to diſcharge every
' duty of our ſtation, in ſuch a manner, that each
' of us may receive that moſt enlivening com-
' mendation, Well done, good and faithful fer-
' vant; thou haſt been faithful over a few
' things, I will make thee ruler over many
' things: enter thou into the joy of thy Lord.
' It will avail us nothing to attain to riches or to
' honour here, if we are ſtill the enemies of God.
' O give us grace to ſeek firſt the kingdom of
' God, and his righteouſneſs, and all needful
' things ſhall be added unto us.

' O God of grace, let thy bleſſing reſt upon
' us at all times. May this houſe be a houſe for
' God. May we be bleſſed in him in whom all the
' families of the earth are bleſſed. Bleſs us in our
' baſket and in our ſtore. Bleſs us in our out-
' going, and in our incoming: but, above all,
' may our fouls be in health and profper.

' May the good Lord pardon whatever we
' have done amiſs this day. Blot out the ſins of
' our whole lives. We confeſs, that in all things
' we offend, and come far ſhort of thy glory.
' O Lord, we are unprofitable ſervants. Know-
' ing that a man is not juſtified by the works of
' the law, but by the faith of Jeſus Chriſt, we
' deſire to believe in Jeſus Chriſt; that we may
' be juſtified by the faith of Chriſt, and not by
' the works of the law. O grant us grace to

' adorn

'adorn the doctrine of God our Saviour in all
'things. Fill us with thy Spirit. Enable us,
'through the Spirit, to mortify the deeds of the
'body, that we may live. Let the same mind
'be in us, which was also in Christ Jesus; that
'learning of him, who was meek and lowly, we
'may find rest unto our souls. Hide pride from
'our eyes. Clothe us with humility.

'We pray, O Lord, that thou wouldest
'keep us from all danger. Preserve us from
'fear in the night. Let our rest be sweet; and
'in the morning, when we awake, may we be
'still with thee. We pray for all who are in
'sickness and distress. Provide for the poor and
'needy. Make them sensible of their spiritual
'wants; and may they be directed to him in
'whom all fulness dwells. Bless thy church
'throughout the world. Encourage, assist, and
'prosper all the ministers of the everlasting gos-
'pel. Bless our rulers, and enable them to
'rule in thy fear. Grant us whatever thou
'seest to be good for us: and let our prayers
'come up before thy throne, and send us an
'answer of peace; for the sake of Jesus Christ,
'thy well beloved Son. *Amen.*'

A PRAYER for a FAMILY in AFFLICTION.

'Almighty and eternal God, the heaven is
'thy throne, and the earth is thy footstool.
'Thousands of angels surround thy throne; ten
'thousand times ten thousand of these blessed
'spirits minister unto thee. The heavens are
'not clean in thy sight. Behold, God put no
'trust in his servants; and his angels he charged
'with folly. The most exalted of the celestial
'hosts

‘ hosts veil their faces in thy presence, and rest
‘ not, day and night, saying, Holy, holy, holy
‘ Lord God Almighty! Just and true art thou
‘ in all thy ways, and holy in all thy works.
‘ Day unto day uttereth speech, and night unto
‘ night sheweth knowledge of thee.

‘ O Lord, although thou hast not left thyself
‘ without a witness, in that thou dost good, and
‘ givest us rain from heaven, and fruitful seasons,
‘ filling our hearts with food and gladness; yet
‘ we have forgotten thee. O Lord, we have
‘ often misimproved the bounties of thy provi-
‘ dence, and have abused thy goodness, and have
‘ not remembered or acknowledged thee, the
‘ bountiful giver of all good things. What shall
‘ we say unto thee, O most righteous God? for
‘ we have forsaken thy commandments. Justly
‘ mayest thou say unto us, In the day of your
‘ prosperity, your hearts waxed fat, and ye
‘ kicked against the heavens; now in your dis-
‘ tress ye come unto me.

‘ Lord, we confess, with shame and confusion
‘ of face, our thoughtlessness, our sin, our stupi-
‘ dity, and our folly. Thou mightest justly hide
‘ thy face from us, and turn our prayer into sin.
‘ But, be not wroth very sore, O Lord, neither
‘ remember iniquity forever : Behold, see, we
‘ beseech thee, we are all thy people. Our
‘ fathers trusted in thee, and were not put to
‘ shame. Thou art still the same merciful God;
‘ forgiving iniquity, transgression and sin. Thine
‘ ear is not heavy, that thou canst not hear;
‘ thine arm is not shortened, that thou canst not
‘ save. O Lord, hide thy face from our sins;
‘ and hear us for thine own name's sake. Should-
‘ est thou lay judgment to the line, and righte-
‘ ousness

'ousness to the plummet, none could stand before
'thee. But thou hast given thine own Son, to
'be a sacrifice for sin; and art in Christ recon-
'ciling the world unto thyself, not imputing their
'trespasses unto them. Encouraged by the grace
'and promises of the gospel, we have felt in our
'hearts to pray unto thee this prayer.

'O Lord, we do not ask those things which
'the world calls good. Our heart's desire, our
'most fervent prayer unto thee is, that we may be
'found in Christ Jesus, not having our own right-
'eousness, which is of the law, but that which is
'through the faith of Christ, the righteousness
'which is of God by faith. O may we pass from
'death unto life; and have reason to say, it is good
'for us that we have been afflicted; for before
'we were afflicted we went astray; but now
'have we learnt to keep thy holy law.

'O Lord, we beseech thee, of thine infinite
'mercy, to bless, unto each of us, this afflictive
'dispensation of thy providence. In this day of
'adversity may we consider. Let us not despise
'the chastening of the Lord; nor faint when
'we are rebuked of him. Enable us to possess
'our souls in patience, and to say, whatever thou
'art pleased to order in our lot, the will of the
'Lord be done.

'But, O Lord, contend not with us forever.
'Remember that we are but dust. Deliver us,
'we humbly intreat thee, in thy good time, and
'in thine own way, that we may yet praise thee
'in the land of the living. Grant, O grant unto
'us, the pardon of all our sins. May we be
'washed in the fountain opened for sin and for
'uncleanness. May we receive, from the Prince
'and Saviour exalted, true and unfeigned re-
                                          'pentance

'pentance. Beautify our souls with thy salva-
'tion; and let the consolations of thy Spirit
'abound in us. O teach us so to number our
'days, as to apply our hearts unto wisdom.
'May we daily die unto sin, and live unto righ-
'teousness.

'O Lord God of Hosts, let none of us so
'far deceive our own souls, as to put off prepa-
'ration for eternity to a dying hour. In this
'our day, enable us to attend to the things
'which belong to our peace, before they are
'forever hid from our eyes. For us to live,
'may it be Christ; for us to die, may it be gain;
'that so, when our flesh and our heart faileth,
'God may be the strength of our heart, and
'our portion forever. Now, O Lord, what
'wait we for? Our hope is in thy word: all
'our desires are before thee. O Lord, hear;
'O Lord, forgive; O Lord, hearken and do:
'defer not, for thine own sake, O our God. We
'offer all our supplications unto thee, in the
'name of Jesus Christ, the High Priest of our
'profession, who is God over all blessed forever.

A M E N.

A
SERMON

ON THE

D U T Y

OF

CIVIL OBEDIENCE,

AS REQUIRED IN

S C R I P T U R E.

Delivered in Christ Church and St. Peter's, April 25, 1799, being a day of general Humiliation, *Appointed by the President of the United States.*

By WM. WHITE, D. D.
Bishop of the Protestant Episcopal Church,
In the Commonwealth of Pennsylvania.

𝔓𝔥𝔦𝔩𝔞𝔡𝔢𝔩𝔭𝔥𝔦𝔞:
*P*RINTED BY JOHN ORMROD,
No. 41, Chesnut-street,
1799.

ADVERTISEMENT.

THE following sermon was preached in substance, and the greater part of it in the very words in which it stands, in Chrift Church and St. Peters' on the 5th of November 1775, at the beginning of the revolutionary war; and in the prefence of many members of the Congrefs, then affembled in this city. It is well known, that the aforefaid day was celebrated in this country, as in other parts of the Britifh empire, on the double account of the difappointment of the gunpowder plot in the reign of king James the firft, and of the revolution atchieved by king William the third. In the aforefaid year, the commemoration happening on a Sunday, and one of the events being the failure of a wicked confpiracy againft legal government, while the other was the fuccefs of an honourable refiftance of arbitrary power; and the fervice of the day being full of reference to the two fubjects; it appeared to the preacher a fuitable opportunity, for ftating the ground of civil obedience, as it is laid in Scripture; and for drawing a line of diftinction, of which the events referred to appeared to him an happy illuftration. Not many years ago, the fermon was again preached in the fame churches, on the return of the anniverfary of independence. The author, having preached it the third time on an occafion lately paft, with a fmall addition relating to prefent circumftances, complies with the requeft for publication, prefented to him by many whom he efteems. He can with great fincerity declare, that when the propofal was made, he felt great reluctance in complying with it: And yet, on reflection, this was confiderably leffened by the confideration, that he was delivering to the prefs a ftandard of what are and have been his fentiments on a fubject, on which he has fometimes, from a fenfe of duty, addreffed his hearers: A fubject, on which, perhaps more than on any other, a preacher is liable to be mifunderftood and mifreprefented.

A DISCOURSE, &c,

ROM: Ch. 13, v. 1, 2.

"*Let every soul be subject unto the higher powers:*
"*For there is no power but of God: The powers*
"*that be are ordained of God: Whosoever there-*
"*fore resisteth the power, resisteth the ordinanc* of*
"*God: And they that resist, shall receive to them-*
"*selves damnation.*

THE only way in which a minister of the gospel can adapt his discourse to the civil conduct of his hearers, is by explaining and enforcing certain precepts of scripture, which have a reference to the subject. This falls within his sphere and may be sometimes useful; because those precepts have been variously misrepresented, as it has suited the purposes of faction or of despotism; and thus, doctrines of the most destructive tendency have been founded on a system of divine truth, in itself wholly calculated to give glory to God and to promote peace and good will among men.

You will bear me witnefs, that if, on very few occafions, and when appointments by public authority invited to it, I have applied my fubject matter to the civil concerns of our country, it has gone no further, than to the refcuing of the word of God from fuch abufe. I have conceived this to be one of the opportunities, when, for fo good a purpofe, I might bring before you fentiments, which accomplifh their effect on a future life, thro' their intermediate influence on the civil interefts of the prefent. And as to the duty to which we are principally fummoned, of humiliation under a fenfe of our tranfgreffions, I truft, that it will be perceived to have a near connection with my fubject. For the motive of the chief magiftrate in calling our attention to the duty, is its relation to exifting dangers: which can never bring material injury to the ftate, except through the inftrumentality of licentious paffions, in their refiftance of the divine will. Accordingly, I cannot more properly conform to the defign of our being affembled, than by opening to you the ground of civil obedience, as it ftands in fcripture. And altho' the religious fupport thus to be erected is to fuftain what you will daily hear refted on the nature of the focial ftate; yet let it be remembered, that no fuch theoretical contemplation of the fubject has been found fufficient in practice, for the retaining of men in fubjection to law and government. No; it is nothing lefs than the fenfe of an over-ruling Being, and the conviction of his exercising his administration on earth, thro' the delegated authority of those, who, through his providence, are clothed with power, which can be a sufficient counterpoise to the bad passions of our nature: Passions, which are continually exciting in some members of the community, the expectation of raising private gain and happiness, out of public loss and misery.

I therefore proceed in my design: And this is, 1st. To state to you two opinions, which seem to me unfavourable to civil happiness; and are alleged to be founded on my text and other places like it; altho', as I conceive, not taught in those passages, nor fairly to be inferred from them: 2d. To set before you, what I take to be their true interpretation: And 3d. To establish the leading duty they enjoin:—First, I am to state to you two opinions, which seem to me unfavourable to civil happiness; and are alleged to be founded on my text and other places like it; altho', as I conceive, not taught in those passages, nor fairly to be inferred from them.

The first of these opinions, is the indefeasible right of Princes, to the obedience of their subjects; a right not to be set aside, it is said, nor altered, by any law, for the avoiding of any evil, or for the obtaining of any good to the community. I mean the opinion, which, within the prefent century, and in an empire of which we were a part, produced two rebellions, in fupport of this imaginary right of a lineal fucceffor, in oppofition to the double right of legal fettlement, and of peaceable poffeffion. Far be it from me to abridge any meafure of charity, which it may be thought reafonable to extend to unwarrantable actions, when they flow from a mifguided confcience : And indeed, I think, that in the prefent inftance, much is due. But there can hardly be a principle, more directly tending to kindle and to keep alive the flames of civil difcord ; and that, not for the obtaining of any public good, but to affert the pretended right of an individual, who may happen to be one of the moft weak or the moft wicked of his fpecies.

And as it is a principle full of mifchief, fo alfo, it feems to have no foundation, either in reafon or in the gofpel. It has none in reafon, becaufe, if it were true, we might expect to find the rule of fucceffion as clearly defined by that faculty, as the other rules which are to be the guides of our moral conduct; whereas fucceffion, whether applicable to fovereigns or to individuals, has been various in different nations, and always held to be the fubject of law :—I fay of law; who being allowed to fpeak on the queftion, may be expected to declare herfelf, in a matter of public concern, with a view to the public good; and not to be limited to the narrow scale of individual interest. And it has as little foundation in the gospel; because whatever may be either the limits or the extent of its precepts, they evidently relate to the present possessor of the power; without any reference to the means by which it was obtained.

On this account, I consider the second opinion, as the more consistent, although the more extravagant error of the two. The opinion I mean, is that of the duty of submission to the civil authority, in whatever hands it may be lodged; to whatever extremes it may be abused; and whatever constitutions or laws it may contradict. But this is inconsistent with a universally acknowleged characteristic of Christianity; viz. its not intermeddling with the civil constitutions of countries; and its leaving of their different policies, to the principles on which they have been respectively founded. Whereas, let the opinion mentioned be admitted and acted on in Christian States; and immediately it follows, that all legal boundaries of prerogative are done away; that one simple and absolute dominion supersedes the various modifications of power; that the first Prince, or the first Robber, who will seize all, shall from that moment possess all, to be governed by himself, and by his successors, as their lusts or as their fancies may direct.

I am not contending, either that the scriptures inculcate resistance, or, that the lawfulness of it being supposed, they justify Christian ministers in declaring, at what point it may begin: And if the present were a time when you might be misled by me in this matter, I should be careful, as I was in times not long past, to guard you against the mistake. But at present, my only object is to shew, that the submission due to government does not necessarily extend to a principle, which counteracts its very end; and which would destroy that most amiable property of it, its being an image of the divine government; which, though co-extensive with the universe, and without beginning or end, is yet regulated by the unchangeable law of right.

In order therefore to seek a foundation for the duty before us, which shall be a sufficient check of faction, without upholding despotism, I proceed, 2dly, to set before you, what I take to be the true interpretation of my text and of other places like it.

The most remarkable passages besides that of my text, are those in the 2d chapter of the 1st Ep. of St. Peter; in the 2d chap. of the 1st Ep. of St. Paul to Timothy, and in the 3d of the same Ap. to Titus. They are so much alike, that a comment on the text itself will serve for the rest also: And you will find the sense of the whole to be, that there is inculcated, in general, the duty of obedience to the civil magistrate, without any nice discussions concerning the origin, or the extent or the discontinuance of his power; but leaving the doctrine to be applied, in these respects, according to the nature of the duty and the end for which it was ordained. Nor need we wonder that it should be left on this footing in the scriptures; since it is so, in common with all the other social obligations. Take, for instance, the authority of father and that of master, with the corresponding duties of child and of servant; and you will find the one required and the other asserted, without limitation or exception. Not however that there are no limitations and exceptions, for there are confessedly; and it is the business of judgment and of conscience to ascertain and to regard them, and to apply principles to cases, as they occur. In the enjoining of all the social duties, and especially that before us, it became the apostles to be the more positive, and at the same time the more general, because of the slander that had gone forth, representing the Christians as setting up the licentious plea, that, being the servants of God, they were not subject to the ordinances of men: And there is evidently an eye to this very reproach, in all the passages which I have mentioned to you.

But to attend to that which we took, as the leading paſſage: It ſays—" Let every ſoul be ſubject to " the higher powers." There is a ſpecial uſe in the vague expreſſion here applied to the civil magiſtracy. St. Peter, in his epiſtle, which was addreſſed to the Chriſtians diſperſed through Aſia Minor, a country where monarchical power was the moſt familiar and acknowleged, injoins them " to honour " and obey the king:" But St. Paul, here writing to citizens of Rome, where the government was in the hands, partly of an emperor, and partly of a ſenate, the boundaries of their reſpective juriſdiction being not preciſely drawn, and it being no part of his commiſſion to define the rightful government of the country, adopts the more comprehenſive term, " the higher powers."

He goes on—" for there is no power but of God: " the powers that be are ordained of God:" That is, the viſible poſſeſſors of the power, without any diſtinction as to hereditary right, to which there was not the ſhadow of pretenſion in the then Roman emperor, " are ordained of God." St. Peter, in his epiſtle, calls their authority "the ordinance of men." But there is no inconſiſtency between the two: For although the perſon be appointed and the power be guided by human act and law; ſtill, the neceſſity of government for the conducting of the affairs of the world, and of conſequence the rights which it involves for the accomplishing of that end, flow from the will and the determinations of God. "Who-"foever, therefore, refisteth the power, refisteth "the ordinance of God." Submission being a general duty, refistance muft of courfe be criminal.

" And they that refift fhall receive to themfelves "damnation." Laws would be to no purpofe, without penalties: And we have here the higheft penalty annexed to a crime, which threatens ruin, not merely to an individual, or to a family, but to the community. And this is a fanction which religion will always extend to the fupport of juft government, by adding the terrors of an eternal, to thofe of temporal punifhment. But whether the cafe of an extreme abufe of power be at all in contemplation, will appear from a confideration of the verfes immediately following my text, in which the apoftle goes on thus. "For rulers are not a terror to good "works but to the evil. Wilt thou then, not be "afraid of the power, do that which is good and "thou fhalt have praife of the fame. For he is the "minifter of God to thee for good. But if thou "do that which is evil, be afraid; for he beareth "not the fword in vain: for he is the minifter of "God; a revenger to execute wrath upon him that "doeth evil." Now this is nothing elfe, than reafoning from the nature and the end of Government, which are always good, to the fuitable fubmiffion and

obedience. But what relation it has to a continued courſe of the wanton abuſe of power, or to the perverſion of it from its true end, as here ſet forth, can not be ſhewn from the expreſſions uſed. No, this is a caſe of which the paſſage does not ſpeak; leaving it to what reaſon, under the guidance of religion and of morals, ſhall point out, as the proper means of aſcertaining and ſecuring civil rights. But ſuch extraordinary occaſions being out of the queſtion, the apoſtle repeats his precept, with a ſpecial ſtreſs on the principal motive to it. " Where-
" fore, ye muſt needs be ſubject, not only for
" wrath, but alſo for conſcience ſake;" that is, not merely from the low conſideration of temporal puniſhment, but as ye ſhall anſwer for your conduct to God.

And as this duty of obedience extends to actions generally, ſo eſpecially it requires us to contribute our proportion to the neceſſary ſupport of government, by the payment of all legal dues. " For, for this cauſe, pay ye tribute alſo; for they " are God's miniſters, attending continually on this " very thing." " Pay ye tribute," ſays the apoſtle. To whom? " To the powers that be,"— that is, thoſe who have the acknowledged right and have been in the known practice of impoſing it. Still the ſame ſpirit pervades the whole paſſage; that where prerogative and privilege interfere, there is no determination on that point ; but it is left to be determined by reason and right, according to the respective policies of different states.

Accordingly the passage goes on thus—" For " they are God's ministers, attending continually on " this very thing :" which is still arguing from the ordinary executing of the policy of a state ; and has no relation to any extraordinary prostitution of its powers. And in the spirit which has pervaded the passage all along, it thus concludes—" Render " therefore to all their dues : tribute to whom tribute " is due ; custom to whom custom ; fear to whom " fear ; honor to whom honor." Now what is to be the measure of these dues ? Certainly the most reasonable measure is the venerable authority of constitution and of law. And although, where there is neither constitution nor law, mere power may be a foundation of the claim, on account of the absolute necessity of government to mankind; yet this can be no reason for asserting the cause of power against constitution and against law ; or for the setting at nought of these, in order to give to the other, an exclusive claim to tribute, to custom, to reverence and to honour.

I have set before you what I take to be the true sense of this and of similar passages of scripture : And although I have not and indeed in conscience cannot fo explain them, as to raife the civil magiſtrate above law, yet I truſt, that I have taken ſuch a foundation, as is a ſufficient check to faction; and will affiſt us under the 3d head; which was to eſtabliſh the leading duty which my text injoins.

This duty may be expreſſed as follows—That when the civil magiſtrate is in the exerciſe of his authority, agreeably to conſtitution and to law, it is criminal to refiſt him, on any pretence whatever.

I know but of three principles, on which ſuch refiſtance can, with any colourable plea be founded. Reſentment of private injuries; a ſuppoſed uſe of projected changes; and a motive of religion.—Iſt. It is criminal to oppoſe, or interrupt the lawful authority of the magiſtrate, from reſentment of private injuries; whether we be accidentally expoſed by law to heavier burthens than others; or ſuffer from the infirmities, or from the miſtakes, or even from the vices, which may be the lot of rulers. I ſay, that neither of theſe cares juſtifies refiſtance. For, in the former, the inequality is the reſult of the imperfection inherent to human law; or rather of the imperfection of human reaſon, which finds it difficult to apply the eternal principles of law, to the circumſtances of individuals. And in the other, partial diſtreſs can never be a juſtification for engaging in meafures, which would produce general misfortune. What are public fpirit and the love of country, not to fay Chriftian charity, but mere names, if they will not induce the fuffering of wrong, rather than to fet an example, which tends to the deftruction of all law and government; and may give a beginning to calamities of great extent and duration; and out of all proportion to the injury fuftained?

The fecond pretence, is that of a fuppofed ufe in projected changes. But altho' the door fhould never be fhut againft thofe improvements, which the cultivation of general knowlege may make in the fcience of civil government, yet the introducing of them muft be left, partly to the conviction of the public judgment; and partly to the moral influence, which fuch improvements will filently obtain over the fentiments and the manners of the community. The lawfulnefs of a forcible introduction of them muft be rejected, becaufe of its pernicious confequences. It profeffes to have in view the public good, which cannot confift with a continued ftate of tumult and confufion; the neceffary refult of every one's fetting up his own ideas of perfection; and his feeking of it, thro' the horrors of civil war. The beft of governments may fhew fome traces of human infirmity and imperfection; and while an endeavor to rectify by force, will certainly produce bloodshed; it is uncertain, whether it will accomplish the end proposed. On this subject, there is great variety of opinion: And, if all were to assume a right to model things to their respective fancies, the probability is, that anarchy would prevail for a while; until at last there would follow a general submission to despotism, as the more tolerable grievance.

The 3d pretence is that of religion: which, surely, can never warrant resistance of the just authority of the magistrate. For it is impossible, that a system of duty, which professes to make man peaceable and mild to man, should justify its followers in involving their country in bloodshed and desolation. There has been, indeed, set up the bold pretension of an ecclesiastical authority, to absolve subjects and citizens from their allegiance. But could that amiable Instructor, who taught his apostles to " ren-
" der unto Cæsar the things that are Cæsar's," give to those very apostles and their successors, a commission so inconsistent with his precepts? Or will that excellent system, which dictates the purest morality, admit of a dispensing power, to release its professors from their most solemn obligations? Certainly, no. It was not thus, that the first followers of our Saviour published the glad tidings of salvation. On the contrary, they recommended their

religion, not by perfecuting their fellow creatures, but by enduring perfecutions with patience.

This pretended prerogative over moral duties, is not the only way in which religion has been abufed to the purpofes of faction. There have been other falfe zealots, who have difturbed the public peace, by pretending, that dominion is founded in grace; that the faints are to rule the earth; and that it is lawful to extirpate thofe, whom they call the enemies of Chrift. It was not thus that Chrift fought, either to fubdue his enemies, or to exalt his faints. The latter forfeit all hopes of being acknowleged by him at his fecond coming, when they make his kingdom of this world. Their warfare is to fubdue their paffions: And although their religion is far from prohibiting them from being ferviceable to their country in public ftations, yet it reftrains from an immoderate defire of rule; much more, from feeking it by injurious methods. It gives a fanction to the relation between rulers and the people: And the idea of Chriftians being exempted from obedience, even to unchriftian governors, is the very error, againft which the fcriptures caution us, under the penalty of damnation.

Thus there has been laid before you the foundation of civil obedience, as it appears in fcripture. And your preacher entertains the confcioufnefs that his fentiments, after having been the fruit of his earlieft ftudies, have been continually confirmed in him by reflection; and by obfervation of the great events, which have been acted on the theatre of the world. He alfo knows, that the views of the fubject to which he has been accuftomed, are the moft favorable to the higheft improvements of focial life: For thefe feek the foftering care of a government of laws; which is always in a medium between arbitrary power on the one hand, and mad democracy on the other.

On thefe principles it is, that he never doubted of the lawfulnefs of the great change, which raifed our country to a rank among the nations of the earth: An event that had its origin, not in a defire on our part to remove the eftablifhed landmarks of law or of prerogative; but in an attachment to invaded rights, which had been handed down to us from the firft fettlers of the country; on the faith of which they had left the land of their nativity, and braved the dangers of the wildernefs; and which had become endeared to their pofterity, by opinion, and by long enjoyment. Rights like thefe we might reafonably affert, confiftently with the ties which bound us to the parent ftate. Rights like thefe we might reafonably defend, by breaking thofe ties, when fecurity could no otherwife be obtained. This is one of the great cafes in the hiftory of mankind, which muſt be produced by exiſting circumſtances; but which would be wickedly miſapplied, ſhould it be ſet up as a pretence for the reſiſtance of legal government: eſpecially of a government, which, having been eſtabliſhed by the general will, involves in itſelf a peaceable mean of of remedying any imperfections, ſhould they be diſcovered, in its conſtruction.

Under ſuch a government, to deny the right of expreſſing private ſentiment on the adminiſtration of its powers, would be contrary to the liberal ſpirit which it breathes. But when this freedom is abuſed to the rendering of rulers odious by miſrepreſentation and falſhoods; When recourſe is had to the low artifices of faction, much more to the outrageous violence of ſedition and of treaſon; Or, what is the root of all theſe evils, when there is an intemperate oppoſition, diſdaining ſubmiſſion to public meaſures, however unequivocally ſupported by legitimate declarations of the general will; then it is, that we may apply, without heſitation, the awful cenſure of my text; and affirm of the perſons to whom this belongs, that they " reſiſt the ordinance of God; " and that without repentance and reformation, they will " receive to themſelves damnation."

It is for the preventing and for the correcting of

D

the vicious difpofitions which impel to fuch a conduct, that we are fummoned to the duties of the day. For if government refts on the will of God; and if fubmiffion to it is the demand of reafon and of revelation; there are no fins which fhould not be repented of, and no bad paffions which fhould not be mortified, not only becaufe of their effect on our condition in another world, but as they injure our civil interefts in the prefent. And efpecially it follows, that we fhould deplore an increafing forgetfulnefs of God, which impairs the influence that ought to flow from a conviction of his prefence, a reverence of his perfections, a fenfe of the obligation of his laws and an apprehenfion of his judgements. For thefe have been always the beft cement of focial life and the beft fecurity of public and of private rights; and can never fuffer a lofs of force, without a proportionate neceffity of the arm of power, to accomplifh what had been better done by law, by habit, and by affection.

If ever there was a time, when an extraordinary occafion has occurred, of being awake to fuch truths as thefe, it is the prefent; when a fpirit has gone forth, which feeks the demolition of religious principle in every fhape; and which glories in the opinion of its inutility, in reference to civil interefts and duties. And altho' this licentious theory bears within itfelf the feeds of its deftruction, in the mifchiefs to which it prompts; yet it is impoffible to calculate either the number or the weight of the calamities, of which it may be for a while the caufe; and which are therefore chargeable on the confciences of all thofe, who withdraw themfelves from a religious profeffion and the practice of religious duties.

If indeed the delufive theory were to reft on its pretended evidence alone, we might hope to find a counterbalance to it, in the dictates of fober reafon, in the authority of the wifeft ftatefmen, and in the experience of paft ages. But there has arifen before the aftonifhed world a military defpotifm of a gigantic fize, and republican in name, which patronifes the licentious fentiment in the difaffected and the defperate of every country; making it the engine of an ambition without bounds: and which acts by the novel expedients, of a benevolence that knows no pity; of a patriotifm that has no refpect either to property or to perfon; of a fraternity that proftrates the independence of nations, and gives them up to plunder; and of boafted improvements in public law, which do away all the expedients of former ages, for the preventing, or the moderating of war. What will be the final refult of this united force of hypocrify and of power, time only can unfold. But it is eafy to read the leffon written in it for the inftruction of virtuous citizens; on whom it is an additional call to the love and the fupport of order and an adherence to the ground on which it refts ; viz. the will of God and the fanctions by which he fuftains it in the expectation of a future life. Thus will they contribute to the killing of thofe feeds of difcontent, difunion, faction and infurrection, againft which we are inftructed at this time to pray: And thus alfo will they affift in fortifying every heart and ftrengthening every hand againft the defolating fword of hoftile invaders, fhould it be brought within our borders.

And while we thus prepare by confideration and contrition againft threatening dangers, let us not be forgetful of that other object of the appointment—gratitude to God, for what we enjoy of his undeferved mercies; and efpecially for his continuing to us the bleffings of a free conftitution and an upright adminiftration of its powers; while fo many of the nations are bowed down under an imperious domination, directed to the fubjugation of them all. For although we have no directions in fcripture to determine us, as to many queftions on which wife and good men differ; yet, for whatever civil benefits we undeniably enjoy we fhould be thankful to God, as well as for the other mercies of his providence. And indeed, if it be a duty to thank him for his fun and rain, for the returns of feed-time and harveft, and for the fruits of them conducive to our well-being, much more should we confess his good providence, in that legal security of person and property, on which the enjoyment of the rest so much depends; and above all, for that religious freedom of worshipping him according to our consciences, which is not only in itself a most invaluable blessing, but connected with the advancement of every kind of knowlege, distinguishing man above the brutes.

In regard to different forms of government, men may think differently, according to their respective habits, tempers and education: But as to those other matters, which affect our daily happiness; and which promote, what the apostle mentions as the end of our praying for civil rulers, viz. " the " leading of quiet and peaceable lives, in all God- " liness and honesty;" it is difficult to conceive of a man's being indifferent to such properties of a free government, and yet that he should entertain a love of moral order and a kindness to his species. The object of government is human happiness: And all improvements which have been found to promote this, by curbing the passions, either of arbitrary rulers or of licentious people, are of the number of those " good gifts which come down from the father " of lights."

That in the minds of our fellow-citizens in general, there is an attachment to a government under which ſuch benefits are enjoyed, we have recent evidence in the zeal with which a late public ſummons has been obeyed, and by which the objects of it have been carried into full effect. And while I ſee among you many, whom I welcome on their return from an expedition, honourable alike to the commonwealth and to themſelves, I can refer to it, as an additional reaſon for rejoicing in a conſtitution, by which ſuch a ſpirit has been excited, and for the ſake of which ſuch ſacrifices have been made. Neverthelefs, with all due value for the love of country thus manifeſted, I may predict, that it will not be permanent in its effects, unleſs in union with a ſenſe of that great Being, by whoſe providence our public mercies have been beſtowed, and under whoſe pleaſure they are held. On the preſent occaſion therefore in particular, let them be cheriſhed with thankfulneſs; and let a preparation be made, for their being enjoyed with virtue: And let the ſolemnity be inſtrumental to the exciting in us of ſuch devout ſentiments and affections, as ſhall be to the divine praiſe and to our own benefit, in time and in eternity.

www.ingramcontent.com/pod-product-compliance
Lightning Source LLC
Chambersburg PA
CBHW031425230426
43668CB00007B/443